The Wright Library
Westford Academy
30 Patton Rd.
Westford, MA 01886

Deleted

The Regions of France

THE REGIONS OF FRANCE

The Regions of France

A Reference Guide to History and Culture

Wayne Northcutt

Deleted

The Wright Library
Westford Academy
30 Patten Rd.
Westford, MA 01886

Greenwood Press
Westport, Connecticut • London

Library of Congress Cataloging-in-Publication Data

Northcutt, Wayne.
    The regions of France : a reference guide to history and culture /
Wayne Northcutt.
      p.   cm.
    Includes bibliographical references and index.
    ISBN 0-313-29223-X (alk. paper)
    1. Popular culture—France—Regions. 2. France—
Civilization—1945– 3. Decentralization in government—France—
History—20th century. I. Title.
DC33.7.N63   1996
944.083—dc20   96-5806

British Library Cataloguing in Publication Data is available.

Copyright © 1996 by Wayne Northcutt

All rights reserved. No portion of this book may be
reproduced, by any process or technique, without the
express written consent of the publisher.

Library of Congress Catalog Card Number: 96-5806
ISBN: 0-313-29223-X

First published in 1996

Greenwood Press, 88 Post Road West, Westport, CT 06881
An imprint of Greenwood Publishing Group, Inc.

Printed in the United States of America

The paper used in this book complies with the
Permanent Paper Standard issued by the National
Information Standards Organization (Z39.48-1984).

P

All photos by Wayne Northcutt.

Cover photo: The old port of Marseille.

All maps were produced by Nighthawk Design.

In order to keep this title in print and available to the academic community, this edition
was produced using digital reprint technology in a relatively short print run. This would
not have been attainable using traditional methods. Although the cover has been changed
from its original appearance, the text remains the same and all materials and methods
used still conform to the highest book-making standards.

For my father

CONTENTS

Photo essay follows page 158

PREFACE

The Regions of France: A Reference Guide to History and Culture is intended to make the twenty-two regions of the nation accessible to students and others interested in contemporary France. Foreigners often associate France primarily with Paris, but understanding the individual regions allows us to see their great variety—physical, cultural, linguistic, and so on—and their role in the nation's historical, political, economic, and cultural development. Although almost one-fifth of France's inhabitants reside in the capital, Paris, the majority of the population is found in the regions. Moreover, the French people tend to identify closely with their region. Therefore, in order to better understand France and the French, we must be acquainted with the nation's twenty-two regions.

In this volume, the description of each region is organized around specific categories: regional geography, history, recent politics, population, economy, culture (including cuisine), and architecture and noteworthy sites. A map of each region is found at the beginning of the appropriate chapter. To aid the reader in orientation, each regional map is accompanied by a smaller key map showing the region's location within France. At the end of each chapter is a select bibliography. In addition to a photo essay, two appendixes are included: a chronology and a list of the rulers of France. A general bibliography concludes the book. To date, no other work in the English or French language provides such in-depth and comprehensive coverage of all of France's regions. In France today, scholars are just beginning to publish work on the regions that is large in scope.

Much of the statistical material found in this volume was obtained from *La France et ses régions* (1993), an economic and demographic survey of the twenty-two regions, published by the *Institut National de la Statistique et des Études Économiques* (National Institute of Statistics). *L'État de la France,* an annually updated reference work on the nation and the regions, and *La France dans ses regions,* published by Le Monde, also provided valuable economic and demographic data. A considerable amount of additional material, especially from French repositories, was utilized in preparing this manuscript.

My own scholarly work on contemporary France, my lengthy *séjours* in Paris, Provence, Languedoc-Rousillon, and Alsace, and twenty-five years of regular travel to this country have been invaluable assets in preparing this book. Over the course of the years, I have visited all parts of the nation. This travel experience has given me a "feel" for France and a comprehension of the similarities and differences between Paris and the regions, as well as the similarities and differences that exist among the regions themselves. The regions, as this volume will demonstrate, are key to understanding France in the past, present, and future.

ACKNOWLEDGMENTS

In writing this book I have accumulated a number of important debts and must thank several people. First, I thank Barbara Rader, Senior Editor for School and Library Reference at Greenwood Press, and her colleagues for inviting me to undertake this project. I readily accepted because being a scholar who writes on the "hexagon" (a name given to France because of its shape), it was obvious to me that an understanding of the regions was necessary in order to deepen our understanding of *la France*. Also, the project offered an opportunity to research and write a significant volume that could possibly influence a younger generation seeking to understand the complexities of both France and the French. Niagara University awarded me several academic-year research grants to cover part of the cost involved in researching this study in France and in the United States. I must also thank Niagara University for several reduced course loads, which facilitated completion of the manuscript. Several people helped proofread this manuscript: Linda Schineller proofed the entire final manuscript, and a large debt of thanks is extended to her; Ann Young's assistance in proofing several early chapters should be acknowledged as well. Finally, I must thank Alice Vigliani for her skillful copyediting of this manuscript, and Jean Lynch, Production Editor at Greenwood Press, for her valuable assistance.

The Regions of France

Introduction

REGIONS, HISTORY, AND IMAGES

The regions of France represent a relatively new administrative unit, dating back only to the 1950s. However, the regions reflect centuries of history. In fact, in many ways the rise of the regions contradicts the long history of France, which has witnessed numerous attempts to centralize authority in order to unify and modernize the nation-state. A brief overview of French civilization from its origins to the present reveals the various efforts to centralize authority and demonstrates the regions' importance in the development of contemporary France.

HISTORICAL OVERVIEW

Prehistory

The prehistory of France stretches back thousands of years to the lower Paleolithic period, around 380,000 B.C. Evidence of Cro-Magnon hunters and fishers from about 35,000 B.C. has been discovered in the Dordogne area, where cave paintings reveal the existence of an advanced and creative people. Around 3000 B.C. (long before Stonehenge) mysterious megaliths and dolmens, huge symmetrical rock formations, appeared in Brittany. Relatively little is known about these earliest inhabitants of France.

Arrival of the Gauls, the Romans, the Franks, and the Arabs

Between the seventh and fifth centuries B.C. a horde of Celtic tribes arrived in France from the east. One branch of these tribes became known as the Gauls, considered to be the direct ancestors of the French. The Gauls even established contact with the Greeks who had colonies on the Mediterranean, including Marseille. Following conflict between the Gauls and Rome, Julius Caesar's Roman legions took control of Gaul in 52 B.C., crushing the revolt of the gallic chief Vercingétorix. Lyon became the capital of Roman Gaul. Early in the second century A.D. Christianity was introduced to the area. France remained under Roman rule until the fifth century, when the Franks and other Germanic groups (e.g., Visigoths, Burgundians, and Alemani) invaded the area. (France, of course, derived its name from the Franks.)

From the fall of Rome in the late fifth century until 986, two Frankish dynasties ruled France: the Merovingians and the Carolingians. However, the Frankish tradition of having all the sons share in succession rights weakened the country and made it susceptible to invasion. The Arabs conquered Spain in the early eighth century and ruled there for seven centuries. Yet when the Arabs pushed northward into France, Charles Martel, the grandfather of Charlemagne, stopped their advance at Poitiers in 732. France was thereby saved from Muslim domination.

The Middle Ages

During the rule of Charlemagne, 768 to 814, the boundaries of his kingdom were extended. As a result of France's enlarged position in Europe, Charlemagne was crowned Holy Roman Emperor in 800. A revival of scholarship and education emerged during his reign. Then, in the ninth century, Scandinavian Vikings (known also as the Normans) launched raids on coastal areas and some interior areas as well. The Normans settled in the lower Seine valley and established the Duchy of Normandy in 911.

A new king, Hugues Capet, founded the Capetian dynasty in 987. Yet the royal domains were relatively small, mainly the territory around Paris and Orléans. The kingdom of France faced a powerful rival in William, Duke of Normandy, who in 1066 conquered England. A portion of France fell to the English crown in 1154 when Eleanor of Aquitaine wedded Henry of Anjou, who became King Henry II of England (Eleanor's earlier marriage to the French king Louis VII had been annulled). Subsequently the French and the English fought for three centuries over control of Aquitaine.

During the first half of the thirteenth century, an ascetic Christian sect in southwestern France known as the Cathars challenged papal doctrine. Their stronghold was the town of Albi; their challenge came to be known as the Albigensian heresy. With the support of the king of France, the Church launched an inquisition and a holy war against the Cathars. Known as the Albigensian Crusade, its goal was to eliminate the Cathars.

The early history of France is clearly intertwined with that of the Church. Indeed, France played a significant role in crusades other than the war against the Cathars. For example, the First Crusade of 1095 witnessed the persecution of Jews, who were expelled from France over a period of two centuries. To rekindle the faith, the Church built major new cathedrals—especially Gothic cathedrals—throughout the country between 1150 and the end of the fourteenth century. The French Pope Clement V, facing disorder in Rome and the area now known as Italy, moved the Holy See, the office of the Pope, to Avignon in the south of France, where it remained from 1305 until 1378. During this period Avignon was the home of seven pontificates.

The Hundred Years War between France and England began in 1337 over feudal rights and the line of accession to the French throne. Shortly after the start of the Hundred Years War the plague struck the country, ravaging roughly one-third of the population. In the early fifteenth century when the situation looked bleak for France in the Hundred Years War, a 17-year-old peasant girl (who came to be known as Joan of Arc) rallied the troops at Orléans and contributed to turning the tide of war in favor of her country, making possible the coronation of the Capetian king Charles VII. Shortly thereafter the English were expelled from France. During the conflict Joan was captured by the Burgundians and handed over to the English, who burned her at the stake in Rouen in 1431. Following the Hundred Years War the Italian Renaissance made its impact on France, owing in part to French military actions in Italy.

The Reformation

Early in the 1500s Reformation ideas began to divide France. John Calvin, who resided in exile in Geneva, quickly made a reputation for himself as a Protestant reformer. Between 1562 and 1598 a series of religious and political wars rocked France. Known as the Wars of Religion, these conflicts involved French Protestants (Huguenots); the Catholic League, led by the House of Guise; and the Catholic monarchy. In Paris alone on August 23 and 24, 1572, some 3,000 Huguenots were slaughtered.

To halt the religious conflict and to enhance royal authority, King Henry IV, a former Protestant who had adopted Catholicism, issued the Edict of Nantes in 1598. This proclamation guaranteed the Huguenots equal civil and political rights and a degree of freedom of religious worship. However, King Louis XIII (1610–1643) and his minister, Cardinal Richelieu, were determined to strengthen the monarchy at home and abroad. Consequently Richelieu attacked La Rochelle, a Huguenot stronghold, and more than 20,000 residents died after more than one year of siege.

From Louis XIV to the Revolution

Subsequently the Sun King, Louis XIV, sought to strengthen the monarchy and centralize power in France. Assuming the throne in 1643 at the age of 5, Louis XIV later built the magnificent palace at Versailles outside of Paris. He invited the country's leading aristocrats to reside at Versailles, while at the same time sending his own administrators—mainly from the emerging middle class—to govern the provinces in his name. He also engaged France in a long series of costly wars to promote his glory and that of France. He reveled in his own power, announcing, "*L'État, c'est moi*" (I am the State). Louis XIV revoked the Edict of Nantes in 1685, prompting the flight of more than 50,000 Huguenot families.

The kings that followed, Louis XV and XVI, were relatively weak and ineffectual, and their governments led France to the brink of revolution. State debt, enhanced by the building of Versailles, foreign wars, and French assistance to American revolutionaries, pushed France toward revolution. Of course, informed individuals in France were armed with new ideas from the Enlightenment thinkers (e.g., Voltaire, Jean-Jacques Rousseau, Charles-Louis Montesquieu) that challenged the "divine right" of kings, the theoretical underpinning of the monarchy itself. An all-class attack ensued, led first by a disgruntled aristocracy that was opposed to tax reform, followed by the bourgeoisie, the urban masses, and then the peasants. This led to the creation in 1789 of the National Assembly, which ended feudalism and issued the Declaration of the Rights of Man and Citizen, granting rights to all. In 1792 the revolutionaries created the Republic, followed shortly thereafter by the beheading of the unpopular Louis XVI. These bold actions threatened the institution of monarchy elsewhere in Europe.

When foreign armies led by European monarchs invaded France, the Revolution accelerated and took a more radical course. The National Convention (1792–1795), established after the overthrow of the monarchy, purged its moderates, the *Girondins* (most of whom were from the Gironde area near Bordeaux). Between 1793 and 1794 the Convention engaged in the Reign of Terror. Led by Maximilien Robespierre, the Terror was meant to counter the domestic enemies of the Revolution and to enhance the war effort against France's external enemies. It soon led to excess; approximately 40,000 men and women were guillotined during this bloody phase of the Revolution.

When the Terror ran its course—consuming Robespierre himself and another early supporter of the Terror, Danton—power was transferred to the five-member Directory, which governed France from 1795 to 1799. But as the economy soured and discontent continued to rise, power passed from the Directory to Napoleon Bonaparte, who assumed power as a result of a *coup d'état*. Born in Corsica, during the Revolution he rose quickly through the ranks of the French military. In 1799 he assumed the title of First Consul; after making peace with the Church in the Concordat of 1801, in the following year he became Consul for life. In 1804, with great audacity, he crowned himself Emperor in the Notre Dame cathedral while

Pope Pius VII looked on. During the same year Napoleon issued the Napoleonic Code, the first unified law code in France.

Even though Napoleon had military victories in Europe (e.g., he defeated Austria and Russia at Austerlitz), he also had setbacks (e.g., the Peninsular War against Spain and Portugal, and the disastrous Russian campaign in 1812). A cold winter and a scorched-earth policy pursued by the Russians led to the defeat of the mighty Napoleon and his subsequent abdication and exile. France was now at the mercy of European monarchs.

The Nineteenth Century

At the Congress of Vienna (1814–1815), European monarchs restored the Bourbon line in France and insisted on two guiding principles for the post-Revolution and post-Napoleonic periods—namely, legitimacy and balance of power. But while the Congress deliberated, Napoleon escaped from exile on the small island of Elba off the French coast and mounted an army in France. His "Hundred Days" ended in defeat at Waterloo in Belgium by the British Duke of Wellington. This time Napoleon was sent to the island of St. Helena in the South Pacific, where he died in 1821. (His remains were returned to France in the 1830s and his tomb placed under the dome of *Invalides* in Paris.)

In the wake of the Congress of Vienna, Charles X (1824–1830) sought a return to the divine right of kings. But he was overthrown in 1830 and succeeded by Louis-Philippe, who headed a constitutional monarchy. During the Revolution of 1848 a Second Republic was established, followed by the election of Napoleon III (the nephew of Napoleon I) as president. A *coup d'état* in 1851 by Napoleon III led to the creation of the Second Empire and a new emperor for the French. Although the country experienced a measure of economic growth, Napoleon's foreign policy—including the Crimean War of 1854–1856 against Russia and an attempt to make Maximilian of Austria the emperor of Mexico—weakened France and the new emperor. The Franco-Prussian War of 1870 (by which the Prussian Otto von Bismarck unified Germany) led to a humiliating French defeat at Sedan. In the midst of this disaster, Parisians demanded the creation of a new republic—the Third—and resisted the Germans. National Assembly elections led to a conservative-controlled government after Paris capitulated. When the new National Assembly accepted the harsh terms of the Treaty of Frankfort (loss of Alsace-Lorraine and a 5 billion franc indemnity), the Paris Commune arose to oppose the National Assembly. Karl Marx viewed the Commune as the first great insurrection of the working class against the bourgeoisie, inspiring the myth of a proletarian revolution.

Another crisis for the Third Republic was the Dreyfus Affair. In 1894 a Jewish army captain was unjustly sentenced to life in prison, allegedly for serving as a German spy. A number of intellectuals in France (including the novelist Emile Zola) rallied to his cause and demanded a new hearing, whereas the army, right-wing politicians, and some Catholic groups opposed a re-opening of the case. The Dreyfus Affair deeply divided France. However, Dreyfus eventually received a presidential pardon and in 1906 a civilian court cleared him of all charges. The case exposed the level of anti-Semitism in France, led to greater civilian control over the military, and prompted legal separation of the Church and the state.

The Twentieth Century: World Wars I and II

Tensions in the Balkans, produced largely by the rising tide of nationalism, led to World War I, a war in which France paid a high cost. Although Germany was ultimately defeated and France regained Alsace and Lorraine, 1.3 million French citizens were killed and almost 1 million crippled during the war. At the battle of Verdun in 1916 alone, the French and the Germans each lost 400,000 lives. The material and financial costs of the war were also staggering. The harsh Treaty of Versailles forced Germany to assume responsibility for the war and to pay reparations. Instead of preserving the peace, the treaty only helped to the sow the seeds of yet another world war.

World War II was even more devastating and humiliating for France. Within months after the start of the conflict following the German invasion of Poland, France capitulated. The supposedly impregnable Maginot Line proved useless when the German military machine went around it by passing through Belgium. The Germans proceeded to divide France into a zone of northern Occupation and a southern zone that was unoccupied but run by a puppet government in Vichy headed by General Philippe Pétain. During this divisive and controversial period in French history, more than 70,000 of the 300,000 Jews in France were deported—a number with the assistance of French officials—and sent to their deaths in Nazi concentration camps.

When France fell to the Germans, General Charles de Gaulle fled to London; in a radio broadcast on June 18, 1940, he asked his fellow countrymen and women to resist the Germans. De Gaulle set up a government in exile and created the Free French Forces to resist German control of France. He also fostered the development of an underground movement known as the Resistance. (Former president François Mitterrand, 1981–1995, played a role in the Resistance, although he also had held a position in the puppet regime at Vichy in the early 1940s.)

The Liberation of France began on June 6, 1944, when an Allied force that included U.S., British, and Canadian troops landed on the beaches of Normandy. By late August Paris itself was liberated. At the end of the war de Gaulle returned to Paris and created a provisional government, but he resigned in 1946 because the new Fourth Republic lacked a strong executive. The Fourth Republic (1946–1958) was a "regime of parties" as governments came and went on a regular basis. However, foreign policy setbacks finally doomed the Fourth Republic. The first major setback was at Dien Bien Phu in 1954, when the French military was defeated in Vietnam after a protracted struggle. At this time, too, insurrection occurred in Algeria as nationalists demanded sovereignty from French colonial rule. Complicating this conflict was the presence of 1 million French settlers in Algeria.

Establishment of the Fifth Republic and the Renewal of France

In this context de Gaulle was brought back to power in 1958. Mitterrand and others on the left charged that the general's return represented a *coup d'état*. De Gaulle created a new constitution for a Fifth Republic that would have a presidency with wide-ranging powers, and he began the process of granting independence to Algeria (1962) and other colonies. He shrewdly maintained ties with former colonies by providing them economic and military aid. In 1962 he sponsored a successful referendum to have the president of the Republic elected by direct universal suffrage. In the 1965 presidential contest he experienced an unexpectedly strong challenge from Mitterrand, who was backed by a noncommunist Federation of the Democratic and Socialist Left. In the mid-1960s de Gaulle took France out of NATO, including the military command of the alliance, and developed a nuclear arsenal for his nation to ensure its autonomy and importance on the world stage. Even though de Gaulle rode the crest of an economic boom that enhanced his popularity, a powerful student-worker revolt in 1968 almost toppled him. He resigned a year later after losing a minor battle in Parliament.

Never a formal ideology, Gaullism came to include elements of patriotism, populism, and conservative strongman rule. De Gaulle's tenure was followed by that of another gaullist, Georges Pompidou, and then by the presidency of Valéry Giscard d'Estaing from the center-right Union for French Democracy. Giscard won the 1974 contest over the socialist Mitterrand, his second attempt at the presidency. The energy crisis of the 1970s, coupled with the twin problems of unemployment and inflation, weakened Giscard's chances for re-election in 1981 when he faced the socialist candidate Mitterrand, who was backed by a Union of the Left that included the French Communist party. The 1981 triumph by the socialist Mitterrand and his supporters represented the first time that the left governed under the Fifth Republic, having been out of power for twenty-three years.

In the face of recession in the Western world, Mitterrand launched a spending program that exacerbated the French economic crisis. Consequently in the 1986 parliamentary election voters returned a conservative majority to Parliament, forcing Mitterrand to appoint a gaullist prime minister, the Paris mayor Jacques Chirac. This was the first time that *cohabitation* (a president co-existing with a prime minister of another political persuasion) had been attempted under the Fifth Republic. Yet in 1988 Mitterrand won re-election as president by a relatively wide margin over Chirac. During both his terms a new political development became worrisome: the rise of the extreme right-wing National Front, a chauvinistic, xenophobic (i.e., against foreigners), and anti-immigrant party led by Jean-Marie Le Pen. This party now captures roughly 15 percent of the vote in some national elections.

The socialist Mitterrand proved to be a good European while in office. He backed integration of the European Economic Community and understood the importance of anchoring Germany to the European Community, especially after the fall of the Berlin Wall in 1989 and the reunification of Germany. Although revelations surfaced late in his second term concerning his Vichy experience and Vichy contacts even during his presidency, Mitterrand will likely be remembered as a political modernizer who (1) led France in its experiment with alternating left- and right-wing governments, or *cohabitation,* and (2) helped to decentralize power in France, especially by granting more power to the regions and by easing state control over audiovisual (media) policy. Mitterrand served the longest term—fourteen years—of any president under the Fifth Republic.

In the 1995 presidential elections Jacques Chirac triumphed over the socialist candidate Lionel Jospin by a relatively small margin. Yet Chirac's honeymoon with the public proved short-lived. Worldwide protest emerged in the summer and fall of 1995 following his decision to re-launch French nuclear testing in the South Pacific, and serious nationwide protests erupted in November and December of the same year following the announcement of an austerity budget in the face of mounting deficits. Even worse, a frightening wave of terrorism struck France in the summer and fall of 1995; this was supposedly linked to French support of the military-backed government in Algeria opposed by Islamic fundamentalists. Early in 1996, Chirac announced that France would halt nuclear testing in French Polynesia and that the hexagon would rejoin the military command of NATO, strengthening the Atlantic Alliance in the post–Cold War world. Rejoining NATO permitted Chirac to make cuts in the French military budget and at the same time demand a stronger European pillar in the Atlantic Alliance.

Today, France seeks to maintain its place on the world's stage in the post–Cold War period, to safeguard its leadership role in the Common Market as the organization moves toward a common European currency, and to deal with shifting internal divisions that challenge centralized authority in Paris.

THE REGIONS

To understand contemporary France we must understand its regions. A study of the regions enables us to comprehend the complexities of the nation, why it has had such an illustrious history, and why it will continue to play an important role in our own era. But first it is instructive to discuss the origins of the regions and their significance within the larger French and European context.

Prior to the French Revolution of 1789, about thirty provinces constituted the area known as France. During the Revolution a new administrative unit, the *département* (department), was imposed on France by the government in Paris to break the power of the old historical provinces and to centralize authority. Today, metropolitan France is divided into ninety-five departments; there are four overseas departments as well: Guadeloupe, Martinique, French Guiana, and Réunion. In 1955 twenty-one regions were created, each comprised of a number of departments. (Corsica became the twenty-second region in 1970; this was done in part to appease growing separatist sentiment on the island.) The function of these new units was to produce regional development plans and to aid at the national level in minimizing regional imbalances, economic and otherwise.

In 1964 the regions became an important part of the nation's administrative structure, and more than simply a forum for discussing regional matters. At this time an administrator known as a prefect was nominated by the government in Paris to head each region, along with an advisory commission for regional economic development. This body provided input for the region and to Paris authorities on matters such as social and economic development and spatial planning. Thus, the administrative structure of local government included the regions, the departments, and municipalities.

During the 1970s the regions acquired more power. In July 1972 their political status was acknowledged when they were given the same status as a public authority; each region would be controlled by the prefect, who safeguarded the interests of the central government, and a newly created regional council nominated from the region's *communes* (municipalities) and departments. Each region was also assigned a small budget to aid both communes and departments with such matters as infrastructure. Yet its main function was still to design a regional development plan and advise the national government on developmental issues.

During the 1980s, following the election of a socialist president (François Mitterrand) and Parliament, the regions took on an even greater role. As the socialists made decentralization the cornerstone of their program, the regions' legal status was no longer under the direct control of Parisian authorities. Instead, regional councils would be elected through a system of proportional representation, and council members gained the right to elect the president of the regional council, who would assume the control once exercised by the prefect. Each region's budget also increased, as did its responsibilities for education, vocational training, housing, transportation, tourism, regional parks, strategic planning, and social and economic development. In addition, the regions were mandated to produce regional plans negotiated with the national government. They also acquired the ability to intervene directly in their own economic development, such as obtaining and administering regional grants to aid the creation of businesses and to assist businesses in difficulty.

Another development under the socialists was the emergence in the 1980s of contractual planning. The goal was to produce a combined investment program between the national government and each region over a five-year period. The regions and the national government in Paris were to be cognizant of each other's investment priorities, and the national government was obligated to include the regions' plans in the national plan (*contrat de plan État-région*). Under the first contract plan (1984–1988) the chief areas of investment were communication and transport; development of research and education; and revitalization of urban areas, agriculture, and related industries. Under the second contract plan (1989–1993) the program for each region differed, but major investment priorities included making improvements in infrastructure; enhancing research and vocational training; and promoting economic development and technology transfers.

Over time the regions have become a third level of local government, after the municipalities and departments. Their primary role, however, continues to be one of strategic planning and social and economic development.

The rise of the regions parallels the integration of the European Economic Community (EEC, Common Market). Both the formation of the regions and the Treaty of Rome, which launched the plan for an integrated Europe, emerged during the 1950s. Just as the regions have developed over the past decades, so too has the EEC; it now represents fifteen member states that constitute the largest trading bloc in the world. Within this European context four regional poles—one that is French-based, and another that includes part of France—are attracting significant investments and are demanding greater autonomy. The four poles are centered around Lyon; the triangle formed by Barcelona, Toulouse, and Montpellier; Milan; and Stuttgart. Lyon (capital of the Rhône-Alpes region of France) is building connections with Geneva and Turin and now does twice as much business with northern Italy than with Paris. The economic triangle between Barcelona, Toulouse (capital of the Midi-Pyrénées region), and Montpellier (capital of the Languedoc-Roussillon region) is becoming the crossroads of the Mediterranean.

Thus the regionalization of France has complemented the integration of

Europe, and the integration of Europe has strengthened the importance of the cities. Some observers might even wonder if we are witnessing on one level a return to "city-states" (an ancient form of organization that dates back to the Greeks) as Europe moves toward integration and national boundaries become less important. Obviously the development of the regions is important to France; but it has also strengthened the trend toward European integration, a process that has reinforced the logic of the regions.

IMAGES OF FRANCE

Given its long and colorful history, France as a nation conjures a number of images. For many people it is still a country of old churches, castles, historical monuments, and a grand cultural tradition. It is often viewed as a nation that has inspired artistic and literary sensibilities over the centuries, especially the revolutionary artistic movements of the nineteenth and twentieth centuries. During this period France was the home of Impressionism, post-Impressionism, fauvism, and cubism; as well as great works of literature, philosophy, and history that led to the post–World War II accomplishments of intellectual giants such as Jean-Paul Sartre, Albert Camus, Simone de Beauvoir, Fernand Braudel, Michel Foucault, and many others.

Although France has a traditional image, it also has an impressive modern image. For example, France produced the first supersonic jet passenger aircraft (the Concorde), the fastest train in the world (the TGV, or *train à grande vitesse*), a successful nuclear energy system, and an excellent telecommunications system. Furthermore, over the past few decades France has been the third major arms supplier in the world. Although one can still see signs of *la France profonde* (a rural and traditional France), one can also see a modern France. It is symbolized in many ways by the postmodern architectural projects (*les grand projets*) constructed in Paris during the 1980s and 1990s: the new Opera at the Bastille; the huge, functional, square arch at *La Défense*, or the new national library in the capital. Thus, France today is an interesting mix of the old and the new.

The nation's history, cultural heritage, and rural landscape suggest an image of the old, but its technological accomplishments and public services are forward-looking. This contrast is evident throughout the regions, whether one travels to rural areas or to the nation's leading cities such as Paris, Lyon, Marseille, Lille, and Bordeaux. Today approximately 76.4 percent of the French live in urban settings (municipalities of more than 2,000 inhabitants). Twelve cities have populations of more than 350,000. Moreover, the regions themselves add to the variety of France. Indeed, the French are fiercely attached to their regions, and each region has its own history and traditions—not to mention geography, climatic conditions, and in some cases even its own dialect.

Throughout history, France as a nation has exercised an influence far greater than its size. With a population of approximately 58 million and a surface area roughly 80 percent the size of Texas—but still the largest country in Western Europe—France is ranked as a medium-sized nation. It is the fourth or fifth leading industrial power in the world. Yet France is influential today not simply because of its economic power, nuclear arsenal, and foreign policy that emphasizes good relations with the Third World (especially former colonies), but because of its culture and cultural achievements. France is admired as one of the leading fashion centers of the world. Also, it produces large quantities of luxury goods such as perfumes, glassware, and leather articles. It is also a producer of films that refuses to be dominated by Hollywood, even though the number of American films shown in France is staggering. It has many admirers of its excellent culinary tradition and its superb wines and spirits. The nation's extensive tourism industry reinforces the notion—not just among Americans but among tourists the world over—that there is something special about *la France*.

Years ago when de Gaulle wrote his war memoirs, he said he could not envision France "without greatness." Many French men and women would probably agree with this assessment. The notion of a special mission for France is not just a reflection of a fiercely independent attitude but an assessment based on the nation's accomplishments over time. Both truth and myth reinforce the idea among the French and others that France has a significant role to play in European and world affairs.

SELECT BIBLIOGRAPHY

Ardagh, John. *France Today*. London: Penguin Books, 1988.

Bernstein, Richard. *Fragile Glory: A Portrait of France and the French*. New York: Alfred A. Knopf, 1990.

Braudel, Fernand. *The Identity of France*, 2 vols., trans. Reynolds Sian. New York: HarperCollins, 1990 and 1992.

Corbett, James. *Through French Windows: An Introduction to France in the Nineties*. Ann Arbor: University of Michigan Press, 1994.

Cordellier, Serge, et al., eds. *L'État de la France, 95–96*. Paris: La Découverte, 1995.

Dayries, Jean-Jacques, and Michèle Dayries. *La Régionalisation*. Paris: PUF (Que sais-je?), 1986.

Northcutt, Wayne, ed. *Historical Dictionary of the French Fourth and Fifth Republics, 1946–1991*. Westport, CT: Greenwood Press, 1992.

———. *Mitterrand: A Political Biography*. New York: Holmes & Meier, 1992.

Price, Roger. *A Concise History of France*. New York: Cambridge University Press, 1993.

Schmidt, Vivien. *Democratizing France: The Political and Administrative History of Decentralization*. New York: Cambridge University Press, 1990.

Tiersky, Ronald. *France in the New Europe: Changing Yet Steadfast.* Belmont, CA: Wadsworth Publishing, 1994.

Tuppen, John. "Regions," in Wayne Northcutt, ed., *Historical Dictionary of the French Fourth and Fifth Republics, 1946–1991.* Westport, CT: Greenwood Press, 1992.

Wright, Gordon. *France in Modern Times: From the Enlightenment to the Present.* New York: Norton, 1987.

ALSACE

Chapter 1

ALSACE

REGIONAL GEOGRAPHY

Located in eastern France and situated between the Vosges mountain range and the Rhine River, Alsace borders both Germany and Switzerland. It comprises only 5,111 square miles, or 1.5 percent of the surface area of metropolitan France (metropolitan France does not include the four overseas departments). The region is roughly 125 miles long and 31 miles wide. It is made up of two departments: Bas-Rhin (Lower Rhine) and Haut-Rhin (Upper Rhine). The regional capital is Strasbourg.

The geography is somewhat varied: it includes the Vosges mountains, the foothills, and the plain. Although the Rhine River is an important part of the geography of the region, so too is the Ill River, which parallels the Rhine. Many major towns in Alsace are situated along the Ill. Alsace—*Illsass* in the regional dialect—means "Country of the Ill."

The climate is continental, with wide-ranging temperature variations during the four seasons. Yet there is little difference between the climate in the north and the south; the Vosges mountains act as a barrier to Atlantic climatic conditions. The summer tends to be hot and dry; the autumn is often misty and beautiful; the winter is dry and cold; and the spring is often mild and bright. The climate is such that both tobacco and wine are produced; in fact, Alsace is the most important producer of tobacco in France.

HISTORY

Alsace is rich in history. The region was inhabited by the Celts as early as 1000 B.C. The area came under Roman control in the first century B.C.

when Julius Caesar conquered the region. The Merovingians Christianized the region by the fifth century, and it was part of the Holy Roman Empire from roughly A.D. 800 to the 1600s. During the Middle Ages the city of Strasbourg attracted a sizable Jewish community; yet Jews periodically suffered violent attacks and expulsions. From 1359 to 1791, for instance, they were forbidden to live in Strasbourg or spend the night there. Consequently, many Jews located in the villages surrounding the city (today the Jewish community in Strasbourg numbers approximately 15,000). During the Reformation, Protestantism made strong gains in Alsace—especially in Strasbourg. During the Wars of Religion (1562–1598) and the Thirty Years War (1618–1646), many Alsatian towns caught between Protestant and Catholic forces turned to France. In 1648 the region was officially attached to France by Louis XIV under the Treaty of Westphalia.

Wars during the nineteenth and twentieth centuries saw Alsace changing hands between France and Germany. Enjoying considerable autonomy by the time of the French Revolution in 1789, Alsatians felt attached more to France than to Germany; some upper-class Alsatians were even beginning to adopt the French language. Yet following the Franco-Prussian War of 1870–1871 (one of the wars through which Prussia's Otto von Bismarck achieved German unification), Alsace and part of Lorraine were handed over to the newly united Germany under the Treaty of Frankfort (1871). Not only did France have to cede this territory to Germany, but it also had to pay an indemnity amounting to 5 billion francs. According to some estimates, one-tenth of the region's inhabitants left Alsace following German annexation. For many who remained, German annexation was not popular.

World War I brought changes to Alsace. During the war, Alsatians were conscripted into the German army and forced to fight their French brothers and sisters. Alsatians in France were viewed as enemy aliens and were held in internment camps. Following Germany's defeat in World War I, Alsace was returned to France. Subsequent French efforts to Frenchify the region led to a powerful home-rule movement in Alsace.

A second annexation of Alsace by Germany occurred at the start of World War II in 1940, when France fell to Hitler's German war machine. Hitler imposed a harsh Germanization program on Alsace, banning the Alsatian language and jailing those caught speaking French.

The post–World War II period has been somewhat kinder to the region. At the end of the war, Alsace reverted back to France. However, conflicts erupted among those who returned to the region and confronted compatriots suspected of collaborating with the Germans. Given the region's central position in Europe, efforts were undertaken to make Alsace the symbol of Franco-German and European cooperation. In 1949 Strasbourg was made the seat of the Council of Europe and later was chosen as the site of the European Parliament.

RECENT POLITICS

Alsace is committed to European integration and has seen a swing toward the right in recent years. More than any other region in France, Alsace supported the Maastricht Treaty in the September 1992 referendum on the treaty to expand European integration and to forge an economic, monetary, and political union (including a common currency and a central bank by the end of the decade). Only 52 municipalities out of 894 in Alsace voted against the treaty, with most of these located in the southern agricultural zone.

The parliamentary elections of March 1993 confirmed the swing to the right that had emerged in the 1992 regional elections: the traditional right—the gaullist Rally for the Republic (RPR) and the Union for French Democracy (UDF)—captured fourteen of the sixteen seats from the region and approximately 46.6 percent of the vote. The ruling Socialist party (PS) lost all three of its seats to Parliament from Alsace and won only 10 percent of the vote. The decline of the PS was related to the long tenure in office of President François Mitterrand (a socialist elected in 1981 and re-elected in 1988), the inability of socialist governments to reduce unemployment, and a number of scandals that touched high-level socialist politicians. The other leftist party in the election, the French Communist party (PCF), captured less than 3 percent of the vote in the 1993 parliamentary elections. In the same election the anti-immigrant and chauvinistic National Front (FN) garnered 14.7 percent of the vote, down from the 17.2 percent it won in the 1992 regional contest. The Ecologists, a growing political power in eastern France owing to the pollution of the Rhine River and the high concentration of industry in the region, won 12.8 percent in the 1993 contest.

Then, in the 1995 presidential elections, the right-wing candidates won by a large margin in the first round of a two-round contest over leftist candidates. Moreover, the extremist National Front candidate Jean-Marie Le Pen won approximately 25 percent of the vote in the region during the first round, far above his 15 percent national average. In the second round the gaullist Jacques Chirac, mayor of Paris at the time, won both departments in the region over the socialist candidate Lionel Jospin. Chirac was also victorious on the national level. However, in the municipal elections of June 1995 the socialist Catherine Trautmann won the mayor's office in Strasbourg in the first round of voting. (Trautmann is the first and only woman mayor of a town of more than 100,000 inhabitants.) The socialists, too, won the city hall in Mulhouse, whereas the gaullists were victorious in Colmar. In municipal elections throughout France the national left-right balance remained largely unchanged, with the right (excluding the extreme right) winning a net gain of five towns. Thus, in general, the Socialist party in recent years has lost strength in Alsace, as it has throughout France, and the right has emerged as a major political force. At the same time, the region has witnessed a strong advance by the National Front and the Ecologists.

POPULATION

Over the past two decades the region has experienced a small population increase, climbing from 1,517,000 in 1975 to 1,646,000 in 1993, giving Alsace 2.9 percent of the national population. The region's birthrate is 1.74, approximating the national average of 1.73. Population density is almost twice the national average of 105.7 people per square kilometer, or 171.23 per square mile. In Alsace in 1993 the population density was 198.8 per square kilometer, or 322.05 per square mile.

In some ways the population of the region conforms to national averages. Those 60 years of age and older make up 17.5 percent of the population, whereas those age 19 and younger comprise 26.9 percent (19.7% and 26.8%, respectively, are the national averages). The immigrant population, however, is 7.8 percent, slightly higher than the 6.3 percent national average. On the other hand, the urban population is close to the average for all of France, with 74 percent of the inhabitants of Alsace residing in urban settings (76.4% for France as a whole).

Life expectancy in Alsace is lower than the national average. Alsatians can expect to live 75.7 years, almost two full years below the national average. Approximately 25.1 percent of all households in the region are single-person households.

Although educational levels in Alsace conform to the national average, the percentage of the work force in industry is above national norms. About 10.5 percent of Alsace's population possess a high school diploma, and 10.8 percent hold advanced degrees. Only 2.4 percent of the work force is employed in agriculture, well below the 5.3 percent national average. Yet 35.6 percent of the work force in this eastern region is found in industry, well above the national average of 26.9 percent. The service sector makes up 62 percent of the work force, approximately 6 percent below the national total. In recent years unemployment has been well below the national average, now roughly 7 percent to 8 percent as compared to 12.1 percent for the nation. Among women, unemployment is slightly higher in the region (8.1%) than among men.

ECONOMY

Although Alsace constitutes only 1.5 percent of the surface area of France and the region's population is small (less than 3% of the national total), it possesses strong potential for future development, especially because it borders prosperous areas of Germany and Switzerland (Karlsruhe and Basel) and is located at the hub of the European Common Market. Today, Alsace ranks among the thirty most prosperous regions of the Common Market in terms of gross domestic product per capita and ranks as the third most prosperous region in France. It is estimated that 25 percent of the Alsatians who work in industry are employed by firms that are dependent on foreign capital, with four out of ten working for French-owned companies.

Being situated between two dynamic poles of development across the border is both an advantage and a possible handicap for the region. It is an advantage because the location aids the general prosperity of Alsatians: in this regard, the work force expanded by 6,900 workers each year between 1982 and 1990. Unemployment in the region now hovers between a relatively low 7 to 8 percent. However, the location is a potential disadvantage because inhabitants are increasingly crossing the borders into Germany and Switzerland to find higher-paying jobs. In 1991, for instance, 7.3 percent of the Alsatian work force crossed the frontier daily to travel to their jobs. In the department of the Haut-Rhin, 16 percent of the work force between 25 and 29 years of age cross the border to work.

Because of its location and the presence of foreign capital in the region, Alsace is sometimes viewed as a regional laboratory for European integration. The internationalization of industrial development in the region and the significant portion of the work force that crosses the border to work make this region worthy of study as European integration advances. Indeed, Alsace might find itself as a region without frontiers. Even today the region's economy is closely tied to European and international economic trends. In recent years, a growing demand for employment in the region and industrial layoffs (e.g., the auto maker Peugeot laid off 775 workers in January 1993) suggest that Alsace may no longer be isolated from the general economic trends affecting most of France.

Industry and retail dominate the economy, with each sector comprising approximately 30 percent. Nonretail services represent 15.4 percent of the regional economy, commerce 12.5 percent, construction 5.1 percent, and agriculture and fishing a mere 3 percent.

The three largest towns in the region are Strasbourg with 252,338 inhabitants, Mulhouse with 108,357, and Colmar with 63,498. Roughly 31 percent of the work force is centered in Strasbourg, 15.8 percent in Mulhouse, and 7.1 percent in Colmar. The four largest employers are Rhône Poulenc Chemicals, the Department of the Haut-Rhin, Electricity of France, and Pechiney Rhenalu (aluminum, chemicals).

CULTURE

The culture and traditions of the region reflect Alsatian, French, and European influences. The long history of this contested border region, where the Alsatian dialect has been spoken for centuries, has given the area a unique character and flavor. Alsatian is an Alemmanic dialect of High German that is similar to dialects in neighboring Switzerland and Germany. The dialect has no official written form, and the spoken form varies from area to area. Since the end of World War II the dialect has declined in popularity, owing in part to the rejection of the Nazi occupation and takeover during the war years and a closer identification with France. The region's border location, its changing of hands between France and Germany during the nineteenth and twentieth centuries, and its central position in the Common Market have given the region a European identity. Moreover, Strasbourg, the commercial and administrative center, has become a symbol of Europe—the seat of the Council of Europe, the European Parliament, and the International Court of Human Rights. Thus, in Alsace one can feel Alsatian, French, and European. Some say that Alsace is the most non-French region in France, with its dialect, cuisine, architecture, and history giving it a special atmosphere.

Although Alsace has produced relatively few significant writers, it has attracted a number of well-known figures in and outside the world of literature. One was **Johannes Gutenberg** (1390–1468) of Mainz, Germany, who invented the printing press while residing in Strasbourg between 1434 and 1448. The famous writer, philosopher, and critic **François-Marie Voltaire** (1694–1778) spent a year in Strasbourg in 1753–1754 and criticized the people and area in his *Lettres d'Alsace*. The writer and poet **Johann Wolfgang von Goethe** (1749–1832) also lived for a year in Strasbourg as a university student in 1770–1771. While there he fell in love with a young woman from a nearby village; the relationship, however, did not last. Nevertheless, he mentions this love affair in his memoirs and fondly remembers his lover in one of his famous poems, *Willkommen und Abscheid*.

During the French Revolution the French national anthem was written and composed in Strasbourg by **Claude-Joseph Rouget de Lisle** (1760–1836), a poet and musician who was a captain in the French army. Supposedly the mayor of Strasbourg wanted a rousing tune that the volunteers of the Army of the Rhine could sing while marching. Known first as the *"Chant de guerre de l'Armée du Rhine,"* it became known as *"La Marseillaise"* when revolutionary volunteers from Marseille in the south of France sang the anthem in Paris.

The nineteenth and twentieth centuries brought writers to the region and saw the emergence of native writers as well. The great writer **Victor Hugo** (1802–1885) stayed in Strasbourg in 1839 and included a chapter on the city in his travel book *Le Rhin*. The American poet **Henry Wadsworth Longfellow** (1807–1882) visited Strasbourg in the 1830s and wrote a poem about the city's cathedral, as well as other poems about the region. In the nineteenth century, too, **Emile Erckmann** (1822–1899), in collaboration with **Alexandre Chatrian**, produced stories concerning Alsatian life. Most of their books were published prior to the Franco-Prussian War and are not permeated with anti-German sentiment. Perhaps the best-known book published by Erckmann and Chatrian was *L'Ami Fritz* (1864), a story about a not-so-confirmed bachelor who eventually falls in love and marries. At the dawn of the twentieth century René Bazin (1853–1932), a professor of law at the Catholic university of Angers and a right-wing traditionalist, resided in Strasbourg and completed a novel about an Alsatian family and their divided loyalties toward France and Germany during the period of annexation.

In the contemporary period there has been a revival of interest in village life and traditions. Two Alsatian novelists, **Jean Egen** and **André Weckmann** (b. 1924), try to capture the charm and traditions of Alsatian villages. One of Egen's books, *Les Tilleuls de Lauterbach* (The Lime Trees of Lauterbach), was also made into a successful television series. The book describes life in the Florival valley northwest of Mulhouse. Alsace has also produced the cartoonist and satirist **Tomi Ungerer** (b. 1931), who was born in Strasbourg but later took up residence in Ireland.

An important figure in Alsatian folklore is the stork, a bird that has become a symbol for the region itself. Given the near extinction of the stork in recent years, Alsatians have developed centers to hatch and to raise them in order to ensure a permanent population of the popular birds.

The region is also known for its cuisine and great wines. Food in Alsace is very rich, including numerous pork products such as saveloy (a highly seasoned dry sausage), liver sausage, Strasbourg sausage, black pudding, and Alsatian *foie gras* (livers of specially fed geese). Included among the traditional dishes are *pâté de foie gras, tarte à l'oignon, choucroute garnie* (sauerkraut cooked with white wine sauce and topped with ham and sausages), *baeckaoffe* (a casserole of potatoes, marinated beef, pork, and lamb), and *coq au Riesling* (chicken cooked in a white wine sauce). Near Strasbourg one finds *flammenkueke,* a tart made with onions or fresh fruit. Egg noodles often accompany sauced dishes, such as stews and chicken braised in Riesling (a variety of wine). Riesling is also included in a freshwater fish stew known as *matelote.* Fried carp is another traditional dish. North of Strasbourg, springtime asparagus is a specialty. Popular cheeses found in the region include the Germanic Muenster and the Swiss Emmenthal. A favorite dessert is *kugelhopf,* a yeasty raisin cake; this is sometimes followed by *eau-de-vie* (brandy) flavored with fruit or berries. Alsatians, similar to the Germans and the Swiss Germans, tend to have dinner earlier than most other residents of France; restaurants open at 6:00 or 6:30 P.M. instead of 7:30 or later in other places.

Other well-known products of Alsace are wine, brandy, and beer. The region is considered the third most important wine-producing area in France (after Bordeaux and Burgundy). Wine has been made here since A.D. 300. Today the region produces primarily white wines noted for their freshness and lightening effect on the heavy local cuisine. The four most important grape varieties are Riesling (known for its subtlety), Gewurztraminer (rather pungent), Tokay-Pinot Gris (high in alcohol, and robust), and Muscat (somewhat sweet). A premium wine made from a blend of grapes is Edelzwicker. Wine from the region is usually sold in distinctive tall, slender bottles. The area's *route du vin* (wine route) is a popular attraction for locals and tourists; it begins near Strasbourg and continues southward toward Colmar and Thann. Alsace also produces a variety of brandies (kirsch is quite popular) and beer. In fact, the region produces one-half of France's beer. A recipe for a popular dessert is found below.

TARTE AUX POMMES À L'ALSACIENNE
(Alsatian Apple Tart)

Homemade pastry dough or unbaked prepared deep-dish pie crust	⅓ cup sugar
	¼ tsp. vanilla extract
	¼ tsp. cinnamon
1 lb. tart apples	¾ cup heavy cream
4 egg yolks	

Preheat oven to 425°F. If using homemade pastry dough, butter a 10-inch tart (flan) pan or pie plate, roll out the dough into a 12-inch circle, and line the pan with it. If using an unbaked prepared pie crust, defrost before using. Peel, quarter, and core the apples. Slice each quarter into four slices. Arrange slices evenly over the pastry in overlapping circles. Bake for 15 minutes. Meanwhile, combine the egg yolks, sugar, vanilla, and cinnamon and beat until well mixed. Beat in the cream. After removing the tart from the oven, cover the apples with this mixture and bake for another 35 minutes or until the apples are tender. Serve warm. Serves 6.

ARCHITECTURE AND NOTEWORTHY SITES

Many of the attractive traditional houses in Alsace date from the sixteenth, seventeenth, and eighteenth centuries. In the countryside, dwellings are often clustered. Half-timbered houses on stone foundations are quite common in the towns and countryside; however, stone is the most common building material in the towns. Rural houses are often separated by passages, forming street-villages or cluster-villages. Roofs are steep, usually with an overhang, and covered with a flat brown beaver-tail tile. During the German occupation in the twentieth century, several grandiose building projects were undertaken, such as the railway station and *Place de la République* in Strasbourg.

STRASBOURG (pop. 252,338), whose name in German means "City of

Roads," is the cultural and intellectual capital of Alsace. For centuries its arteries of roads, railways, and waterways have made it a link between northern and central Europe and the Mediterranean. The city is located just a few kilometers away from the Rhine River. Some have said that Strasbourg, of all European towns, is where one can see Europe's past, present, and future. It has an excellent university, founded in the seventeenth century; today nearly 50,000 university students study in Strasbourg. The cathedral, an important historical monument, was constructed between the eleventh and fifteenth centuries from rose-colored Vosges sandstone. Until the nineteenth century it was the tallest monument in Christendom, 466 feet high. The *Musée d'Art Modern* possesses an excellent collection of paintings and sculpture by artists such as Marc Chagall (1887–1985), Paul Klee (1879–1940), and Jean Arp (1887–1966), as well as some Impressionists' works. The *Musée de l'Oeuvre Notre Dame* has an outstanding collection of Romanesque, Gothic, and Renaissance sculpture. The *Musée Alsacien* displays artifacts from Alsatian life over the centuries. The modern *Palais de l'Europe* is the headquarters of the Council of Europe and the meeting place of the European Parliament. The city is also the site of one of the region's largest fairs, the Strasbourg Christmas Market, held during the month of December. During the summer months Strasbourg sponsors an International Festival of Music.

MULHOUSE (pop. 108,357) is important to the region because of its traditional industries, such as textiles and potash mining, and its dynamic cultural life. In addition to its *Fine Arts Museum* there is the *Musée Français du Chemin de Fer* (the largest railway museum in Europe), the *Musée National de l'Automobile,* and the *Musée de l'Impression sur Étoffes* (a museum for textile painting).

COLMAR (pop. 63,498) is a picturesque town that serves as the capital of its department. It is located 47 miles from both Strasbourg and Basel, Switzerland. The center of town has cobblestone streets and restored Alsatian buildings from the late Middle Ages to the Renaissance. The *Musée de Unterlinden,* with its famous Issenheim altarpiece (considered one of the most dramatic works of art ever created), is found in Colmar. The *Musée Bartholdi* features the life and work of a native of Colmar, Fréderic August Bartholdi (1834–1904) the sculptor. (Bartholdi gave New York City the Statue of Liberty.) In August the town hosts the Regional Wine Fair of Alsace, which attracts thousands of people.

RIQUEWIHR (pop. 1,075) is described as a "pearl" amid the vineyards that surround it. The eccentric Dukes of Wurtenberg owned the village for centuries. The village itself and the sixteenth- and seventeenth-century wine growers' houses are well preserved. High-quality Riesling wine is produced in Riquewihr.

MOUNT SAINTE-ODILE, located in the department of Bas-Rhin, is the patronal shrine of Alsace. It was probably a sacred place even before the rise of Christianity in the region. Today it is a pilgrimage site for the pious and for tourists. Sainte-Odile, born in the seventh century, was the daughter of a cruel duke of Alsace who eventually became resigned to the divine will interpreted by his daughter. She was canonized in the eleventh century and in 1946 was proclaimed the patron saint of Alsace.

THE MAGINOT LINE, named after Minister of War André Maginot (1929–1931), is a subterranean defense network built during the 1930s. It stretched from the Swiss border and along the Franco-German frontier to Belgium. Although it was thought that the Line would offer France protection from future invasions, at the start of World War II Hitler simply went around the Maginot Line by circling through Belgium and then attacked the Line from the rear. One can visit sections of the Maginot Line in Alsace and Lorraine. In Alsace, it is possible to visit it at Schoenenbourg, about 28 miles north of Strasbourg.

SELECT BIBLIOGRAPHY

Denis, M. N., and C. Veltman. *Le Déclin du dialecte alsacien.* Strasbourg: Presses Universitaires de Strasbourg, 1989.

Reitel, François. "Alsace," in Andre Gamblin, ed., *La France dans ses régions,* vol. 1. Paris: SEDES, 1994.

Vogler, B., et al. *L'Alsace, une histoire.* Strasbourg: Oberlin, 1990.

Chapter 2

AQUITAINE

REGIONAL GEOGRAPHY

Aquitaine is located in the most southwestern portion of France and stretches from the Pyrenees mountains along the Spanish border in the south to the Poitou-Charentes region in the north. The western edge of the region borders the Atlantic Ocean. Aquitaine comprises 25,499 square miles; it constitutes 7.6 percent of the surface area of metropolitan France, making it the third-largest region. Aquitaine includes five departments: Dordogne, Gironde, Landes, Lot-et-Garonne, and Pyrénées-Atlantiques. The Gironde and the Landes are two of the largest departments in France. Aquitaine has been referred to as the French "Far West." Its capital is Bordeaux.

The geography varies from broad sand beaches along the coast, to fertile wine-growing areas around Bordeaux, to large forested areas in the south, to agricultural areas in the Dordogne. The highest elevations are found near the Pyrenees and the Spanish border, where the region rises to 6,500 feet. The Gironde estuary, formed by the Dordogne and the Garonne Rivers, connects Bordeaux to the Atlantic. Bordeaux is both an ocean port and a river port, and it serves as the capital and dominating city in the region.

The climate is mild with a relatively warm and early spring. The coastline west of Bordeaux, the Côte d'Argent (Silver Coast), obtained its name because in the spring there is a perceptible haze that softens both the contours and the colors of the seascape. In autumn, the period of the grape harvest, the days are quite beautiful. Along the coast the winter is mild; inland the weather is far from severe. The French Basque section in the Pyrénées-

AQUITAINE

ATLANTIC
OCEAN

Lesparre-
Médoc

Nontron

PÉRIGUEUX

DORDOGNE

Gironde

Blaye

BORDEAUX

Libourne

Les Eyzies-de-Tayac

Sarlat

Dordogne

Garonne

GIRONDE

Bergerac

Arcachon

Marmande

Langon

Villeneuve-
sur-Lot

LANDES

LOT-ET-
GARONNE

Lot

AGEN

Nérac

*MONT-DE-
MARSAN*

Dax

Bayonne
Biarritz

St.-Jean-de-Luz

Hendaye

PAU

PYRÉNÉES-
ATLANTIQUES

Oloron-
Ste-Marie

SPAIN

Atlantiques is known for its summer showers, which are particularly common in the western portion of the Basque area.

HISTORY

During the first millennium B.C., Iberians from Spain settled between the Garonne River and the Pyrenees. In the sixth and fifth centuries B.C., invading Celts forced the Iberians to move back to the mountainous south. Then, in 56 B.C., Julius Caesar's armies won a major campaign against the Celts. By the first century A.D., Roman colonization was well under way in the area. A brilliant cultural elite flourished here in the fourth century; this group included the grammarian and poet Ausonius (309–394).

A massive wave of barbarian invasions in the fifth century saw the Emperor Honorius ceding the Visigoths an empire in the southwest, where Toulouse served as the capital. However, in the sixth century the Frankish King Clovis defeated the Visigoth Alaric, and Aquitaine became part of France. In the mid-seventh century an alliance between the Aquitaines and the Iberian Vascons led to the restoration of the kingdom of Toulouse, ruled at the time by the dukes of Aquitaine. In the eighth century Charles Martel, viceroy of the kings of the Franks, defeated Arab invaders at Poitiers (in 732). Martel occupied the Bordeaux region and his son, Pepin the Short, completed the conquest of Aquitaine. In 780 Charlemagne made Aquitaine a kingdom for his son, Louis the Pious.

Anarchy spread throughout the region in the tenth century, and it broke up into independent baronies. Monastic orders spread during the eleventh century when a period of security returned. This development led to clearing the land and increasing agricultural production. A large number of pilgrims traveled through the region on their way to visit the shrine of St. Jacques de Compostelle in Spain. The tomb of the martyred apostle St. James (Santiago in Spanish) is found near present-day Santiago de Compostela, which became a focus of faith for Spain and other European countries, including France.

After the area came under the control of the counts of Poitiers, the marriage of Eleanor of Aquitaine brought the region into contact and rivalry with England. Eleanor, the sole heiress and daughter of Duke Guillaume X, married Louis VII, King of France. When he repudiated her in 1152 she married Henry Plantagenet, heir to the English throne who held Anjou, Touraine, and Normandy. Meanwhile, King Henry ceded Aquitaine to his son, Richard the Lionheart. Following the deaths of Richard and Eleanor a period of instability returned to Aquitaine. King Henry III appointed Gascon stewards to return order to the region; this they did with assistance from the Church. Meanwhile, the king of England granted significant liberties to towns in the region in order to consolidate his control.

During a period of relative peace, 1250–1350, numerous walled towns, or *bastides,* emerged in the region.

Early in the Hundred Years War, the son of Edward III of England defeated French forces at Poitiers in 1356. Following his death the city government of Bordeaux and the Bordeaux (Guyenne) parliament emerged as the true centers of power in the region. In 1451 Bordeaux recognized the suzerainty of the French king but one year later rallied to the English army sent by Henry VI. The French King Charles VII defeated the English in 1453 at the battle of Castillon, thereby ending three centuries of English domination and conflict with France over the control of Aquitaine.

The sixteenth century witnessed political centralization and religious protest. When Francis I came to the throne in 1515, he attempted to strengthen the monarchy by centralizing state power. Beginning roughly in 1550 Protestantism made numerous converts and religious wars raged, even though the mayor of Bordeaux tried to serve as a peacemaker. The Edict of Nantes (1598) issued by Henry IV, a native of Aquitaine, helped to restore religious peace. However, the subsequent revocation of the edict by Louis XIV led to a large emigration of the Protestant middle class (the Huguenots).

The eighteenth century was one of expansion and prosperity as well as challenges to centralized authority in Paris. During this century vineyards and maize cultivation grew, and new farmland was cultivated. Simultaneously the wine trade with England increased, as did the slave trade. The Enlightenment philosopher Montesquieu (1689–1755), known for his tracts on the separation of powers, was a member of the Bordeaux parliament. In 1787 the Bordeaux parliament refused to register royal edicts, indicating discontent with the monarchy. The revolt of this parliament and other regional parliaments was one of the first stages of the French Revolution of 1789. During this time the revolutionary government in Paris divided France into departments, creating a new administrative structure to break the power of the old provincial areas. Moderates among this group were called *Girondins,* because their most noted speakers came from the Gironde (Bordeaux) area. The Gironde represented for the most part the shipping interests and the upper middle class. When Napoleon came to power in 1789 and subsequently introduced the Continental System (1806) to blockade trade with Great Britain, Bordeaux's maritime trade suffered.

At the end of Napoleon's reign when the Bourbon monarchy was restored, many of Aquitaine's politicians were either liberals or moderates. The July Monarchy of Louis-Philippe (1830–1848) found ready acceptance. The Second Empire of Napoleon III (1852–1870) ushered in economic change, with many landowners focusing on vineyard cultivation. Aquitaine in general welcomed the beginning of the Third Republic following the Franco-Prussian War of 1870. Although the economy and the political scene looked bright for Aquitaine, its vineyards were destroyed by an outbreak of phylloxera. The disease in the vineyards stimulated a rural exodus.

Since World War I, various governments have tried to encourage industrial development in Aquitaine. This effort was more successful after World War II, however. Agriculture has changed drastically in the region, with crops other than the grape playing a role in agricultural production. New crops include maize, vegetables, and fruit.

RECENT POLITICS

Aquitaine has recently expressed divisions over an important vote on the 1992 Maastricht Treaty, which called for accelerated integration of the European Economic Community (EEC). Of the region's total population, 50.74 percent voted against the treaty. The departments closest to the Spanish border, Pyrénées-Atlantiques and Landes, voted in favor of it. The heavily agricultural Dordogne voted an overwhelmingly 56.86 percent against the measure. Nevertheless, the treaty was approved by a small margin on the national level, and Aquitaine and France are now committed to fuller integration with the EEC.

Legislative elections in 1993 saw the triumph of the right, which won twenty-six seats in Parliament as compared to a mere four for the left (the socialists). Among the right, the gaullist Rally for the Republic (RPR) dominated by winning sixteen of the twenty-six seats captured by the right. An embarrassing defeat for the Socialist party (PS) was the re-election failure of Roland Dumas, friend and former minister of foreign affairs under the presidency of the socialist François Mitterrand (1981–1995).

In the 1995 presidential elections, three of the five departments—Dordogne, Landes, and Gironde—voted for the left in the first round of the contest. Also in the first round the right-wing extremist Jean-Marie Le Pen (representing the National Front) captured 9.8 percent of the vote, below his 15 percent national average. In the second round the departments of Dordogne, Landes, and Gironde gave a majority of their votes to the socialist Lionel Jospin, with the gaullist Jacques Chirac winning Lot-et-Garonne and Pyrénées-Atlantiques. Chirac won the presidential contest.

The capital of the region (Bordeaux) has been the fiefdom of the gaullist Jacques-Chaban Delmas (b. 1915), who was first elected mayor in 1947. He served as prime minister from 1969 to 1972 and then as president of the National Assembly in 1958–1969, 1978–1981, and 1986–1988. In the 1995 municipal elections, however, another gaullist took control of Bordeaux: Alain Juppé was elected mayor. Juppé was appointed prime minister of France under President Chirac.

POPULATION

Although the region's population has increased since 1975, rising from 2,550,000 to 2,841,000 in 1993 (making Aquitaine the sixth most populous region), it is underpopulated as compared to the nation as a whole. For example, the population density is a mere 64.3 inhabitants per square kilometer (104.16 per square mile), as compared to the national average of 105.7 per square kilometer (171.23 per square mile). Moreover, the rural population is in decline, especially in the mountainous area. Aquitaine's birthrate is 1.58, well below the 1.73 national average. The region's population is centered around three urban poles: Bordeaux, Pau, and Bayonne.

Compared to the national norm, Aquitaine's population is elderly. Those 60 years of age and older comprise 23.3 percent of the region's population (19.7 percent is the national average). On the other hand, those age 19 and younger make up 24.3 percent of the population (26.8% is the national average). Immigrants represent 4.1 percent of the total population, below the 6.3 percent national average.

The urban population is well below the average for the nation, with 65.5 percent residing in urban settings (76.4% is the national average). Residents of Aquitaine can expect to live 77.3 years, approximately the national norm. Roughly 26.1 percent of all households are single-person households, slightly below the national average.

Educational levels in Aquitaine approximate national averages with one exception, but the composition of the work force does not mirror that of the nation. Approximately 10.3 percent of the region's population possess only a high school degree (10.5% for the nation) and 10 percent hold an advanced degree (11.2% for the nation). The agricultural population of Aquitaine is large as compared to national averages: 8.5 percent work in agriculture as compared to 5.3 percent for France as a whole. The industrial work force is less than the national average: 25.3 percent work in industry (26.9% is the national average). The service sector is also slightly smaller than the national average: 66.2 percent work in this sector in Aquitaine (67.8% for the nation). Unemployment runs at approximately 13.6 percent, slightly above the national rate, which is a little over 12 percent. As in many other regions of France, unemployment among women is several percentage points above the national rate. In Aquitaine, 14.7 percent of the female work force is unemployed.

ECONOMY

The region's economy is relatively diverse. Approximately 7 percent is derived from agriculture and fishing, with vegetables and animal husbandry playing an important role. Yet the pillars of Aquitaine's agricultural production are maize and quality wine. Agriculture is oriented toward the exterior: 35 percent of the region's agricultural exports are in the agro-food sector, where wine is a major component.

Industry has been slow to progress in the region, but in recent years it has developed progressively. To the traditional industries—lumber and shoes—have been added more modern industries such as aeronautics, chemicals, and pharmaceuticals. The defense policy of France under President Chirac will have an important bearing on the continued development or decline of the region's aeronautical industry. One reflection of the strong weight of tradition in the region is the large number of artisans in Aquitaine: there are 20 artisans for every 1,000 inhabitants (15 is the national average).

The region's service sector is developing, mainly owing to new urban industries and activities and to the growth of tourism along the region's long coastline. In 1990 six jobs out of ten were found in the service sector as compared to two out of ten in industry, one out of ten in agriculture, and less than one out of ten in the building trades. Consequently, jobs have increased in the food, hotel, and restaurant business. Between 1982 and 1990 the work force increased by 5 percent, with 1,067,000 people working (i.e., 53% of the population engaged in the work force). Between 1982 and 1990 the number of salaried positions jumped 10 percent in the region. The geographical areas hurt most by unemployment have been those surrounding Bordeaux and the southern and rural part of the region.

According to some, Aquitaine itself does not exist; only Bordeaux exists. After all, Bordeaux is the dominating metropolis of the region. Its population is 210,336 (the greater Bordeaux population is 696,364), whereas the next two largest cities have much smaller populations: Pau (82,157) and Bayonne (40,051). Moreover, 30.1 percent of all jobs are located in Bordeaux; only 6.3 percent are in Pau, and 6.2 percent in Bayonne. The four largest employers in Aquitaine are Ford France, Elf Aquitaine, Turbomeca, and Aérospatiale.

The character of Aquitaine is changing, especially with the introduction of more modern industries. Yet future prosperity and further economic development may well depend on several factors. First, the defense policy of the French govenment will certainly influence the region's economy, as well as that of other regions tied directly or indirectly to the military-industrial complex. Second, the state of the world's wine market and the intensity of international competition will undoubtedly affect the region's economy. The Bordeaux wine region, roughly 625 square miles, produces roughly 500 million bottles of wine each year and includes some of the world's best vintages, such as Château-Lafite-Rothchild, Château-Latour, Château Margeaux, Château-Mouton-Rothchild, Château-Haut-Brion, and Château-Yquem. Wine is an essential part of the region's economy and image. Third, Spain's entry into the EEC in 1986 has increased trade opportunities and challenges for neighboring Aquitaine. Like other parts of France, Aquitaine is in the process of change and is developing increasing contacts with the rest of France, Europe, and the world. With the high-speed train known as the TGV (*train à grande vitesse*) serving Bordeaux, the capital of the region is less than three hours from Paris.

The airport at the coastal resort of Biarritz serves the Spanish interior as well. Thus, Aquitaine is a region with a traditional character (especially its agricultural sector and wine industry) but is becoming more modern and confronting the advantage and disadvantages of international competition.

CULTURE

Aquitaine contains the French Basque country, an area that gives this region a special character. The Basque country is located north of the Pyrenees, and the western portion borders the Atlantic. Its two main cities are Bayonne, the cultural capital, and the affluent beach resort of Biarritz.

The early history of the Basques is unknown. Early in the sixth century they took over southwestern France; in the tenth century they converted to Christianity. Basque nationalism flourished in the area before, during, and after the Spanish Civil War of 1936–1939. During the civil war, German aircraft supporting Francisco Franco's Fascist movement bombed the city of Guernica in 1937, a symbol of Basque nationalism. During Franco's reign as dictator (1939–1975), a number of Spanish Basques and anti-government guerrillas took refuge in France. Even today, some Basques wish to see a Basque state carved out of the Basque areas in France and Spain. A group known as Basque Homeland and Liberty (ETA), which has sponsored terrorist activities, agitates for the creation of an independent Basque state.

Both the language and the cuisine of the Basque country are distinctive. In earlier centuries the Basque language withstood the onslaught of Latin, the only language in southwestern Europe to do so. Until the Middle Ages it was an unwritten language. The first book printed in Basque appeared in 1545. The food is also unique. One of the basic ingredients in Basque cooking are red chilies. Also characteristic is goose fat, which is used in many dishes.

A popular sport in the Basque area is *pelote,* a game played with a hard rubber ball (*pelote*) and either bare hands or a scoop-like racquet made of wicker, leather, or wood. A popular variety of *pelote* is *cesta punta,* known too as *jai alai* and considered the fastest game in the world of sport. It is played on a three-sided court that is normally more than 164 feet long. Spanish-style bull fighting, in which the bull is killed, is also popular.

The Basque country has produced a few writers of note, such as **Pedro de Axular** (seventeenth century) and **Francis Jammes** (1886–1938). De Axular, a parish priest in a small village, wrote *Gero,* a collection of religious folk tales that have become part of the Basque cultural revival. Jammes wrote topographical poems about towns and places in southwestern France. Some of the best descriptions of the Basque country and its inhabitants are provided by the writer **Pierre Loti** (1850–1923) in his work entitled *Ramuntcho* (1897). Loti first became acquainted with the area when he was a captain stationed on a naval vessel at Hendaye across from the Spanish border. Later he built a vacation house near the port in Hendaye.

The remainder of Aquitaine, especially the Bordeaux area, has produced famous writers. The three standouts from Bordeaux are Montaigne, Montesquieu, and Mauriac. **Michel de Montaigne** (1533–1592), son of a wealthy Bordeaux merchant, was a moralist who created the essay as an art form. Not only did he write, but he served for a time as mayor of Bordeaux and as magistrate in the parliament of Bordeaux. His great masterpiece was entitled *Essais;* it explored a wide variety of subjects dealing with human affairs.

Charles-Louis de Secondat Montesquieu (1689–1755), like Montaigne, engaged for a while in politics and law in Bordeaux. Like Montaigne, too, he preferred life on his country estate near Bordeaux. His masterpiece was *L'Esprit des lois* (The Spirit of Laws), a treatise that argued in favor of the separation of powers in government. His ideas influenced the founders of the United States as well as the leaders of the French Revolution.

François Mauriac (1885–1970) is known in France as one of the best regional writers, a man who possessed a strong Catholic faith. Born in the old section of Bordeaux, after the age of 20 he lived in Paris but returned regularly to the Gironde area. His well-to-do family was involved in Bordeaux shipping, the timber industry, and forestry. Mauriac stressed among other things a spiritual dimension, but also the influence of landscape on his characters. *Thérèse Desqueyroux* (1927), considered by some his finest work, reflects his interest in nature and human character. Former French president François Mitterrand considered Mauriac his favorite regional writer; Mitterrand himself had a vacation house in Aquitaine in the department of Landes.

The best-known writer focusing on Périgord, the Dordogne, is the leading novelist of this area, **Eugène LeRoy** (1836–1907). He spent his entire life in the region and was close to the local people. He was a man of the left; his most noted novel, *Jacquou le croquant* (The Revolutionary), is a tale of a peasant revolt that took place around 1830 against an unjust landowner.

A number of foreign writers wrote about Aquitaine or parts of the region. The American poet and critic **Ezra Pound** (1885–1972) wrote about the Dordogne and even devoted a study to Bertrand de Born (1140–1215), one of the great troubadours who battled Henry II of England and Richard the Lionheart. The English travel writer **Arthur Young** (1741–1820) once wrote that Bayonne was the prettiest town he had seen in France and its women the most beautiful. The American author **Ernest Hemingway** (1899–1961) in *The Sun Also Rises* also praised Bayonne. The Anglo-French writer **Hilaire Belloc** (1870–1953) wrote about his walks in the Pyrenees. Furthermore, both the Irish-born playwright **George Bernard**

Shaw (1856–1950) and the English author **Rudyard Kipling** (1865–1936) stayed in Biarritz.

Gascony, an ancient area centered around Pau, has been the homeland not of great writers but of a number of important literary characters. The three musketeers in **Alexandre Dumas's** (1802–1870) famous novel were historically from Gascony (Dumas himself came from Paris). Another celebrated literary character, the satirist and duelist Cyrano de Bergerac, was given Gascony identity. In Edmond Rostand's 1897 play, the Parisian Bergerac is transformed into a chivalrous Gascon knight.

The food of Aquitaine is typified by the cuisine of Bordeaux and the Basque country. In the Bordeaux area one can enjoy superb food and wine. Many dishes derive from the sea, such as fish, oyster, lamprey, shad, and eel. A salt-meadow lamb is also served, as well as mushrooms *à la bordelaise* (cooked in oil with garlic and parsley). Other dishes prepared *à la bordelaise* use shallots and wine, including the *entrecôte* steak. Additional food products are *foie gras* (goose and duck livers), *confit* (any meat preserved in its own fat), *magret* (the breast meat of goose or duck), and yellow chicken fed high-quality maize only. Salmon and excellent beef are also available.

Basque cuisine features *jambon de Bayonne,* a ham that is cured by being rubbed with salt. It is often fried with eggs and used in cooking Basque-style, which includes the use of red chili peppers. Goose and duck livers and *confits* are also served here. A green vegetable soup savored by the Basques is *garbure.* Fish dishes are also served, such as tuna, sea bream, turbot, and whiting. Fish specialties include fried sardines with egg yolks, fish stew (*matelote*), and baby squid (*chipirones*). Salmon can be found in mountain streams. One excellent cheese is made of ewe's milk. A favorite sweet is *touron* (marzipan with nuts). Below is a delightful recipe for lunch or a light dinner meal.

SALADE DE HADDOCK AUX EPINARDS L'AQUITAINE
(Aquitaine's Spinach Salad with Smoked Haddock)

2 tbs. lemon juice

pinch of salt

1 tsp. Dijon mustard

⅓ cup olive oil

2 tbs. heavy cream

salt and freshly ground black
   pepper to taste

½ lb. scrubbed small new potatoes

2 cups milk

1 lb. smoked haddock fillets

1 lb. spinach leaves, stems removed

To make the dressing, whisk together the lemon juice, salt, and mustard in a small bowl. Slowly whisk in the oil and then the cream. Season with salt and pepper and set aside.

Cook the potatoes in salted water until tender. Drain and cut into thin slices. Put the potatoes in a bowl and toss with several tablespoons of the dressing. Set potatoes aside.

Pour the milk into a skillet and bring it to a simmer over medium-high heat. Add the smoked haddock, cover, and reduce heat; simmer for 10 minutes.

Wash and dry the spinach leaves. Cut the spinach into 1-inch strips and place in a salad bowl.

Remove haddock from skillet, draining and removing the skin. Add haddock to the bowl of spinach and then add potatoes. Add remaining dressing and toss the salad, adding freshly ground pepper to taste. Serve accompanied by a baguette and white wine. Serves 4 to 6.

ARCHITECTURE AND NOTEWORTHY SITES

In some areas of Aquitaine there are numerous chateaux; in the Gironde alone, roughly 3,000 names of chateaux are linked to wine production. Around Bordeaux and in Landes, houses include half-timbered walls. In Landes one often finds a single-storey house under a hayloft and a double-sloped tile roof. The loft opens to the front, where there may be a gallery-verandah. On the right bank of the Garonne are many *bastides,* with right-angled streets leading off a central square with arcaded galleries.

In the Basque area the typical house, the *etché,* is white-washed and timber-framed. The roof ridge is often offset, giving it an asymmetrical appearance. In some parts of the area the houses have wooden balconies. At higher altitudes the roofs are steeper and slate rather than tile is used. In the mountains the houses are grouped in hamlets; at higher elevations thick walls and smaller doors and windows are common.

BORDEAUX (pop. 210,336; greater Bordeaux 696,364) is a river port and ocean port characterized by eighteenth-century architecture. It is also a university center with approximately 60,000 students. Three times it served briefly as the capital of France: during the Franco-Prussian War of 1870–1871, at the outset of World War I, and for two weeks in 1940 before the creation of the Vichy government. The *Esplanade des Quinconces* is a large square where a sizable fountain-monument is dedicated to the Girondins of the Revolution. There are also large statues of Montaigne and Montesquieu. The public gardens, designed from 1746 to 1756, are a favorite retreat for residents of Bordeaux. The *Place Gambetta* is considered the city's loveliest square; it has a garden and is surrounded by Louis XV–style houses. During the Reign of Terror of the French Revolution, a guillotine functioned on the Place Gambetta and ended the lives of several hundred suspected counter-revolutionaries. The *Musée d'Aquitaine* displays artifacts of the history and ethnography of the region from as far back as 25,000 years. The *Musée d'Art Contemporain* exhibits works of present-day artists. The *Musée des Beaux-Arts* possesses a large collection of Flemish, Dutch, Italian, and French paintings from the nineteenth century. A maritime museum houses a large collection of model ships. The *Musée des Arts Décoratif* displays porcelain, silver, glass, furniture, and faience (earthenware). The *Musée Jean Moulin* features the history of the Resistance movement against the Nazis. The *Cathédrale Saint André* is where Eleanor of Aquitaine married the future king of France, Louis VII. In May the city hosts a classical music festival. In late June there are numerous concerts as Bordeaux participates with other cities and towns in France in the national *Fête de la Musique* to usher in the summer season. During this celebration the streets of many cities and towns throughout France are filled with live music.

PAU (pop. 82,157) is known for its mild climate and stunning views of the Pyrenees mountains. It serves as an excellent base for exploring the Pyrenees. In the nineteenth century the wealthy from England made this city a notable retreat. Part of its prosperity can be attributed to natural gas fields discovered in the area in 1970. The *Musée des Beaux-Arts* includes works from the seventeenth to the twentieth centuries by artists such as Rubens (1577–1640), El Greco (1541–1614), and Edgar Degas (1834–1917). The *Musée Béarnais* displays artifacts of the history of this area, known as the Béarn. The *Musée Bernadotte* features the history of a Pau-born general who abandoned Napoleon for Sweden (helping to defeat Napoleon in 1813 at the battle of Leipzig) and became king of Sweden. The chateau, built in the thirteenth and fourteenth centuries, once served as the home of the Kings of Navarre. Today it can be visited to view not just the chateau itself but also its fine collection of sixteenth- to eighteenth-century Gobelins tapestries, considered a treasure of craftsmanship.

BAYONNE (pop. 40,051), the capital of Basque country, is a picturesque tourist resort. It is also the center of the region's aeronautical and space industries. The city is known for its smoked ham as well as its chocolate and marzipan. According to some, the bayonet was invented here in the early 1600s. The *Musée Basque* is a superb ethnographic museum. The *Musée Bonnat* holds thirteenth- to twentieth-century works collected by Léon Bonnat (1833–1922), who was also a painter. In this museum is an entire room filled with paintings by the Flemish artist Peter Rubens (1577–1640). *Le Carré* shows exhibits of contemporary art. In Bayonne one can visit the distillery that produces *izarra,* a local liqueur made with exotic herbs. The *Cathédrale Sainte Marie* is a Gothic church that dates to 1258, when the area was under English rule; it was completed under the French. The ornamentation reflects these political changes: there is an English coat-of-arms as well as the French fleur-de-lis. The most famous festival here is the five-day *Fête de Bayonne* in early August; it includes a *course des vaches,* a running of the cows, which is a parody of the running of the bulls in Pamplona, Spain. Basque music, bull fighting, and rugby matches are popular in this area.

PÉRIGUEUX (pop. 30,280) is the capital of the Dordogne area, one of the cradles of civilization. Nearby are a number of ancient caves such as the one at Lascaux, where cave paintings and other signs of Neanderthal and Cro-Magnon peoples are evident. The food of the region, with its wonderfully fresh locally grown products, is considered superb. Périgueux was built more than 2,000 years ago on the banks of the Isle River. The *Musée du Périgord* is considered the second most important prehistory museum after the one at Les Eyzies, a major prehistoric center in the Dordogne. The Musée du Périgord also contains a superb Gallo-Roman collection. The *Cathédrale Saint Front,* a conglomeration of styles, was an important stopping place for pilgrims visiting Santiago de Compostela in Spain. The twelfth-century *Église Saint Étienne de la Cité* served as the city's church until *Saint Front* was built in 1699. It was badly damaged in 1577 by the Huguenots during the Wars of Religion (1562–1598). There are also remnants of a Roman amphitheater and temple in the town.

BIARRITZ (pop. 28,742) is an upscale beach resort that was made famous when Napoleon III and his wife, the Empress Eugénie, began coming here in 1854. It soon developed as a resort for the European aristocracy, becoming popular with Queen Victoria and Edward VII. Today it is sometimes referred to as "the California of Europe." Because of its gentle climate, Biarritz has attracted a large number of retired people, who now make up 20 percent of the population. The centerpiece of Biarritz is the *Grande Plage,* one of several beaches. The *Musée de la Mer* is an aquarium that also has exhibits on commercial fishing and whaling. At one time Biarritz was a whaling port. The *Musée du Vieux Biarritz* displays the history of the town. The *Église Sainte Eugénie* was built in 1864 for the Empress Eugénie. There is also a Russian Orthodox church, the *Église Alexandre Newsky,* constructed to serve Russian aristocrats who visited the resort prior to the Russian Revolution of 1917.

ST.-JEAN-DE-LUZ (pop. 13,031) is a pleasant beach town that is perhaps the most Basque of the area's seaside resorts. Once a whaling station, fishing is still important here; its port brings in large catches of sardines, tuna, and anchovy. The composer Maurice Ravel (1875–1937) was born here. In the *Église Saint Jean Baptiste,* the largest Basque church in France, Louis XIV married the infanta Marie Thérèse of Austria in 1660 (she was the daughter of King Philip IV of Spain). The marriage, part of the Treaty of the Pyrenees (1659), ended more than twenty years of war between France and Spain. The *Église Saint Vincent,* with its unusual bell tower and wood interior, is typically Basque. In June the city celebrates the *fête patronale* of Saint Jean Baptiste. Other festivals center around the sardine and tuna, with music, folklore, and dancing.

LES-EYZIES-DE-TAYAC (pop. 853) is a famous village in the Dordogne known for its proximity to prehistoric caves inhabited by Neanderthal people as early as the middle Paleolithic period, 90,000 to 40,000 years ago. In some cave sites one can view cave paintings from the upper Paleolithic period; some paintings date back more than 10,000 years, and others may be more than 15,000 years old. In Les Eyzies is the *Musée National de la Préhistoire,* which displays some of the oldest artwork in existence. Here one also finds information about prehistoric sites near the village. The *Musée de l'Abri Pataud,* once a rock shelter for Cro-Magnon people, focuses on the life-style of its ancient population. The village is one of the most important prehistory centers in the world.

SELECT BIBLIOGRAPHY

Duboscq, P., and J. Pailhe. "Aquitaine," in Y. Lacoste, ed., *Géopolitiques des régions françaises,* vol. 2. Paris: Fayard, 1986.

Lerat, Serge. "Aquitaine," in André Gamblin, ed., *La France dans ses régions,* vol. 2. Paris: SEDES, 1994.

Roudie, P. *Le Vignoble bordelais.* Toulouse: Privat, 1973.

Savary, G. *La Dérive des régions. L'Aquitaine de la décentralisation à l'Europe.* Bordeaux: Vivisques, 1990.

Viers, G. *Le Pays basque.* Toulouse: Privat, 1975.

Chapter 3

AUVERGNE

REGIONAL GEOGRAPHY

Little known to tourists, Auvergne is located in the center of France and covers most of the Massif Central mountain range. It comprises an area of 16,057 square miles, or 4.7 percent of the surface area of France. The region includes four departments: Allier, Cantal, Haute-Loire, and Puy-de-Dôme. To the north is Burgundy and the Centre; to the east, the wide Rhône valley; to the south, Languedoc-Roussillon and the Midi-Pyrénées; and to the west, Limousin. Clermont-Ferrand is the regional capital.

Auvergne's geography is dominated by the large mountain range known as the Massif Central. Among other things, the region is known for its awe-inspiring volcanic relief. Formed millions of years ago, the volcanic Massif Central predates both the Alps and the Pyrenees. It is best known for its volcanic cones, called *puys*. Water is also a dominant characteristic here. A large number of lakes have filled the volcanic craters. Moreover, some of France's best-known rivers originate in the Auvergne: the Dordogne, Allier, Lot, and Loire. Many of its rivers, including the powerful Loire, flow into the Atlantic Ocean. Auvergne is also known for its hot mineral springs, one of the benefits of its volcanic character. Thus, it is a mountainous region with an abundance of water and scenic valleys, where most of the population is settled.

The region has harsh winters with cold temperatures and snow in the mountains. In the spring the temperature varies. Summer tends to be hot and humid. Fall is considered the best season of the year.

AUVERGNE

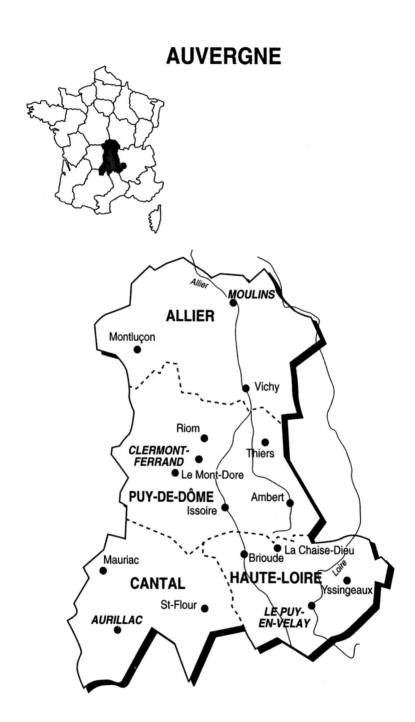

Allier

MOULINS

ALLIER

Montluçon

Vichy

Riom

**CLERMONT-
FERRAND**

Thiers

Le Mont-Dore

PUY-DE-DÔME

Ambert

Issoire

Mauriac

Brioude

La Chaise-Dieu

HAUTE-LOIRE

Loire

CANTAL

Yssingeaux

St-Flour

**LE PUY-
EN-VELAY**

AURILLAC

HISTORY

Human life in Auvergne began thousands of years ago. By around 800 B.C. the Auvergne people, pastoral nomads, settled the plains of the Allier River area and their dominance spread from the Rhine to the Atlantic. Under the leadership of Vercingétorix, chief of the Celtic Arverni tribe, the Roman conqueror Julius Caesar almost failed in his attempt to dominate the region. Vercingétorix organized various tribes and mounted a formidable resistance to the Roman army, yet the Celtic chieftain eventually fell to Caesar's military forces. He was taken to Rome, imprisoned for six years, and then put to death by strangulation. (Vercingétorix is a national hero today in France, with a famous comic-book character—Astérix le Gaulois—and series based on his exploits.) Once in control of the region, the Romans began building roads and baths and encouraged agricultural development.

Following the fall of Rome in the fifth century A.D., private struggles between warlords fragmented the region. During the Middle Ages, Clermont-Ferrand was the meeting place of the synod, the ecclesiastical council of the Church. It was here that Pope Urban II proclaimed the First Crusade in 1095. During the eleventh and twelfth centuries the region witnessed the rise of Auvergnat Romanesque architecture as the Church increased its influence in Auvergne. The French King Philippe Auguste united Auvergne with the rest of the country during his reign.

The period from the fourteenth through the seventeenth centuries saw death, religious wars, and revolt in the region. In the fourteenth century, during the Hundred Years War with England, the plague took many lives in Auvergne. In the first half of the fifteenth century the Protestant Reformation was felt at many levels of society. When a tax increase led to a serious rebellion in the region, one that the prelate and political leader Cardinal Richelieu could not quell, Louis XIV sponsored the *grand jours d'Auvergne* in 1665–1666, during which time the Parliament of Paris reorganized the affairs of the region.

In recent centuries Auvergne has witnessed interesting developments. The region showed little support for the Revolution and Empire. In fact, some mountainous regions became a refuge for nonconformists. In the early nineteenth century the region was still basically agricultural, with some industrial centers such as Clermont-Ferrand and Thiers (at Clermont-Ferrand, a rubber products factory was established in 1832). Migration out of the region increased in the late nineteenth century owing to the phylloxera blight that destroyed the vineyards, so local people sought work in industrializing regions. In the twentieth century, electrification schemes on the Truyère and upper Dordogne Rivers and the creation in 1964 of the Association for Enhancing Auvergne and Limousin have aided the region's development.

RECENT POLITICS

The politics of Auvergne have paralleled the trend elsewhere in France. In the 1993 parliamentary elections the left lost five deputies, with only one socialist deputy remaining in the National Assembly. Although the French Communist party (PCF) played a major role in the region after World War II, it has declined dramatically (as elsewhere in France). On the other hand, the Ecologists have made headway. In the 1993 parliamentary elections the right-wing coalition of gaullists and Independent Republicans obtained 30.5 percent of the vote in the first round, surpassing slightly their 1988 score of 29.5 percent. In the first round of the 1995 presidential elections the left- and right-wing candidates each won two departments in the region. The right-wing extremist Jean-Marie Le Pen of the National Front (FN) won 12.5 percent of the vote in the first round of voting in Auvergne, below his 15 percent national average. In the second round the gaullist candidate Jacques Chirac was victorious against the socialist candidate Lionel Jospin in all departments of the region except for Allier. Chirac became the fifth president of the French Fifth Republic. One surprise in the 1995 municipal elections was that former president Valéry Giscard d'Estaing failed to oust the veteran socialist mayor Roger Quilliot in Clermont-Ferrand. In general, although the left has lost ground here, the right has picked up electoral strength owing in large measure to the plight of the economy in the 1980s and early 1990s.

POPULATION

Since 1975 the region's population has fallen slightly: in 1975 it stood at 1,330,000, whereas in 1993 it was 1,319,000—approximately 2.3 percent of the national total. Auvergne's birthrate is 1.54, considerably below the national average of 1.73. Population density is only 50.6 people per square kilometer (81.97 per square mile), less than half the average for France as a whole.

In past decades there has been migration out of Auvergne to other areas, especially large cities. Paris has attracted a number of the region's natives, who have opened cafés and bars or sold wood and domestic coal as profitable concerns. In Paris, Auvergne is known as an area that has produced café owners and politicians.

The population of the region is slightly older than the national norm, with 23.5 percent being 60 years of age or older. Youth age 19 or younger represent 24.1 percent, more than two percentage points below the national average. In recent years many young people have left the area in search of employment. The immigrant population is approximately 4 percent, less than the national average of 6.3 percent.

The urban population in Auvergne is 58.8 percent of the total, considerably below the 76.4 percent national average. Educational levels are slightly below the national norm, with 9.8 percent of the inhabitants holding only a high school diploma and 8.8 percent possessing advanced degrees. Of the work force, 10 percent are in agriculture (almost twice the national average), 28.1 percent in industry, and 61.9 percent in the service sector. Most of the population is located in the center of the region in the plains and valleys, notably around Clermont-Ferrand. Unemployment currently runs at approximately 11.5 percent (more than 12% for France as a whole), with almost 13 percent of females out of work.

ECONOMY

Although unemployment in Auvergne has been slightly below the national average in recent years, the recession of the 1980s and early 1990s hit the area hard. Between 1982 and 1990 the region lost thousands of jobs: 25,000 in industry, 8,000 in the building trades, 20,000 in agriculture. Yet during the same period 25,000 jobs were created in the service sector. To a large degree, the flight of the young out of Auvergne has contributed to an unemployment rate below the national norm.

Agriculture has suffered greatly over the past decade. Nevertheless, 10 jobs out of 100 in Auvergne are in agriculture—the national average is 5.3 percent. Roughly 80 percent of agriculture involves the production of meat and milk. The region exports corn seed worldwide. The agro-food industry also specializes in the production of cheese and mineral water. The region also produces a large quantity of blueberries. Other industries include beauty products and pharmaceuticals.

Industry as a whole represents one-quarter of the work force. The best-known industry in Auvergne is the Michelin tire production center at Clermont-Ferrand. Also present in the tire production industry is Dunlop-Sumitomo. Smelting works and metal works in general are found in the region as well.

Because forests cover one-fourth of Auvergne, the lumber industry and furniture making are important. Whereas the region is weighted toward agriculture and other important industries, high-tech or highly developed industries such as aeronautics, computers, and nuclear energy production are underrepresented.

The three largest towns are Clermont-Ferrand with a population of 136,181 (the greater Clermont-Ferrand population, 254,416, is nearly 20% of the entire population of the region), Montluçon with 44,248, and Vichy with 27,714. As might be expected, a large part of the work force (26.8%) is centered in Clermont-Ferrand. The four largest employers are Michelin (roughly 19,000 work in the tire industry), CHRU Hôpital St. Jacques in Clermont-Ferrand, the city hall of Clermont-Ferrand, and the French national railroad (SNCF).

Although the traditional character of Auvergne's work force has not been well suited for the present-day economy, the extension of new highway systems and a new airport at Clermont-Ferrand-Aulnat (which can accommodate 700,000 passengers per year) may well open up this isolated region to tourists and outdoor enthusiasts seeking to exploit the beauty of the natural surroundings, whether it be skiing, hiking, cycling, or hang-gliding.

CULTURE

The region is known for its scenery, outdoor activities, and thermal baths, as well as its role during the Nazi occupation of France. Outside of Clermont-Ferrand and the other large towns, a rural culture dominates. Mountainous terrain and forests have made this region attractive to outdoor enthusiasts. Two large parks are located here, including the dramatic Regional Park of the Volcanoes of Auvergne. Moreover, for more than a century Auvergne has been known for its thermal bath establishments, especially at Vichy. During *la belle époque,* the end of the nineteenth century, the rich and famous flocked to Vichy spas. Although the baths prospered prior to World War II, in the postwar period they have not regained their status with health-conscious French and European visitors. Nevertheless, Auvergne has five of the ten leading thermal resorts in France. The region is also known for being the seat of the Vichy government during World War II. It was here that Marshal Philippe Pétain set up his puppet government in what became known as the "unoccupied zone" of France after the nation fell to the Nazi war machine at the start of the war.

The region also has a reputation for its contribution to art and architecture. In the twelfth century Auvergne was the home of an original and important school of Romanesque art where architecture and sculpture dominated. There are a number of well-preserved Gothic and Renaissance dwellings. The region also possesses a number of castles and country homes.

Auvergne has a reputation for producing political leaders. Not only was the hero Vercingétorix from this region, but two modern presidents of the Republic were born here: **Georges Pompidou** (1969–1974) and **Valéry Giscard d'Estaing** (1974–1981).

Auvergne has inspired little in the way of literature. However, it was the home of **Blaise Pascal** (1623–1662), a mathematician and physicist who contributed to society's understanding of atmospheric pressure, hydraulics, and the theory of probability. Moreover, the famous engineer **Gustave Eiffel** (1832–1923), known for the famous Eiffel Tower in Paris, built several bridges and viaducts in Auvergne.

The cuisine of the region is simple and hearty, with cooking based on long and gentle simmering. Soups (especially cabbage-based) and stews are popular; both blend local produce with lentils, chestnuts, or mushrooms. Among the meats, *charcuterie* is important—such as sausages and, especially, Auvergne ham. Charolais beef is another specialty. Mouton and tripe, as well as poultry, game (rabbit, boar, pheasant, partridge, and quail), and lake fish (trout, char, and salmon), are favorites. Cheese is the great specialty of Auvergne: famous ones include Cantal; the blue-veined Bleu d'Auvergne; the smooth, creamy Saint-Nectaire; and a number of cheeses made from cow's milk and goat's milk. Locally produced fruit often follows a meal; sometimes the fruit is in the form of a tart or a *clafoutis* (flan). Rye bread is a regional favorite. Local wines (although not rivaling wines produced elsewhere) are also consumed, such as Boudes, Chateaugay, Corent, and Dellet. *Gentiane* is often served as a before-dinner drink, or *apéritif,* and *marc d'Auvergne* or *prunelle du Velay* is offered as a *digestif* to finish a meal. Below is a recipe for a lunch dish that can be served with a tomato salad.

LA PATRANQUE
(Auvergne Rarebit)

6 thick slices of white bread, cut into chunks	8 cloves of garlic, peeled, then chopped or pressed
milk to moisten bread	a pinch of salt
3 oz. butter	
6 slices Cantal cheese or aged Gruyère, cut into slivers	

Place chunks of bread in milk and moisten. Melt butter in a large frying pan and add bread. When bread sizzles, add cheese, garlic, and salt. Mash the mixture together until it forms a sticky dough. Wait until it is golden on the bottom, then place under the broiler until it is golden on top. Serve immediately. Serves 6.

ARCHITECTURE AND NOTEWORTHY SITES

Building materials in Auvergne tend to be of schist (layered rock), sandstone, or dark lava. Houses are seldom isolated; normally they are grouped in villages or hamlets. They usually face southeast. Chimneys are important because of the climate, and often there is an enormous hearth. Windows tend to be small and located on the least-exposed side of the house. At higher elevations, roofs are steeply pitched. Away from the mountains, houses take on the character of neighboring regions. Auvergne also possesses a number of shepherd's cottages with tiny doorways and windows.

CLERMONT-FERRAND (pop. 136,181), often referred to simply as Clermont, is the largest city in the region. It is France's major producer of rubber and the headquarters of the Michelin tire industry. It is also a university center. In the old town, many buildings are constructed of black lava rock. Just a few miles outside of Clermont-Ferrand are a series of *puys* called *Monts Dômes,* the highest of which is 4,805 feet. In the city itself, the *Cathédrale Notre Dame* is considered one of France's greatest Gothic structures; it was built in the thirteenth century from dark volcanic stone. The *Musée des Ranquet,* one of the more interesting museums in Clermont-Ferrand, contains a Pascal exhibition. Near the city one can visit the *Puy de Dôme,* where the Celts and the Romans worshipped gods from the summit. It sometimes serves as one of the most difficult stages in the famous *Tour de France* bicycle race.

VICHY (pop. 27,714) is known for its spas and its role as the seat of the Pétain government during World War II. Napoleon III, the nephew of Napoleon I, partook of the waters of Vichy; and the triangular *Parc des Sources* was created in the middle of the city to impress the emperor of the Second Empire, Napoleon III. At one end of the Parc des Sources is a glass *Hall des Sources* where four of Vichy's springs originate; the temperature range of the springs is 64.4° to 107.6° Fahrenheit.

LE PUY-EN-VELAY (pop. 21,743) is a beautiful little town in a fertile valley of Haute-Loire that has attracted visitors for centuries because it is ringed by volcanic mountains and because during the Middle Ages it was one of the stops on the pilgrimage to Santiago de Compostela in Spain. By the end of the seventeenth century Le Puy became an important center as well for the making of fine lace (*dentelle*); much of the lace production was for religious purposes. In the town one can see a huge red statue of the Madonna and a small chapel sitting atop a volcanic plug. A number of festivals are held here, including a pre-Lent carnival, a summer international folk music festival, and an autumn *Fêtes Renaissance du Roi de l'Oiseau* that portrays seventeenth-century Le Puy.

LE MONT-DORE (pop. 2,000), located 31 miles southwest of Clermont-Ferrand, is a small spa town at an elevation of more than 3,000 feet. It attracts spa seekers, skiers, hikers, and hang-gliders.

LA CHAISE-DIEU (pop. 953) is located in the heart of a huge forested area in Haute-Loire. The name of the town literally means "the throne of god." It was once the seat of a significant abbey; one of its monks even became Pope. The *Église St. Robert* is a superb fifteenth-century Gothic structure constructed at the order of Pope Clement VI.

PARC DE VOLCANS, officially known as the *Parc Naturel Régional des Volcans d'Auvergne,* stretches for 75 miles and displays numerous cone-shaped volcanoes. Volcanic activity first began here roughly 20 million years ago. Many of the towns and villages within the park are constructed of dark volcanic stone.

SELECT BIBLIOGRAPHY

Bouet, G., and A. Fel. *Le Massif Central.* Paris: Flammarion, 1983.
Mazataud, P. "Auvergne," in Y. Lacoste, ed., *Géopolitiques des régions françaises,* vol. 3. Paris: Fayard, 1986.
———. *L'Auvergne. Géopolitique d'une région.* Paris: Fayard, 1988.

Chapter 4

BRITTANY
(Bretagne)

REGIONAL GEOGRAPHY

Located on the western tip of France where it reaches out into the Atlantic, Brittany comprises 16,795 square miles, or 5 percent of the surface area of the nation. Four departments make up the region: Ille-et-Vilaine, Côtes-d'Armor, Finistère, and Morbihan. Given its coastal location, the region is a popular holiday spot. Rennes is the regional capital.

Geographically there are two Brittanies—the Brittany of the long 685-mile coast, known as *L'Armor* (Land of the Sea); and the interior, *L'Argoat* (Land of the Woods). The western coastline is swept by the rough Atlantic Ocean, and the northern coastline is washed by the calmer waters of the English Channel. The coastline is known for its rocky coves and numerous lighthouses. Sandy beaches and intriguing inlets leading to picturesque small ports are also common. *Abers,* or deep inlets, are quite common along the northern coast. A number of beautiful and well-preserved islands lie offshore—especially along the southwestern coast, such as Belle-Île. The inland area is known for its forests, moorlands, and fields enclosed by hedges.

The climate is maritime and variable. Owing to the influence of the Gulf Stream, a current that flows from the Gulf of Mexico toward northwestern Europe, the climate is normally quite mild. There is little frost in the region, even inland. During the summer months there are few hot spells, with temperatures ranging roughly between 65° and 75° Fahrenheit. There is also a high rate of sunshine—roughly 2,000 hours per year, equal to that along the Mediterranean. Nevertheless, the region has high levels of precipitation, especially in January to May.

BRITTANY
(BRETAGNE)

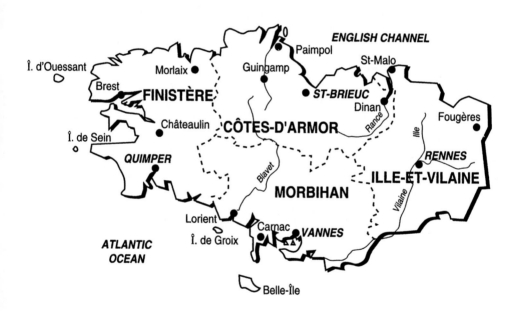

HISTORY

Brittany's first inhabitants were Neolithic tribes, whose menhirs and dolmens (large stones arranged symmetrically) can still be seen. In the sixth century B.C. a first wave of Celts, originally from central Europe, settled in Brittany. The Romans under Julius Caesar conquered the region in 56 B.C., and it remained under Roman control until the fifth century A.D. When the Romans departed, another wave of Celts from Britain and Ireland settled in Brittany. This wave of Celtic settlers had been driven across the channel by Anglo-Saxon invaders. Celtic missionaries Christianized the region in the fifth and sixth centuries. Several towns in Brittany are named after these missionaries, such as Saint Brieuc and Saint-Malo.

The region did not become a permanent part of France for almost 1,000 years. In the ninth century, a warrior known as Nominoë—Brittany's national hero—led a revolt against Frankish rule in the region and captured control of Rennes and Nantes. Following this success, the Bretons were able to protect their region from the Norman (Viking) invasions. During much of the Middle Ages the rulers of France sought control over Brittany, especially because of its access to the sea. Following a series of royal weddings, Brittany became a part of France in 1532. From the sixteenth through the nineteenth centuries, the shipping industry of coastal Brittany prospered during a period of colonial and commercial expansion. During the Revolution of 1789 the liberal ideas of the age were first hailed; but during the period known as the Convention (1792–1795), which saw the introduction of military conscription and religious intolerance, the Bretons revolted. In the nineteenth century the arrival of the railroad contributed to the decline of the region, because rail lines brought competition from industrialized areas. Subsequently the region suffered the ravages of World War II, especially heavy German bombardment. Since the late 1960s the development of maritime and tourist activities and increasing industrialization have spurred economic development in Brittany.

Given its history, Brittany has retained a strong regional identity. In recent decades there has been an attempt to revive cultural and linguistic traditions in the region. In this regard, ties have been established with other Celtic cultures in Ireland, Wales, Cornwall, and Galicia in Spain. An independence movement has survived in the region; Breton separatists launched violent actions in the late 1960s and 1970s, including a daring bomb attack on the Versailles Palace in 1978.

RECENT POLITICS

The Ecologists (Greens) and pro-Europe forces have gained in Brittany during recent years. In the 1992 regional elections the Ecologists, as well as the ultra-nationalist National Front party (FN), made headway, with the

Ecologists winning twelve new seats and the FN capturing seven. The Ecologists have become the third most powerful political force in Brittany owing to a growing consciousness of environmental problems. Water pollution in the interior caused by nitrates, coupled with oil spills along the coast, have made the Ecologists a force. In the September 1992 referendum on the Maastricht Treaty, which called for increased integration in the European Economic Community (Common Market), 60 percent of the region's voters marked their ballots for Europe, nine percentage points ahead of the national average. During the first round of the 1993 legislative elections, the right-wing coalition comprised of the gaullist Rally for the Republic (RPR) and the Union for French Democracy (UDF) won 42.67 percent of the vote, the Socialist party (PS) and its supporters garnered 22.17 percent, and the Ecologists won 10.82 percent. The socialists lost ten seats in the region (maintaining only three seats), including the seat held by the mayor of Rennes, Edmond Hervé. He had been the minister of health and was implicated in a scandal concerning distribution of contaminated blood containing the AIDS virus. During the first round of the 1995 presidential elections, right-wing candidates came out on top in all departments of the region except for the Côtes-d'Armor. In the first round, too, the extreme-right wing candidate Jean-Marie Le Pen—born on the coast of Brittany—captured 10.2 percent of the vote in the region (13.78% in Morbihan). Le Pen's score in his native region was below his national average of 15 percent in this election. The second round of the presidential contest saw the gaullist Jacques Chirac, the eventual victor, win three departments in Brittany, with only the Côtes-d'Armor going to the socialist candidate Lionel Jospin. Then, in the June 1995 municipal elections, the socialists made gains—especially in the Côtes-d'Armor and Finistère. In the regional capital of Rennes, the socialist Hervé won re-election as mayor.

POPULATION

The region is ranked seventh in terms of population, with 2,826,000 inhabitants, 4.9 percent of the national total. In 1975 the population stood at 2,595,000. The region's birthrate is 1.54, less than the 1.73 national average. The population density of 103.8 people per square kilometer, or 168.15 per square mile, approximates the national average.

Young people—age 19 or less—comprise 26.7 percent of the population, as compared to 21.8 percent for those age 60 or older. Although the percentage of those age 19 and younger mirrors the national average, those age 60 and older are two percentage points above the average for France as a whole. The immigrant population is very low: 0.9 percent, as compared to 6.3 percent for the nation. The small number of immigrants is due, in large measure, to the lack of extensive industry in the region.

The urban population constitutes 57.3 percent of Brittany's total population, well below the 76.4 percent for France as a whole. Moreover, life expectancy in the region is 75.8 years, roughly one and one-half years below the national average. Approximately 27.9 percent of all households are single-person households, slightly above the 27.1 percent national average.

In terms of educational levels, approximately 10.3 percent (about the national average) have high school degrees and 9.2 percent have advanced degrees. Of the work force, 9.6 percent are employed in agriculture (almost twice the national average), 23.5 percent in industry, and 66.9 percent in the service sector. The unemployment rate stands at 11.6 percent, lower than the national average of over 12 percent. Approximately 11.6 percent of females are out of work.

ECONOMY

Agriculture dominates the productive sectors of Brittany's economy. (Its agricultural production ranks third in France, the service sector seventh, and industry twelfth.) Brittany contributes 12 percent of the total national agricultural production; this includes 19 percent of the nation's milk, 54 percent of its pork, 30 percent of its poultry and eggs, and 10 percent of its vegetables. The fishing industry is also strong, producing 45 percent of the total value of all fish sold on the market and 70 percent of all shellfish. It is not surprising that agricultural production and the fishing industry represent 13 percent of all employment in the region.

Industry is becoming diversified in Brittany. The strongest is the agro-food industry. Mining in the region is focused principally on granite. Other industries include shipbuilding, leather, textiles, automobiles (e.g., Citroen), electronics, and chemicals. Brittany produces paper for cigarettes and insulation for condensers. There are three universities in the region, as well as research centers that focus on telecommunications, agro-food production, and oceanography. Tourism—principally along the coastal area and essentially family-oriented—has developed over the years. Health spas, too, contribute to the region's economy.

Even though extension of the high-speed TGV rail line has broken the isolation of the region, Rennes and the Ille-et-Vilaine in the western sector of the department must guard against becoming simply an extension of the Paris Basin. Concerning the region in general, one authority on Brittany has said that although it has traditionally been a region of production it must now become a region of "intelligence," meaning more research and a more technological orientation.

The three largest towns are Rennes with 197,536 inhabitants, Brest with 147,956, and Lorient with 59,271. Rennes employs 9.8 percent of the work force, as compared to 6.9 percent for Brest and 4 percent for Lorient. The four largest employers are Citroen, Arsenal de Brest (naval construction), Arsenal de Lorient (naval construction), and CIT Alcatel (electronics).

CULTURE

The historian Jules Michelet once called Brittany the "resistant element of France." Here one finds a distinctive culture and language influenced by centuries of independence and isolation from the rest of France. Breton customs are most evident in the western portion of the region. Thus, Brittany can be divided into Breton Brittany in the west and Gallic Brittany in the east. Traditional Breton costumes, such as the lace headdress worn by women, are still seen at festivals and religious celebrations. The traditional costume for women also includes a bodice laced over a linen blouse, an apron over a wide and gathered skirt, and a neckerchief. The traditional costume for men includes baggy trousers, a jacket, and a round hat. Two of the most important cultural festivals take place at Quimper and Lorient on the Atlantic coast. The August festival at Lorient is an Inter-Celtic Festival. Part of the festival tradition in Brittany includes Breton pilgrimages known as *pardons,* which date to the Middle Ages. These are religious festivals in which participants wearing traditional costumes beg for forgiveness for their sins. Often beginning with a pilgrimage, followed by a celebration of the mass, the event concludes with a popular festival known as *fest noz.* At the *fest noz,* music is provided by bands playing traditional instruments such as the *biniou* (Breton bagpipes), and the *bombarde* (oboe). Other traditional instruments that are popular in the region include the bardic harp with thirty metal strings, and the Celtic harp with thirty-two gut strings. The well-known contemporary musician **Alain Stivell** includes many traditional instruments in his work and has contributed to the popularity of Breton music not just in Brittany but in France in general.

The regional dialect is known as Breton, a Celtic language related to both Cornish and Welsh, and to some extent to Irish and Scottish Gaelic. Following the Revolution of 1789, Parisian authorities attempted to suppress Breton as they did other regional languages. As recently as several decades ago, students were punished if they were heard speaking Breton. The decentralization program under President François Mitterrand's socialist government in the early 1980s made it easier for Breton culture and language to flourish. It is estimated that roughly 800,000 people speak Breton, most living west of a line running from Paimpol in the north to Vannes in the south. In recent years there has been a revival of interest in Breton literature and theater.

A regional flag and various symbols are important to Brittany. The flag comprises nine horizontal stripes, representing Brittany's nine ancient regions. Often seen throughout the region is the Triskell, a symbol used by the Celts since 450 B.C. (The word "Triskell" is taken from Greek and means "on three legs.") A round symbol, it includes three wavy lines and suggests images of the sun and/or the cycle of life and death.

Legends and fairy tales abound in Brittany's history. The most famous is the story of King Arthur, a fairy tale associated since the Middle Ages with both Brittany and Cornwall in England.

Moreover, Brittany is the home of Astérix the Gaul, probably the most famous cartoon character today in France (Astérix was inspired by the valiant story of Vercingétorix.) Created by **René Goscinny** and **Albert Uderzo**, Astérix has entertained young and old alike since the 1950s. Each Astérix comic book begins by telling the reader that the year is 50 B.C. and that all of Gaul, with the exception of one village, has been captured by the Romans. The inhabitants of this single village are independent, eccentric, and warrior-like. They cannot be defeated because their druid, Panoramix, brews a magic potion that makes them invincible in battle. In the stories, Astérix and his loyal friend Oblex have comical adventures as they travel throughout the Roman Empire helping local warriors rebel against the Romans. Slapstick routines, puns, word plays, and visual jokes make this comic series very humorous. Astérix also pokes fun at what his creators consider national characteristics. By the end of the 1980s, 200 million copies in 40 languages had been sold. Outside of Paris today is a theme park called *Village d'Astérix,* indicating the powerful hold of Astérix on French popular culture.

One of the most fascinating and mysterious aspects of the culture of Brittany is the presence of megaliths, especially around the small town of Carnac near the Atlantic coast. Megaliths are large stones used in prehistoric architecture or monuments in various parts of Western Europe. The megaliths date from between 4,500 and 2,000 B.C. and are associated with Neolithic farmers and herders. The huge rock formations include menhirs (stones between 1 and 20 meters in height and weighing between 2 and 200 tons, and positioned in an upright manner in the ground); dolmens (stone burial chambers); and tumuli (earthen mounds that cover the dolmens). There is still a great deal of mystery surrounding the true significance of these incredible rock formations. Some scholars think they have astronomical and religious significance.

Somewhat surprisingly, Brittany has not produced many great writers, unlike the Celts in Ireland. The two most renowned authors from this region are **François-René de Chateaubriand** (1768–1848), sometimes labeled the first great French romantic, and **Ernest Renan** (1823–1892), a biblical scholar. Some have suggested that the lack of writers may be related to the oral tradition of the Breton language, which French authorities in Paris prohibited from being taught in schools or universities or spoken in public. Others argue that many Bretons refused to write in the language of their colonizers; thus, a great body of Breton literature in French never developed.

Two twentieth-century Breton writers are **Per-Jakez Hélias** (1914–1995) and **Henri Queffélec** (b. 1910). Hélias produced a work on Breton peasant culture, an autobiographical account entitled *Le Cheval d'orgueil* (1975, The Proud Horse). First written in Breton and then translated into French by the author, this work is considered the best account of twentieth-century rural Brittany and one of the most important books to emerge from the region since 1945. The book has sold over 2 million copies and was made into a film. Queffélec, born in Brest, tells the story of sailors whose lives revolve around the sea. His best-known work, *L'Île de Sein* (1944), was also made into a film.

Brittany has influenced several well-known authors. **Pierre Loti** (1850–1923), who was born in the region of Poitou-Charente, lived for a while in Brittany. His works generally relate the stories of brave Breton sailors confronting the cruel sea. One of Loti's best-known novels is *Pecheur d'Islande* (1886, An Iceland Fisherman). The infamous **Jean Genet** (1910–1986), who lived in Brittany in the 1930s, featured the region in his 1953 novel *Querelle de Brest* (The Quarrel of Brest). The famous female writer **Colette** (1873–1954) also spent time in Brittany and wrote *Le Blé en herbe* (The Ripening Seed) in 1923 while residing in the region; the book relates the story of young adolescents on vacation who discover their sexuality. Several other well-known writers discussed Brittany in their works after spending some time there. These include the eighteenth-century English traveler **Arthur Young** (1741–1820) and **Honoré de Balzac** (1799–1850), who visited the region a few years after Young. Both described Brittany as backward at the time.

Several famous people have sought refuge in Brittany throughout the centuries. In the twelfth century the French theologian and philosopher **Pierre Abelard** (1079–1142), known for his radical views and his famous love affair with Héloise (which led to his castration), became abbot at a remote abbey on the Morbihan coast. In the 1970s the Czech writer **Milan Kundera** (b. 1929) left Prague because of political harassment by Czech authorities and took up residence in Rennes, where he taught at the university and authored *The Book of Laughter and Forgetting*.

The cuisine of Brittany features quality and freshness rather than a tradition of *haute cuisine*. Vegetables are normally locally grown and the seafood freshly caught. In terms of regional gastronomy, oysters, crabs, prawns, and numerous fish compete with the famous *crêpes* (thin pancakes made of wheat flour and filled with a variety of ingredients) from the region and *galettes* (a thick variety of *crêpes* made of buckwheat). *Crêpes* and *galettes* are often accompanied by a locally produced cider. *Crêperies* (restaurants that serve *crêpes*) abound in Brittany. In recent years, traditional preparations besides *crêpes* and *galettes* have become known outside of

Brittany, such as *kauteriad* (a fish soup differing from *bouillabaisse* of the south) and *kouign* (a sweet fried cake of wheat flour, eggs, and honey). Below is a popular recipe from the region.

COQUILLES SAINT-JACQUES À LA BRETONNE
(Baked Scallops with Butter and Bread Crumbs)

12 large scallops	½ cup dry white wine
6 tbs. butter	pinch of cayenne
3 large shallots, finely chopped	salt and freshly ground black
2 or 3 cloves of garlic, finely	pepper to taste
chopped or pressed	¾ cup fine bread crumbs
handful of finely chopped parsley	

Rinse the scallops and pat dry. Cut each in half.

Melt half the butter in a large skillet over low heat. Add the shallots and garlic, and sauté until transparent. Add the parsley and scallops, and stir. Add wine to skillet. Stir and add cayenne, salt, and pepper. Cook over medium heat, stirring frequently, for 8 to 10 minutes or until wine has evaporated.

Preheat oven or broiler to 450° Fahrenheit. Rub ovenproof casserole with remaining butter and fill with scallop mixture. Sprinkle with bread crumbs. Dot top of mixture with remaining butter. Heat in oven until bread crumbs are brown, 5–10 minutes. Serve immediately. Serves 6.

ARCHITECTURE AND NOTEWORTHY SITES

The typical Breton house is constructed of granite or schist, with a slate roof. In past years many roofs were made of thatch. Normally there are few openings in the facade. Many houses in the region have a central ridge line and chimneys on the gables. Most Breton houses tend to blend into their surroundings, especially with their low outlines and somber colors.

RENNES (pop. 197,536) has been the capital of Brittany since the sixteenth century. This ancient city was destroyed by fire in 1720 and then rebuilt. Its architecture tends to be more classical than Breton. Over the past fifteen years the population of the city has doubled, with 40,000 students now attending the university in Rennes. In July the city hosts the *Tombées de la Nuit* festival that features music, theater, and medieval costumes. At the *Musée de Bretagne* one can see an overview of the region from Gallo-Roman times to World War I and a display of local costumes.

BREST (pop. 147,956), a major naval port, was France's main naval dockyard in World War II and was heavily bombed. It is not a traditional tourist town. Its principal museums house paintings from the seventeenth-through the nineteenth-century Dutch, Flemish, and Italian schools. A naval museum is also located here.

ST.-MALO (pop. 48,057), although almost completely rebuilt after World War II, is a beautiful oceanside town that is a favorite of tourists. It is known for its walled city, beaches, and vast tidal variations (some of the highest in the world).

VANNES (pop. 45,644) is a quiet country town with charming old half-timbered buildings and narrow winding streets. A small port leads to the *Golfe du Morbihan*. Before the Romans dominated the area, Vannes was the capital of the Veneti, a Gallic tribe of sailors. In the ninth century, under the Breton hero Nominoë, Vannes emerged as the bastion of Breton unity. The *Musée Archéologique* in Vannes is rich in prehistoric items.

DINAN (pop. 11,591) is an attractive, fortified medieval town with cobblestone streets and old houses. Located 20 miles south of St.-Malo and sitting above the Rance River valley, Dinan has long been on the tourist map. The *Musée du Chateau* features the history of the town.

BELLE-ÎLE (pop. 4,500) is a beautiful island located 9 miles off the southern coast. It is the largest of the Breton islands, measuring 12 miles long and 5.5 miles wide. In the summer months the population swells to approximately 35,000 as tourists and vacationers descend on Brittany and its islands.

CARNAC (pop. 4,243) is a popular seaside resort, especially for families, on the southern coast. Besides its beaches, it is known for its almost 3,000 mysterious menhirs that date back several thousand years to the middle Neolithic period and the early Bronze Age.

SELECT BIBLIOGRAPHY

Flatres, P. *La Bretagne*. Paris: PUF, 1986.
Le Guen, Gilbert. "Bretagne," in André Gamblin, ed., *La France dans ses régions*, vol. 2. Paris: SEDES, 1994.
Philipponeau, M. "Bretagne," in Y. Lacoste, ed., *Géopolitiques des régions françaises*, vol. 2. Paris: Fayard, 1986.
Sainclivier, J. *La Bretagne de 1939 à nos jours*. Rennes: Ouest-France, 1989.

Chapter 5

BURGUNDY
(Bourgogne)

REGIONAL GEOGRAPHY

Known for its fine wines, gastronomy, and architectural treasures, Burgundy is situated in east-central France between the Paris Basin and the Rhône valley. Burgundy comprises four departments: Côte-d'Or, Nièvre, Saône-et-Loire, and Yonne. It represents a total of 19,495 square miles, 5.8 percent of the surface area of France, and the third largest region. Dijon is the region's capital.

The northern part of Burgundy is a plateau of Jurassic limestone, an area known especially for its wines. The southern part is very scenic; the fertile basin of the Saône is the heart of this area. Geographically, the region is known for its rolling hills, forests, and waterways. Not only do three major rivers flow through Burgundy—the Loire, the Yonne, and the Saône—but there are also 600 miles of canals. In general, the region is pastoral in appearance.

The climate is temperate, yet it tends to be colder in the Morvan, a hilly area near the center of the region. The mountainous regions are relatively wet; west of Dijon, however, there is considerable sun. Winters are often cold but clear. Spring is variable, and summer is often wet. Autumn, the grape harvest season, is usually mild and clear. Autumn is considered the most beautiful season.

HISTORY

Human history began in Burgundy roughly 100,000 years ago. In past centuries Burgundy represented a transit route, especially between the Med-

BURGUNDY
(BOURGOGNE)

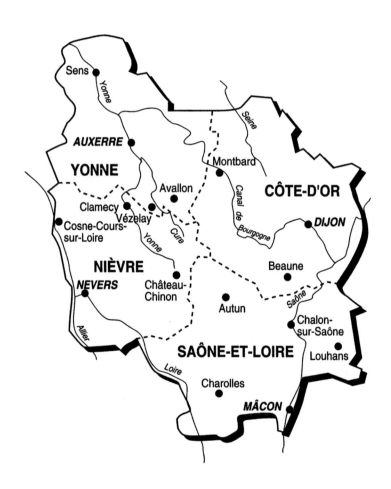

Sens

Yonne

AUXERRE

YONNE

Montbard

Seine

Avallon

CÔTE-D'OR

Clamecy

Vézelay

Cosne-Cours-
sur-Loire

Canal de Bourgogne

DIJON

Yonne

Cure

Beaune

NIÈVRE

NEVERS

Château-
Chinon

Autun

Saône

Chalon-
sur-Saône

Allier

SAÔNE-ET-LOIRE

Louhans

Loire

Charolles

MÂCON

iterranean and northern Europe. The Romans under Caesar first entered the area between 60 and 50 B.C., and in 52 B.C. they broke the resistance of the Gallic chieftain Vercingétorix at Alésia. Roman occupation encouraged trade and spurred the development of Celtic settlements, such as Autun. Eventually Roman civilization and Christianity spread throughout the region. In A.D. 470 the Burgundians along the Baltic shore, fleeing from the advancing Huns, settled in the region. In 534 the neighboring Franks occupied Burgundy. After the death of the Frankish Emperor Charlemagne and a long conflict over control of the area, it was divided into an eastern and a western sector. The east was ruled by Charlemagne's grandson Lothaire; the west was ruled by Charles the Bald, Lothaire's brother and enemy. In 1032 the Kingdom of Burgundy was incorporated into the Holy Roman Empire. Yet the western portion of the territory became linked to the west Frankish Kingdom and evolved into the area now known as Burgundy. The region developed as a stronghold of the Christian Church. Cluny became the headquarters of the Benedictine Order, which controlled more than 1,200 monasteries across Europe during the twelfth century. (Cluny was virtually destroyed during the Revolution of 1789.) The establishment of religious foundations aided the development of both agriculture and viticulture, which in turn strengthened trade. Under Philip of Valois, the region expanded toward the North Sea and the Jura mountain range near the Swiss border. Following the death of Charles the Bold in 1477, the Duchy of Burgundy became part of France.

At its height in the fourteenth and fifteenth centuries, Burgundy was more powerful and wealthy than the Kingdom of France. Much of the region's prosperity derived from the sale of wine and timber to both Paris and the Court. During this period there was a possibility that Burgundy might absorb the Kingdom of France; it was the Burgundians, one might recall, who captured Joan of Arc and sold her to the English. At its zenith the Burgundian capital of Dijon attracted artists, musicians, and architects from other parts of Europe, especially Flanders.

The modern era is said to have begun in Burgundy in 1794, when the Centre canal opened—a canal that linked the Saône and Loire Rivers. Not only did the canal enhance the transport of trade, but it also coincided with the exploitation of iron-ore deposits at Creusot.

RECENT POLITICS

Following World War II Burgundy became the base of former French president François Mitterrand (1981–1995), who began his political career in the Nièvre shortly after the war. However, Burgundy is also known as a region of political contrasts. Small working-class towns have traditionally voted for the left, whereas those associated with the wine industry have voted for the right. Fearing for its wine and agricultural industries, in September 1992 Burgundy voted against the Maastricht Treaty, which proposed further integration of the European Common Market. The parliamentary elections in the spring of 1993 were a debacle for the left, where the presidential majority of Mitterrand won only three seats as compared to the ten it had previously held in the region.

One month after these parliamentary elections, Mitterrand's former prime minister, Pierre Bérégovoy—who was elected mayor of the Burgundian town of Nevers in the 1980s—committed suicide along a canal in the region. Supposedly Bérégovoy took his own life because of the humiliation of the crushing defeat of the Socialist party and because several scandals touched him and his party. His suicide unleashed an outpouring of emotion in the region and throughout France.

In the first round of the presidential elections, the right-wing candidates collected more votes than the left in all departments except for Nièvre, the home base of former president Mitterrand. In the same round the right-wing extremist Jean-Marie Le Pen of the National Front party (FN) won 14.5 percent of the vote, 1 percent less than his national average in this election. Then, in the second round of the contest, the gaullist Jacques Chirac won all departments in the region except for Nièvre, where the socialist Lionel Jospin was victorious. In the June 1995 municipal elections the gaullist Rally for the Republic party retained the mayorship in Dijon and Chalon-sur-Saône, but the Socialist party retained control of city hall in Nièvre and Mâcon.

POPULATION

In recent decades Burgundy has seen a slight population increase. In 1975 the population stood at 1,571,000, and in 1993 it was 1,613,000. Nevertheless, over the past decade the population has grown at a rate one-quarter less than the national average. The region's population represents 2.8 percent of the national total, making Burgundy the seventeenth largest region in terms of population. The region's birthrate is 1.76, slightly above the national average of 1.73. Population density is a low 51.1 inhabitants per square kilometer (82.78 inhabitants per square mile), well below the 105.7 average for France (171.23 per square mile). In the north and west of the region there are often less than 20 inhabitants per square kilometer (32 inhabitants per square mile).

Burgundy has a large rural population, with 42.6 percent living in rural settings. Two departments, Saône-et-Loire and Nièvre, are losing population. Dijon, the regional capital, and its surrounding area account for a large percentage of the population of Burgundy—two out of three in the region live here.

As a whole, the region has an elderly population. Those age 60 and over make up 22.9 percent of the population (19.7% is the average for France).

The Nièvre, especially, is aged and is sparsely populated. Those age 19 and under constitute 25.8 percent of the total population. Immigrants represent 5.1 percent of the population, well below the 6.3 percent average for France. The urban population stands at 57.4 percent; this is far below the 76.4 percent average for France. Life expectancy is 76.8 years, slightly below the national average of 77.2 years.

In terms of educational levels, slightly more than 9 percent hold high school diplomas and 8.4 percent hold advanced degrees. Of the work force, 7.8 percent work in agriculture (down from 27% in 1962), 30.7 percent in industry, and 61.5 percent in the service sector. The unemployment rate is 12.3 percent (approximately the national average), with 12.7 percent of women out of work. Because Burgundy is situated relatively close to Paris and Lyon, the young and others seeking employment often go there to look for work if they are not attracted to Dijon.

ECONOMY

Burgundy's four departments are quite different in terms of economic development. The most prosperous is the Côte-d'Or, which has not only superb vineyards but also a developed service sector. Dijon, the principal city in this department, is both the regional capital and the largest population center in the region. It also has a large university. Further south, Beaune lies at the crossroads of an autoroute network that is important to French and European transportation.

The Saône-et-Loire has suffered a great deal in recent decades. For example, Le Creusot, an industrial conglomeration, has been hit hard by recession. Not surprisingly, the department is losing population as young people seeking work gravitate toward the large city of Lyon nearby. Around Mâcon one finds a large number of vineyards. The area known as the valley of the Loire is known for animal husbandry, which has suffered from an economic crisis in recent years.

The Nièvre and the Yonne are also varied. The Yonne is known for its cereal production. Sens, in the north of the Yonne, is now benefiting from demographic growth owing in large measure to its proximity to Paris and its location near an autoroute. The Nièvre, on the other hand, is the poorest department. In the eastern part of the Nièvre is the relatively mountainous and undeveloped area known as the Morvan; in the west is an active and industrial area, especially around Nevers.

Although Burgundy's economy is diversified, its economic identity is changing. This is due in large measure to the recent recession and the establishment of important communication links in the region, notably autoroutes and the high-speed TGV train that make Burgundy easily accessible.

In 1992 there were 690,000 people in the region's work force. Although the number of agricultural workers has declined to less than 8 percent, Burgundy continues to produce cereals, cattle, and, of course, wine. The average farm in the region is 116 acres, as compared to 69 acres for the national average. Although the region is not known for its industry, almost one-third of the work force is found here. Metallurgy, especially engineering work, is important. The metal industry benefits from access to both wood and coal. A large portion of the salaried employees in industry (70%) work for business whose parent company is located either in Paris or abroad. This is not surprising given Burgundy's geographical location in relation to Paris, Lyon, and the South. Other significant sectors of the economy include electronics, the agro-food industry, and textiles (namely clothing). Chemical and pharmaceutical industries are developing as well.

The three largest towns in the region are Dijon with 146,703 inhabitants, Chalon-sur-Saône with 54,575, and Nevers with 41,968. The four largest employers are Kodak Pathé (chemical), Ugine (iron and steel metallurgy), Creusot Loire (iron and steel metallurgy), and Dim (textiles).

Several factors will likely affect the region's future economic development. First, the economic integration of the Common Market may impact negatively on the agricultural base as Burgundy faces European competitors. Second, the development of autoroutes and the high-speed TGV train will ensure that Burgundy remains an area of transit, a zone of passage, along a north-south axis and an east-west axis. It has been referred to as "a crossroad next to the vineyards." Third, the proximity to Paris (which has a population of 10 million) makes the region a favorite get-away spot for Parisians, many of whom own a second residence in Burgundy. Fourth, the region is capitalizing on its rich history and culture and is promoting tourism.

CULTURE

Much of the culture and traditions of Burgundy center around the region's wines, gastronomy, and architectural heritage. Burgundy, along with Bordeaux, produces France's greatest wines. When the Romans first arrived in the region more than 2,000 years ago, they found grape vines already flourishing. Yet Burgundian wines came into their own during the Middle Ages, thanks to Cluniac and Cistercian monks who cultivated and improved wine production techniques. Today roughly 5,000 vineyards cover 52,500 acres—38,000 of these have superior status and carry the A.O.C. (*Appellation d'origine controlée*) label; less than 300 wines in all of France carry this label. The Côte-d'Or produces the most famous Burgundy wines; the two great vineyards here are the Côte de Nuits and the Côte de Beaune. In addition to its prestigious red wines, the region produces other wines of good quality, such as white wines from Mâcon and Chablis. As in other wine-producing areas of France, during the nineteenth century there was a devastating outbreak of phylloxera vastatrix, which destroyed the vines at the roots. The serious problem was solved when French vines were grafted onto root stocks of resistant American varieties. Without wine, Burgundy would not be the famous region that it is today. In the fall, Dijon hosts a major festival that celebrates wine and folklore: troupes of dancers and musicians from various parts of Europe participate in this celebration, which is known as *Folkloriades Internationales et Fêtes de la Vigne.*

The cuisine of the region rivals the reputation of its wine. Burgundy is known for its excellent restaurants and superb chefs. One authority has noted that *escargots* (snails) are essentially the symbol of the region. In addition to snails, the best-known regional dish is *boeuf bourguignon,* beef cooked in red wine sauce that usually includes mushrooms, onions, and bacon bits. Other dishes described as *á la bourguignon* are prepared with the same or similar red wine sauce. A number of regional dishes are also made with cream. Burgundy is known as well for its production of mustard and *crème de cassis,* a liqueur. Dijon is the mustard capital of the world, producing many varieties of the famous condiment. (Mustard was first introduced to France by the Romans.) Black currants produced in the region are used to make *crème de cassis,* the sweet liqueur that is added to white wine to make the *apéritif* known as *kir.*

Some purely visual treasures are also found in Burgundy, home of a number of masterpieces of Romanesque architecture—especially at sites such as Vézelay, Autun, and Cluny. Many of these architectural treasures, notably the churches and monasteries, date to the Middle Ages and are associated with the Catholicism of the period. For example, the center of medieval Catholicism was at Cluny, where in 910 a Benedictine abbey was founded. (The Benedictines controlled more than 1,200 monasteries across Europe.) Consequently, the church architecture of the region reflects the power and influence of the Benedictines. In Burgundy one can also find a number of medieval and Renaissance-era private residences, many having the multicolored tiled roofs that are typical of the region.

Burgundy is the home of several well-known writers. The Romantic poet **Alphonse de Lamartine** (1790–1869) was born at Mâcon into a family of land-owning minor aristocrats. Much of his poetry reflects the natural surroundings of his youth.

Two writers from the twentieth century have left portraits of their childhoods in Burgundy. **Henri Vincenot,** who was born in Dijon in 1912, wrote novels about local country life. Whereas Vincenot is not known outside of France, another Burgundian, **Sidonie-Gabrielle Colette** (1873–1954), is known around the world. Colette was born near Auxerre; her father was an invalid and former army captain. Her best-known works—*La Maison de Claudine* (1922, The House of Claudine) and *Sido* (1929; Sido was the name of Colette's mother)—focus on her relationship with her adored mother, life in Burgundy, nature, and animals.

Burgundy is also the home of an ancient tradition, "The Race for the Ring." Every year since at least 1639, the residents of Sémur-en-Auxois turn out for a horse race of about a mile and a quarter. This race is held on the Sunday closest to May 31. Supposedly the tradition began when Crusaders returned from Jerusalem bearing a ring that was hailed as the Virgin's wedding ring. At the race, the prizes remain the same as in centuries past: a golden ring engraved with the arms of the town, a gold-embroidered scarf, and a pair of gloves.

As mentioned earlier, excellent cuisine is central to the culture of Burgundy. Wine is used in much of the cooking of the region. *Escargots,* the best of which are fed grape leaves, are particularly delicious when prepared with chablis. Red wine is used in *boeuf bourguignon,* in a dish known as Charolais beef, and in *coq-au-vin.* Fish stew (*pauchouse*) with white wine is a specialty of Verdun-sur-le-Doubs. In the Morvan area, a dish of ham served with a cream sauce and white wine is popular. Ham with parsley as well as grilled tripe sausage served with mustard from Dijon are other appetizing regional dishes. A chicken dish known as *poulet de Bresse* is also well known.

Cheeses are produced in Burgundy. Near the Champagne border excellent cheeses are found: Chaource, Soumaintrain, and St. Florentin. The king of Burgundy cheeses, however, is Epoisses, a strong cheese that is often matured in brandy. In the south of the region, goat cheese is produced.

A Burgundian dinner might conclude with a tart or pudding made with cherries or black currants. One eats well in Burgundy. Below is a typical recipe from the region; the secret of this dish is to use a good quality red wine, ideally a Burgundy wine.

BOEUF BOURGUIGNON
(Beef Burgundy)

2 finely chopped onions

2 tsp. finely chopped garlic

2 finely chopped carrots

2 finely chopped celery stalks

3 tbs. olive oil

3 lbs. beef, such as round, top-side, or chuck steak, cut into 2-inch cubes

bouquet garni composed of 1 bay leaf, 1 sprig thyme and 5 sprigs parsley, bound together

salt and freshly ground black pepper to taste

1 bottle of good quality red wine, preferably from Burgundy

3 tbs. cornstarch

¼ cup water

2 tbs. chopped parsley

Mix together onions, garlic, carrots, and celery. In a large stewing pot or saucepan, heat oil and brown the meat with chopped vegetables for 6 minutes over high heat; stir frequently.

Add bouquet garni and salt and pepper, and pour in red wine. Bring to a boil, reduce heat, cover with lid, and simmer gently for 3 hours.

Mix cornstarch with water; thicken gravy with this mixture and stir until blended. Cook uncovered for 10 minutes. Remove bouquet garni. Add parsley and serve with boiled potatoes. Serves 8.

ARCHITECTURE AND NOTEWORTHY SITES

The Burgundy landscape is crisscrossed with stone walls, mostly dry-built. In the north are massive rectangular houses built of trimmed stone. Near Auxerre the stone is whitish, and the houses are often built on top of cellars. In the same area the family quarters, barn, and stable are under a common roof. Dwellings in areas with higher elevations differ little from houses in the surrounding countryside. In the vineyard areas, the cellar entrance is sheltered by a staircase leading to the living quarters. There is normally an overhanging roof. Because space is limited, village houses are situated close together. Wealthier landowners have houses with striking entrances and dormer windows. Glazed tile is sometimes used as a roofing material. Vine-growers' houses in the Mâcon area have a Mediterranean appearance, with rounded terra-cotta tiles and a first-floor gallery under a roof overhang. The stone used here is pink or russet. Houses in Mâcon are considered the most beautiful in the region. In the Morvan there are granite houses, normally roofed with slate.

DIJON (pop. 146,703) is an elegant city that once served as the capital of the Grand Dukes of Burgundy, who brought artists from Flanders to grace the city. Despite its many buildings dating to the Middle Ages and the Renaissance, the city has a youthful atmosphere owing to the presence of a large university. In Dijon, the palace of the Dukes and the States-General of Burgundy was once the palace of the duke of the region. The *Église Notre Dame* is an extraordinary church that was built between 1220 and 1240 in Burgundian Gothic style, the same style as the *Cathédrale Saint Bénigne* (supposedly constructed above the tomb of St. Benignus, who brought Christianity to Burgundy). The *Musée Rude* houses the works of sculptor François Rude (1784–1855), who was born in Dijon. The city also has an archaeology museum and a museum devoted to Burgundian life. The most outstanding museum is the *Musée des Beaux-Arts,* considered one of the richest in all of France. It houses many works and treasures from the fourteenth century. Seventy-five miles south of Dijon are the ruins of the enormous abbey of Cluny, the former headquarters of the Benedictines.

NEVERS (pop. 41,968) is situated on a bend in the Loire River. It is known for its medieval and Renaissance architecture, such as the *Église St. Étienne* from the late eleventh century and the *Ducal Palace* from the fifteenth and sixteenth centuries. The municipal museum has collections of earthenware, ivories, enamels, glass, and modern paintings.

AUXERRE (pop. 38,819), located between Dijon and Paris, is situated on a beautiful site on the left bank of the Yonne River. Since Gallo-Roman times, it has been a thriving commercial center. The Abbey St. Germain, founded during the sixth century, became an influential Benedictine abbey in the Middle Ages, attracting students from various parts of Europe. There is also a small but important Gothic cathedral, *Cathédrale St. Étienne,* which was constructed between the thirteenth and sixteenth centuries. The *Musée Leblanc-Durvernoy* houses eighteenth-century tapestries from Beauvais, faience from Burgundy and other places, and a collection of paintings.

MÂCON (pop. 37,275) is a busy commercial town and a wine center on the banks of the Saône River. The *Musée Municipal des Ursulines* contains archaeological finds; exhibits of ethnography; Dutch, Flemish, and French paintings; and contemporary art. Mâcon is the birthplace of the poet and politician Alphonse Lamartine (1790–1869). The *Musée Lamartine* has momentos of Lamartine and nineteenth-century furniture and art. Near Mâcon is *Solutré,* where archaeologists in 1866 discovered the skeletons of approximately 100,000 horses. It is at this site that prehistoric men and women disposed of the horse skeletons after eating the animals. Horse meat is still consumed in France.

BEAUNE (pop. 21,289) is a wonderful place for wine tasting; it lies in the heart of the Côte-d'Or and is dedicated to the production of fine wine. The old city is surrounded by ramparts, part of the medieval fortification system. An architectural gem is the *Hôtel-Dieu,* a Flemish-Burgundian Gothic charity hospital with a roof of multicolored glazed tile. There is also the *Basilique Collégiate Notre Dame,* which was begun in 1120 and was affiliated with the Benedictine monastery at Cluny. Beaune also has a wine museum, with exhibits on the various stages of wine production.

AUTUN (pop. 17,906), located 53 miles southwest of Dijon, was founded in 10 B.C. and was one of the most important towns in Roman Gaul. The city was repeatedly sacked during the third century by barbarian tribes, but its fortunes improved in the Middle Ages owing in large measure to the construction of a Burgundian Romanesque cathedral, *Cathédrale Saint-Lazare.* The *Musée Rollin* has an important Gallo-Roman collection as well as works from later centuries. Autun possesses a number of important Roman vestiges: several Roman gates leading to the original town, and a Roman arena. Autun is surrounded by medieval ramparts that gave added protection to its residences in past centuries. Napoleon and his brothers studied briefly at the Jesuit college here.

VÉZELAY (pop. 500) is considered one of the architectural gems of France. This medieval walled village is perched on a hill, originally situated for defensive reasons, and is surrounded by beautiful countryside. The village was founded in the ninth century when a monastery was constructed on the hilltop. The abbey reportedly harbors relics of Christ's disciple St. Mary Magdalene. In 1100 and 1200 it became an important site for pilgrimages. During the height of its power and influence in the Middle Ages, several Crusades began here. UNESCO has proclaimed Vézelay an international treasure.

SELECT BIBLIOGRAPHY

Chapuis, Robert. "Bourgogne," in André Gamblin, ed., *France dans ses régions,* vol. 1. Paris: SEDES, 1994.

Fried, Eunice. *Burgundy: The Country, the Wines, the People.* New York: Harper & Row, 1986.

Plet, F. "Bourgogne," in Y. Lacoste, ed., *Géopolitiques des régions françaises,* vol. 3. Paris: Fayard, 1986.

CENTRE

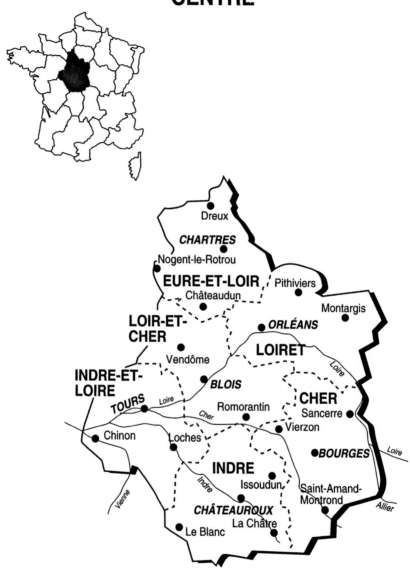

Dreux

CHARTRES

Nogent-le-Rotrou

EURE-ET-LOIR

Châteaudun

Pithiviers

Montargis

LOIR-ET-CHER

ORLÉANS

LOIRET

Vendôme

Loire

INDRE-ET-LOIRE

TOURS

Loire

BLOIS

Romorantin

Cher

CHER

Sancerre

Vierzon

Chinon

Loches

●BOURGES

Loire

INDRE

Indre

Issoudun

Saint-Amand-Montrond

Vienne

CHÂTEAUROUX

La Châtre

Le Blanc

Allier

Chapter 6

CENTRE

REGIONAL GEOGRAPHY

The Centre is situated directly below the Île-de-France, where Paris is located. The southern boundary of the Centre is formed by Poitou-Charentes, Limousin, and Auvergne. The Centre is one of the largest regions of the Paris Basin. It is more or less in the center of France, with several of its villages claiming to be the exact center of the hexagon. The region comprises 24,167 square miles, 7.2 percent of the surface area of France, and includes six departments: Cher, Eure-et-Loir, Indre, Indre-et-Loire, Loir-et-Cher, and Loiret. Orléans is the capital of the Centre.

Geographically the region is one of plateaus and valleys, especially around the Loire River. In the northeastern and southeastern portions of the Centre the elevation rises to nearly 980 feet above sea level; there are lower elevations in and along the Loire valley, which stretches across the region. Forests cover one-fourth of the Centre, with some areas much more heavily wooded than others. Roughly 42 percent of the area known as the Sologne in the middle of the region and south of Orléans is forested; it includes the *Forêt d'Orléans,* one of the largest forests in France. The area north of the *Forêt d'Orléans* includes a number of open fields. Farmland subdivided by hedges and trees can be found in the south. Besides the Loire, numerous rivers flow through the region, such as the Vienne, the Creuse, the Indre, the Cher, the Souldre, the Loing, and the Loir.

The climate varies. Along the Loire valley it is relatively mild, with the influence of the Atlantic Ocean making for mild winters. Temperatures rarely fall below 50° Fahrenheit. Indian summer truly exists in the Centre; consequently autumn is a beautiful season for visiting this area. South of the Loire valley the climate is dominated by a mixture of continental and coastal influences. In general, winters are relatively cold and spring is late; however, summers and autumn are long and sunny.

HISTORY

The Centre is an amalgamation of three ancient provinces—Touraine, Orléans, and Berry. It is instructive to examine first the area along the Loire valley, from roughly Tours to Orléans, and then the southernmost section that was once Berry.

Regarding the northern half of the region, a Mediterranean people known as the Ligurians overran Brittany and the Loire during the Neolithic period. Between 1200 and 800 B.C. the Celts arrived from central Europe and colonized the Loire valley. They founded both Orléans and Blois and established a port town at Tours, controlling trade on both the Loire and Cher Rivers. Julius Caesar's legions arrived in the area in 52 B.C. In the first century A.D. Christianity was introduced, with Saint Martin of Tours (316–397) playing a leading role in promoting the new religion.

Following the fall of the Roman Empire in the fifth century and the arrival of the barbarians and then the Arabs, the abbeys of the Loire valley attempted to preserve Christian teachings and Greek and Roman knowledge. The Germanic Merovingians under Clovis in 448 initiated the conquest of Gaul and settled in the Loire valley. In 451 the Huns were turned back at Bordeaux. In 732 Charles Martel defeated the Arabs at Poitiers as the invaders were marching to the gates of Tours.

Charlemagne's reign brought stability. The first university in the region was established at Orléans by Bishop Theodulfe. The Loire valley became a significant part of the struggle between the Plantagenets and the Capetians beginning in the twelfth century when Henry Plantagenet became King of England. This ushered in a long period of conflict. Then followed the Hundred Years War (1337–1453). When the English captured Paris, the ancient province of Touraine became the seat of royalty. At the end of the Hundred Years War, the French kings retained their hold over the Loire and remained there. Louis XI's reign saw the revival of trade and the start of the silk industry at Tours. Moreover, following the example of his father, Louis XI utilized the middle class and craftsmen instead of feudal lords as his chief administrators. These administrators built beautiful townhouses in Blois and Tours and the chateaux of Chenonceaux, Azay-le-Rideau, Villandry, and Blésois. During the first half of the sixteenth century, France maintained a presence in Italy (which was only a geographic expression at that time; it was united in the nineteenth century). This resulted in Italian artists and artisans working in France and spreading the Italian Renaissance along the Loire. Subsequently the Wars of Religion broke out in the Loire valley. At this time, the Protestant Henry IV converted to Catholicism and moved the central government to Paris.

The southern part of the region, what was once Berry, has a different history. In the eighth century B.C. two Celtic tribes inhabited this area. Later, the city of Bourges was reputed to be the most beautiful city in Gaul. Yet Gaul was partitioned in 27 B.C., and this area was considered part of Aquitaine. With the spread of Christianity in the third century A.D., Bourges became the office of the bishop for the diocese of Aquitaine. Germanic tribes began invading as early as A.D. 279, but neither the Visigoths nor the Franks imposed their authority over the area. The Duchy of Aquitaine, formed in 614, remained independent of Frankish Merovingian kings until 761. At this time, the rise of the feudal system helped to break up the area.

In the tenth century the former county of Bourges was divided into two units. One was the viscounty of Bourges, which was sold to France in 1101 and then given status as a duchy. The second was the viscounty of Déols, which was attached to Aquitaine until conquered by Philippe Auguste.

The best-known duke of this area was Jean (1340–1416), brother of Charles V. Jean had an elegant court and patronized the arts. He left behind, among other things, a glimpse of the Middle Ages in the famous book of hours known as the *Très Riches Heures du Duc de Berry*. During the Middle Ages, Bourges was an important center for the arts. King Charles VII of France resided there until Joan of Arc helped to drive the English occupiers out of France. In 1601 the area was annexed by France and became an integral part of the nation.

RECENT POLITICS

The 1992 regional elections were won by the right, claiming thirty-two elected officials as compared to twenty-five for the left. In the same elections the Ecologists won nine representatives. The extremist right-wing National Front (FN) party, led in the Centre by Marie-France Stirbois of Dreux, won eleven representatives.

The 1993 parliamentary elections were a disaster for the left in the Centre. Jack Lang, former minister of culture under President François Mitterrand (1981–1995) and currently the mayor of Blois, was the only candidate on the left to win a seat. On the right, the gaullist Rally for the Republic (RPR) won ten seats and the Union for French Democracy (UDF) captured eleven seats.

Then, in the first round of the 1995 presidential elections, voters in all departments of the Centre favored right-wing candidates over the left. During the first round, too, the extremist National Front candidate Jean-Marie Le Pen won 14.82 percent of the vote in the Centre, close to his national average of 15 percent. In the second round of the presidential contest, voters supported the gaullist mayor of Paris, Jacques Chirac, who captured 65,000 more votes than the socialist candidate, Lionel Jospin. In the June 1995 municipal elections, Marie-France Stirbois of the National Front made a strong showing in Dreux but was defeated in the second round of voting by a gaullist candidate who had the support of the left.

POPULATION

The population of the Centre has increased over the past twenty years; today its birthrate approximates the national norm of 1.73. In 1975 the population was 2,153,000; in 1993 it was 2,418,000, or 4.2 percent of the population of France. However, the population increase has been more drastic in the area closest to Paris, namely, the departments of Eure-et-Loir and Loiret. Between 1962 and 1990 Eure-et-Loir witnessed a 43 percent population increase and Loiret saw a 49 percent increase. The southern portion of the region is less populated and less dynamic; in fact, it is losing population. Although the Centre is one of the largest regions of France, it is also one of the least populated, with a density of 61.8 inhabitants per square kilometer (100.11 per square mile), as compared to a national average of 105.7 per square kilometer (171.23 per square mile).

Although the region's population is keeping pace with the national average, the age of the population is elevated owing in part to retirees who have discovered the region. Those age 60 and older make up 21.5 percent of the population (the national average is 19.7 percent). Young people, those age 19 and younger, comprise 26.4 percent of the population, slightly below the 26.8 percent national average. Immigrants make up 5 percent of the region's population (6.3 percent is the average for France).

The urban population is 64.8 percent, below the 76.4 percent national average. Life expectancy is 77.4 years, roughly the national norm. Approximately 25.9 percent of all households in the region are single-person households.

Educational levels are below national norms. In the Centre only 9 percent hold a high school degree and only 8.4 percent possess an advanced degree (10.5 percent and 11.2 percent, respectively, are the national norms). Yet over the past five to seven years 50 percent of high school students have obtained degrees, and the universities at Orléans and Tours each have roughly 30,000 students. However, many young people are attracted to Paris because of the training and jobs available in the capital. Of the work force, 7.7 percent are employed in agriculture, 29.2 percent in industry, and 63.1 percent in the service sector. The unemployment rate is approximately 12 percent, with nearly 13 percent of women out of work.

ECONOMY

The region is ideally situated adjacent to the Île-de-France, literally at the door of the nation's capital. At the same time, it is one of the least populated regions in France. The Centre is easily accessible from Paris and is attracting young workers from the capital who are seeking work outside of France's largest city. Today the region is ranked eighth in gross domestic product per inhabitant.

Economically, the Centre is diversified. Since 1945 it has benefited from the decentralization of Parisian industry. Its proximity to Paris and its attractiveness for foreign investors are assets. Moreover, its industrial work force is well qualified. For example, between 1982 and 1990 regional industry in the Centre lost only 6 percent of its salaried positions, half the national norm during the same period. The region produces electrical equipment, household electronics, rubber, plastics, chemicals, and pharmaceuticals. It also plays an important role in the French nuclear energy system, with nuclear reactors in Loiret, Loir-et-Cher, and Indre-et-Loire.

The Centre, too, is an agricultural region, with almost 8 percent of its work force in this domain (5.3 percent is the average for France). In fact, 7.5 percent of French agricultural production comes from the Centre. It is the largest producer of cereals in France and in the European Economic Community (Common Market). The region produces 18 percent of the nation's wheat, 12 percent of its corn, and 7 percent of its beets.

Perhaps the greatest weakness of the Centre's economy is the insufficiently developed service sector. Yet the economic crisis in France in recent years—especially in Paris—has seen service sector workers from the capital assuming positions in the Centre. This region, with its peaceful countryside, rural character, and welcoming villages, offers possibilities for further development in the area of tourism, even though its famous chateaux at Chambord and Chenonceaux and its magnificent cathedral at Chartres are well-recognized architectural treasures. Today the hotel industry is strong in the Loire valley.

The three largest towns are Tours with 129,509 inhabitants, Orléans with 105,111, and Bourges with 75,609. Approximately 14.1 percent of the work force is found in Tours, 13.1 percent in Orléans, and 5.3 percent in Bourges. The four largest employers are the General Hospital in Tours, the Mayor's Office in Tours, Michelin Tire Company, and Aérospatiale (aerospace).

One obstacle to development has been the name of the region itself. On the one hand, there is a debate within the region about where the exact center of France is located. On the other hand, the Centre is often incorrectly associated with the Massif Central, a rural backwater that has a negative image with respect to economic development. The desire to change the name of the region reveals the fragility of the Centre's identity. Since 1990, four names have been officially advanced: "Centre-Val de Loire," "Coeur de France," "Val de Loire," and "Val de France." In November 1994 the region decided to opt for Centre-Val de Loire; but the change, requiring a vote of Parliament, has not yet been made.

Like other regions near the Île-de-France, the Centre has trouble maintaining its own identity. With the extension of the autoroute and the high-speed TGV rail line, parts of the region must be careful not to simply become a suburb of Paris.

CULTURE

In the Centre the Loire valley is known for its splendid chateaux, such as Chambord, Chaumont, Chenonceaux, and Azay-le-Rideau. These architectural gems reflect the Renaissance in arts and letters that once blossomed in the Loire. Following the Hundred Years War, the last part of the fifteenth century saw the emergence of the first French Renaissance period. In the Loire valley a school of thought arose that was marked by humanist architects whose inspiration came from Italy and from classical antiquity. Many of the chateaux of the Loire reflect these influences.

The Loire valley, too, is the "garden of France." Flowers, vegetables, and fruits thrive here in the rich alluvium deposited by the Loire and its tributaries. In this "garden" the light is different from that of other nearby regions, such as the Île-de-France and Normandy. Artists such as **Leonardo da Vinci** noted this centuries ago. In 1516 King François I invited da Vinci to France and to Amboise in the Loire valley, where they discussed art and science. Da Vinci died in 1519 in the castle of Cloux near Amboise. He left behind the masterpiece the *Mona Lisa*, a portrait of a Florentine merchant's wife, a woman with an enigmatic smile. This famous painting is now on display in the Louvre in Paris.

The Centre is also known for its pottery, especially that of Gien in the Loiret. Pottery first appeared here in 1820. Gien ceramics often draw inspiration from allegories, proverbs, riddles, and military scenes. The pottery center in Gien is the largest ceramics works in France.

The first writer to call this area "the garden of France" was **François Rabelais** (1494–1553), the rebellious Renaissance humanist who was born in Tours. His satirical novels *Gargantua* and *Pantagruel* mention the villages and chateaux of his native region.

A contemporary of Rabelais was **Pierre de Ronsard** (1524–1585), who was born north of Tours. Ronsard was a lyric poet who passionately loved nature. Many of his poems display his intense feeling for the native countryside.

The Loire must also be given credit for inspiring an enduring fairy tale. Along the Loire near the border separating the Centre and the Pays de la Loire, one finds the chateau of Ussé. This chateau served as a model for the castle in **Charles Perrault's** (1628–1703) *Sleeping Beauty*. (Perrault was also the author of *Mother Goose* and other stories.)

Emile Zola (1840–1902), although born in Provence, used the Beauce (a monotonous plain that is today a wheat-growing area in the Centre north of the Loire near Orléans) as the setting for his novel *La Terre*. Although he admired the beauty of the area, he was critical of its peasant inhabitants as being brutish, malicious, and suspicious. The Beauce also appears in other works by Zola. Other writers, too, have described the Beauce and its inhabitants in their works—writers such as Rabelais, Péguy, and Proust.

Charles Péguy (1873–1914), born in Orléans, not only wrote about the Beauce but also described the cathedral at Chartres, which is visible for miles across the plain. Péguy visited the cathedral frequently and helped to renew the medieval tradition of pilgrimages to Chartres. One of his poems, "*Présentation de la Beauce à Notre-Dame de Chartres,*" celebrates one such pilgrimage.

Marcel Proust (1871–1922) was born in Paris but featured an area near the Beauce in his monumental 3,300-page *À la recherche du temps perdu* (Remembrance of Things Past). He spent part of his childhood holidays with his aunt and uncle at Illiers-Combray. In his work Proust examined the concept of time, the drive for time regained, and the notion that periods of one's life coexist forever within a person. The rediscovery of these things, said Proust, is what gives meaning to life itself. His youth at Illiers-Combray played a significant role in his *temps perdu.*

The southeastern part of the Centre, in what was once Berry, was the home of **Georges Sand** (1804–1876). Born Aurore Dupin in Paris, this noted writer used a pen name after the publication of her first novel. Following the death of her father when she was 5 years old, she was taken to Nohant (southwest of Bourges) to live. She married the Baron Dudevant but remained close to peasant friends from her childhood. Nohant was her home for forty years; here she entertained the cultural elite of the period—personalities such as the Polish-born French composer (and her lover) Frédéric Chopin (1810–1849), the Hungarian pianist and composer Franz Liszt (1811–1886), the French author Honoré de Balzac (1799–1850), the French painter Eugène Delacroix (1798–1863), the French author Gustav Flaubert (1821–1880), and the Russian novelist Ivan Turgenev (1818–1883). A bohemian to the core, Sand smoked, wore trousers, wrote under a masculine pen name, and espoused left-wing views. In part, her work attempts to rehabilitate the peasantry, whom Balzac and other earlier writers had criticized, and to dignify manual labor. She celebrated traditional life instead of technological change. Her social life, however, was anything but traditional.

Near Sand in the village of Epineuil-le-Fleuriel lived the writer **Alain-Fournier**. Although his real name was Henri Fournier (1886–1914) and he was born north of Bourges, he lived at Epineuil from the age of 5 to 12. His novel *Le Grand Meaulnes* (The Wanderer) captures the landscape of the Sologne area of forests and lagoons. The book has seen various translations and is relatively well known in France.

The cuisine of the Centre is wonderfully rich. Around Tours and Orléans, fruits and vegetables are specialties. Excellent salmon, carp, shad, and other fish come from the Loire. Pork and poultry are used in various forms of *andouillette, andouille* (chitterling sausage), *rillettes* (potted meat), black or white *boudin* (blood sausage), and *noisette de porc* and poultry. The Sologne is known for its pheasant, boar, lark, and game *pâtés,* as well as for a variety of wild mushrooms. Around Tours country breads, goat cheese, and red wine are common staples. The area around Orléans, too, produces a wide variety of goat cheese as well as cheeses such as Saint-Benoit, Patay, and Cendré d'Olivet. Traditional recipes dominate the confectionery of the Loire valley, with recipes for Prunes of Tours, crystallized fruit, and quince marmalade from Orléans. The white wines are of excellent quality, especially the Vouvray and the Sancerre (produced principally in the department of Cher).

In the southeastern portion of the Centre, simple country food made with local produce is the norm. Yet great skill has been developed over the centuries in many farm kitchens. One finds, for example, *oyonnade* (chicken in a wine sauce), braised chicken *à la Berry* (cooked with the blood and liver of the bird), and *poulet en barbouille* (a daub). Chicken is sometimes prepared with unsweetened grape juice, and in pies. Also popular are *pâtés* and meat pies with crackling. Berry claims to have invented the *sanciau,* a cross between a pancake and an omelet. Other area specialties are braised beef in wine, braised head of beef, superb local beef, and many kinds of local game. The area also produces goat cheese, including one that is pyramidal in shape and charcoal-dusted, as well as *crottins of Chavignol.* Below is a pleasant accompaniment for many dishes; goat cheese is a specialty of the Centre and makes a flavorful addition to salads.

SALADE DE CONCOMBRES ET CHÈVRE
(Cucumber and Goat Cheese Salad)

2 cucumbers, peeled and thinly sliced	2 tbs. water
1 tomato, cubed	salt and freshly ground black pepper to taste
¼ lb. goat cheese, crumbled	2 tbs. olive oil
1 tsp. Dijon mustard	2 tbs. chopped parsley
1 tbs. red wine vinegar	

Combine the cucumber, tomato, and goat cheese in a salad bowl. In a separate container mix mustard, vinegar, water, salt, and pepper; whisk in olive oil slowly. Add this vinaigrette to salad and toss. Sprinkle with parsley. Serves 4.

ARCHITECTURE AND NOTEWORTHY SITES

The Loire valley is known for its string of magnificent chateaux along the famous river and its tributaries. During the Renaissance, and especially during the eighteenth century, the bourgeoisie and civil servants built elegant mansions in towns such as Tours and Blois. These houses, similar to the chateaux and churches of the area, are constructed of tufa—a fine white limestone from the hillsides. In the countryside and on ordinary buildings, the use of tufa goes back only to the nineteenth century; before this date, brick and stone coated with plaster was used. Roofing was similar. Angers slate was used exclusively for chateaux prior to the nineteenth century but began to appear on smaller buildings in the twentieth century. The combination of blue slate and white stone gives the region a luminous and cheerful character.

Traditional houses are oriented toward the south or southeast to gain protection from the winds. Windows tend to be tall and narrow. Dormer windows are often found in the area around Tours and Orléans. Also, chimney stacks can be of imposing dimensions. In the Loire valley, too, the *fuie* (dovecote) is a characteristic feature. This structure is either circular, square, or hexagonal; it may be attached to a farmhouse or it may be separate. In the Sologne, brick is a typical building material. Here brick replaced cob in the nineteenth century; cob was used to fill in timber-framed structures.

TOURS (pop. 129,509) is often a stopping point or base for those visiting the chateaux of the Loire. Here the wealthy bourgeoisie built elegant Renaissance and neo-classical mansions. Tours twice served as France's capital. In 1870, in the midst of the Franco-Prussian War, the provisional government of national defense fled from Paris and established itself in Tours. (Interior Minister Léon Gambetta fled Paris by balloon.) Later the city fell to the Prussian army. Then, during World War II when France was falling to the Germans, once again the government located in Tours before moving to Vichy. Subsequently the city was damaged by German bombardments. The city was restored after the war. Today Tours is the center of light industry, research, and data processing. It also has a university. In May and September it is the site of important international fairs, and in late June and early July a well-known music festival is held here. The Old Town of the city is centered around *Place Plumereau,* the main square since the Middle Ages. In the Old Town are many half-timbered houses, some dating from the 1400s. The Old Town is a pedestrian area where cafés and restaurants come to life at night. The *Cathédrale Saint Gatien,* built between the thirteenth and sixteenth centuries and with fine flying buttresses at the rear, shows the evolution of the Gothic style. The *Musée des Beaux-Arts* houses a good collection of paintings, *objets d'art,* and furniture from the fourteenth to the twentieth centuries. Several of the paintings were taken from Italy by Napoleon. The *Musée Campagnonage* displays the crafts of artisans, offering a good example of life before the Industrial Revolution. The *Musée Archéologique de Touraine,* housed in a magnificent Renaissance residence, displays a collection of prehistoric, Gallo-Roman, medieval, Renaissance, and eighteenth-century artifacts. The *Musée des Vins de*

Touraine focuses on the significance of and traditions associated with the wines of the area.

ORLÉANS (pop. 105,111) is a town that Joan of Arc helped to make famous; she made a triumphal entrance into the town after the English had been driven out. Orléans celebrates the *Fête de Jeanne d'Arc* in early May of each year. Although the city was damaged during World War II, it has been carefully restored. Today it is a commercial center. The *Rue d'Escures* has beautiful seventeenth-century mansions. The *Cathédrale Ste.-Croix* is a Gothic church rebuilt during the seventeenth and eighteenth centuries after destruction in the Wars of Religion. The *Musée des Beaux-Arts* has an exquisite collection of seventeenth- and eighteenth-century portraits from the French school, as well as other important pieces. There is also a History Museum in a charming Renaissance building, *Hôtel Cabu.* Nearby is a wonderful floral park (5 miles to the southeast) and the *Forest of Orléans,* where one can stroll and picnic.

BOURGES (pop. 75,609) is a beautiful and historic town. In the fifteenth century Charles VII's finance minister, Jacques-Coeur, chose Bourges as his official residence; the residence can be viewed today. John Calvin, the Reformation leader, studied law in Bourges. The *Cathédrale St.-Étienne* was built between 1192 and 1324 and is considered one of the great cathedrals of France; it is known, among other things, for its five doors surrounded with carvings. One of the most attractive streets in Bourges is *Rue Bourbonnoux,* lined with fifteenth- and sixteenth-century houses. The *Musée de Berry* has prehistoric, Gallo-Roman, and medieval artifacts. The *Musée Estève* houses the works of the twentieth-century local artist Maurice Estève and the paintings of other modern artists. The fifteenth-century *Hôtel Lallemant* displays furniture, tapestries, and other items from the seventeenth and eighteenth centuries. A spring music festival held in Bourges features a variety of music, and in late June and July a celebration of traditional music known as the *Fête de Jacques Coeur* takes place. From mid-July through August the town hosts the *Ballades à Bourges,* a grand celebration of music, dance, and theater. Near Bourges is the *Route Jacques Coeur*—a series of eighteen chateaux, many owned by the former finance minister himself. Although not as famous as the chateaux of the Loire, they do present an intriguing variety of architectural styles.

CHARTRES (pop. 39,595) is the home of the famous thirteenth-century *Cathédrale Notre Dame,* with its two soaring spires (one Gothic and one Romanesque) that are visible from miles away across the farmland. Besides a Romanesque bell tower dating from the 1140s and other exquisite features, the cathedral is known for its stunning stained-glass windows. During World Wars I and II the windows were hidden away for safe-keeping. In the city itself there is an Old Town worthy of a visit, plus a *Musée des*

Beaux-Arts that possesses sixteenth-century enamels made by Léonard Limosin for François I. The museum also displays wooden sculptures from the Middle Ages, paintings from the sixteenth through the nineteenth centuries, and a prerevolutionary harpsichord (a harpsichord festival is held here in May). The *Centre International du Vitrail* shows the history, production, and restoration of stained glass. *Le Compa* displays agricultural implements and machinery.

AZAY-LE-RIDEAU (pop. 3,053) is the site of one of the most beautiful chateaux of the Loire valley, a chateau that is surrounded by trees and reflected in its own lake. The chateau is a good example of Renaissance architecture in the Loire valley. A replacement for a smaller fortress, it dates from the early 1500s. It offered both comfort and security to its occupants. The paintings, furniture, and tapestries help to make this chateau a Renaissance museum.

SANCERRE (pop. 2,059) is a small town and a wine-growing district in the department of Cher near Burgundy; it is known for its white wines. The town has small twisting streets and several fifteenth- through sixteenth-century houses. There is also a nineteenth-century pseudo-Renaissance chateau. Points in the town and nearby offer magnificent views of the rolling hills of the countryside covered with vineyards.

SAINT-BENOIT-SUR-LOIRE (pop. 1,880) is known for its abbey and the history behind it. The abbey has been a pilgrimage site since the time of the druids in ancient Gaul. During the Middle Ages the relics of Saint Benedict, the father of Western monasticism, were transferred here. During the reign of Charlemagne in the late eighth and early ninth centuries the influence of the Benedictine abbey spread throughout Christendom. The abbey church, built between 1067 and 1218, is one of the best examples of Romanesque architecture in France. The eleventh-century crypt contains the relics of Saint Benedict.

CHENONCEAUX (pop. 313) is known for its famous chateau built in 1515. An alley of trees leads up to the chateau. It contains fine Flemish tapestries, Renaissance and seventeenth- and eighteenth-century paintings, and period furniture. One can also see the bedrooms of François I and Diane de Poitiers.

CHAMBORD (pop. 200) is the site of a chateau that is one of the gems of the French Renaissance. The chateau marked the beginning of François I's reign. The king adored this residence because of his love of hunting. A former hunting lodge that was rebuilt in 1519, it is based on the plan of a feudal chateau and has a four-tower central keep and enclosing walls. It is surrounded by a 33-square-mile park. From the terraces of the chateau the Court could watch the royal hunt. According to some, this chateau was the first sign of architectural megalomania that eventually led to the construction of Versailles by Louis XIV.

SELECT BIBLIOGRAPHY

Bachelard, A. "Centre," in Y. Lacoste, ed., *Géopolitiques des régions françaises,* vol. 1. Paris: Fayard, 1986.

Gaspard, Françoise. *A Small City in France,* trans. Arthur Goldhammer. Cambridge, MA: Harvard University Press, 1995.

Verrière, Jacques. "Centre," in André Gamblin, ed., *La France dans ses régions,* vol 1. Paris: SEDES, 1994.

———. *La Loire et Paris. La France essentielle de Clovis à nos jours.* Paris: Flammarion, 1990.

Chapter 7

CHAMPAGNE-ARDENNE

REGIONAL GEOGRAPHY

This region, made famous by history and champagne, stretches from the Belgian border in the north to Burgundy in the south. The western border is contiguous with the regions of Picardy and the Île-de-France; the eastern border is formed by Lorraine. The southeastern corner borders Franche-Comté. Champagne-Ardenne comprises 15,806 square miles, 4.7 percent of the surface area of France, and includes the departments of Ardennes, Marne, Aube, and Haute-Marne. The region's capital is Châlons-sur-Marne.

Perhaps the most characteristic feature of the region's geography is its chalky soil. "Chalky Champagne," as one area is called, is the western part of the region around Reims, Épernay, Châlons-sur-Marne, Ste.-Menehould, and Vitry-le-François. The sunny slopes of the valleys produce the vines that give this region its name. An area known as "wet Champagne" forms an arc to the east of Ste.-Menehould and Vitry. This area is wooded and relatively wet. In the northeast is the Ardennes, a hilly and mountainous area with elevations rising to more than 1,600 feet. The Ardennes is known for its forests of beech and fir trees and its abundance of game. Through the Ardennes flows the Meuse River. Champagne is sometimes referred to as a region of forests (Ardennes, Saint-Gobain, and Villers-Cotterets), of lakes, and of fertile valleys.

The climate in Champagne-Ardenne is more temperate in the western portion of the region, with average temperatures ranging from 36° to 64.4° Fahrenheit and with an annual rainfall of 22–28 inches. Both the Ardennes

CHAMPAGNE-ARDENNE

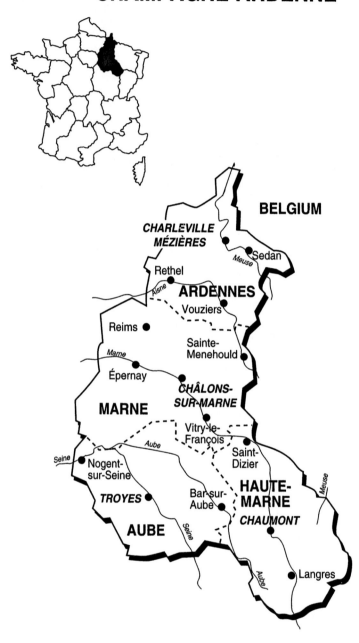

BELGIUM

CHARLEVILLE
MÉZIÈRES

Sedan

Meuse

Rethel

Alsne

ARDENNES

Vouziers

Reims ●

Sainte-
Menehould

Marne

Épernay

CHÂLONS-
SUR-MARNE

MARNE

Vitry-le-
François

Aube

Saint-
Dizier

Seine

Nogent-
sur-Seine

Meuse

HAUTE-
MARNE

TROYES

Bar-sur-
Aube

CHAUMONT

AUBE

Seine

Aube

Langres

in the north and the Haute-Marne in the southeast are colder and wetter, with an average of 39–47 inches of rainfall annually.

HISTORY

A considerable portion of French history has been written in Champagne-Ardenne. In 3,000 to 4,000 B.C. the region was a crossroads that witnessed territorial disputes between the Celts and Danubians. When Julius Caesar conquered Gaul in 57 B.C., the Romans introduced a period of peace and prosperity. Moreover, Caesar made the local capital at a chief town of a Belgic people known as the Remi. Eight trade routes met in this town, which eventually became known as Reims (Anglicized as "Rheims" but pronounced *rance* in French). During the Roman occupation, invading Franks and Teutons stayed and settled and lived in a tenuous coexistence. Yet in A.D. 451 when Attila the Hun invaded the region, the Romans, Franks, and Visigoths joined forces to defeat Attila at the battle of Champs Catalauniques, 12.5 miles north of Troyes.

After the fall of Rome in the fifth century, Christianity received legitimacy in the region and elsewhere in France. In 496 the king of the Franks, Clovis, was baptized in Reims. From this time forward, Reims became the place of coronation for French kings. This gave added importance to the Archbishop of Reims and to the region. When Clovis died the kingdom was divided among his three sons and partitioned again among their heirs. Following Charlemagne's death in 814, the empire that he had established disintegrated and Champagne-Ardenne became a buffer region that witnessed various invasions from the east and the west; the Normans invaded in 883 and the Hungarians in 926 and 954.

During the Middle Ages, however, the region became a hub of European commerce. Its important geographical position made it a center of trade fairs, dealing principally with luxury goods such as silks and spices. The fairs enhanced the region's prosperity, which is reflected in its architecture. In 1147 the Church launched its call for the Second Crusade in Châlons-sur-Marne, a town in the region. The thirteenth-century cathedrals built at Reims and Troyes served as an inspiration to Christendom.

In the fourteenth century the Duke of Burgundy, Jean "the Fearless," attempted to annex Champagne in order to forge a link between his lands in Flanders and Burgundy. He formed a military alliance with the English, who desired to seek their claim to the French throne. The long conflict that followed, part of the Hundred Years War (1337–1453), halted economic prosperity in the region. However, the French rallied around the banner of Joan of Arc, and eventually the English were driven out in 1429; Charles VII was crowned king of the French at Reims (Champagne-Ardenne had come under the control of the French crown in 1361).

Following the termination of this conflict the region saw prosperity again, at least until the sixteenth century when the Holy Roman Emperor Charles V invaded eastern France. In the latter half of the sixteenth century the Wars of Religion between Catholics and Protestants tore France apart. The Edict of Nantes in 1598, giving religious freedom to Protestants, helped to settle the internal conflict. Yet from 1635 to 1643, France was at war with Spain. The region did not experience genuine peace until the 1650s. The region returned to French rule once again following the coronation of Louis XIV at Reims in 1643.

Economic revival in the region began in the nineteenth century but was stymied by the beginning of three wars with Germany: the Franco-Prussian War of 1870–1871 and World Wars I and II. Much like the region of Lorraine to the east, Champagne-Ardenne witnessed a great deal of fighting in these wars. In the Franco-Prussian War there were major battles for Sedan and Metz (Lorraine). In World War I the front was fixed in Champagne-Ardenne. Germany made a considerable effort to capture Verdun in 1916 but was thwarted. In 1918 the Germans advanced toward Reims and the Marne but were pushed back in a bloody battle. In September 1918, the Allied army freed the Ardennes. The war devastated the region, as did World War II. In May 1940 during World War II, the French front was pushed back to Sedan. When France fell, the region was occupied by the Nazis for four years. The German invasion, coupled with the bombings brought forth before and after the Allied landing in 1944, caused heavy damage. Today one can see trenches and military cemeteries near Reims that serve as reminders of the horrors of this and other wars. The Maginot Line, too, is a sad symbol of the ravages of war.

RECENT POLITICS

The right and the extreme right have gained in Champagne-Ardenne in recent years. In the 1992 regional elections the Socialist party (PS) won only 16.79 percent of the vote and the French Communist party (PCF) captured a mere 7.75 percent, whereas the Ecologists garnered 16.20 percent and the extremist and anti-immigrant National Front (FN) received 14.92 percent. The traditional right—the gaullist Rally for the Republic (RPR) and the Union for French Democracy (UDF)—won 33.11 percent of the vote. In the autumn 1992 referendum on the Maastricht Treaty to extend and to accelerate European integration, only the department of the Marne voted in favor of the measure. In the March 1993 legislative elections the RPR and the UDF were the victors, taking seven seats from the socialists who had previously held fourteen seats in Parliament. In the 1994 European Parliament elections the right continued its hold on the electorate, especially among voters with fears and concerns about the position of France in the New Europe. The nationalist Philippe de Villiers obtained 14.3 percent of the vote, his third best performance after the Pays de la

Loire and the Centre. The FN won 12.5 percent. The PS, on the other hand, captured only 12.45 percent of the vote. In the first round of the 1995 presidential elections, three out of four departments voted for the gaullist Jacques Chirac over the socialist Lionel Jospin. Jean-Marie Le Pen, head of the FN, won 18.5 percent of the vote in Champagne-Ardenne, 3.5 percent more than his national average in this election. The department of the Haute-Marne gave Le Pen 20.35 percent of its vote. In the second round of the presidential race only the department of Ardennes favored the socialist candidate Lionel Jospin; the other three departments were won by the gaullist candidate Jacques Chirac, who emerged as the victor. Then, in the June 1995 municipal elections that followed, the right maintained its strength in the city halls of the region.

POPULATION

Although the birthrate (1.83) is slightly higher in Champagne-Ardenne than the national average, the population has grown slowly over the past decades. Moreover, the migration out of the region (especially to nearby Paris) outnumbers newcomers to Champagne-Ardenne. In 1975 the population stood at 1,337,000; in 1993 it was 1,346,000. The population density, 52.6 inhabitants per square kilometer (85.21 per square mile), is less than half the national average (105.7 per square kilometer/171.23 per square mile). Some areas of the region are more stable demographically than others. In the center of the region the population is relatively stable; but in the east, in the Haute-Marne, it is not. Moreover, the population of the region is younger than the national average. For example, those age 60 and older make up 18.9 percent of the population, as compared to 19.7 percent for France as a whole. Those age 19 and younger comprise 28.2 percent of the region's population, whereas the national average is 26.8 percent. Immigrants make up 4.8 percent of the population, below the 6.3 percent average for France.

The urban population of Champagne-Ardenne is 62.2 percent of the total, well below the 76.4 percent national average. Life expectancy is below the average for France as a whole; in the region one can expect to live to be 76 years of age (77.2 years is the national average life expectancy). Approximately 26.1 percent of all households are single-person households.

Educational levels in Champagne-Ardenne are below the national norm, and the agricultural sector dominates the work force. Only 8.8 percent of the inhabitants hold a high school diploma and 7.7 percent have an advanced degree (10.5% and 11.2%, respectively, are the national averages). Of the work force, 12.3 percent are employed in agriculture, well above the 5.3 percent national average. Industry employs 28.3 percent of the work force, slightly above the national norm. Yet the service sector employs 59.4 percent, less than the national average of 67.8 percent. The unemployment rate is 12.8 percent, slightly above the national average. The unemployment rate among women is the same as the general rate in the region, 12.8 percent.

ECONOMY

Agriculture dominates the economy of Champagne-Ardenne. The period 1950–1980 saw thirty years of expansion that transformed the rural landscape. Development of modern fertilizers have helped the region to blossom, especially chalky Champagne. Over roughly a forty-year period the champagne industry has grown enormously, from producing 30 million bottles per year to approximately 250 million bottles of the bubbly beverage. Champagne production is found principally in the departments of the Aube and the Marne, but these two departments also produce wheat and sugar beets.

Thanks to fertilizers, the chalky soil of the region has been made highly productive. The region in general is the second most important agricultural region in France. It is one of the top cereal producers in Europe, and it produces one-fourth of the nation's sugar and one-third of Europe's lucerne (used for cattle fodder). The region also produces maize, poppy seed, beet root, and cabbage. Agricultural production, especially of wheat, is highly mechanized.

Although the Ardennes and the Haute-Marne have traditionally had a strong metallurgy industry, these areas are now turning to mixed farming and breeding. Agriculture as a whole represents 11 percent of the region's economy. Furthermore, the gross domestic product per inhabitant in the region is 109,500 francs, which places it fourth overall among the twenty-two regions of France. To a large degree, the "riches" of the region are related to the strength of the agricultural sector.

Generally speaking, industry is diversified in Champagne-Ardenne; there is a strong tradition of smelting works as well as metalworks and textiles. In terms of the number of salaried employees, the agro-food business is the third largest industrial activity in the region. Other industrial activities include the production of electric material, household electronics, glass products, steel, rubber, and plastics. The industrial sector is also characterized by a large number of small to medium-sized industries. For example, outside the agriculture, food, and energy industries there are only 27 companies that employ more than 500 salaried workers.

The three largest towns are Reims with 180,620 inhabitants, Troyes with 59,255, and Charleville-Mézières with 57,008. Roughly 13.8 percent of the work force is centered in Reims, 8.5 percent in Troyes, and 4.3 percent in Charleville-Mézières. The four largest employers are Automobiles Citroen, CASE Poclain (industrial equipment), Kleber Colombes (tires), and Champagne Moët et Chandon.

In terms of the future development of Champagne-Ardenne, several problems must be addressed. First, the region must arrest the long tradition of outward-bound migration. Although a number of Parisians have secondary residences in the southwestern portion of the region because of its proximity to the capital, the population drain has been a long-standing problem. During the first half of the twentieth century, for example, the region lost 16 percent of its population, with many migrating to Paris or to the steel and coal industries in Lorraine. Second, tourism should be developed in Champagne-Ardenne. This frontier region, close to Belgium and Brussels, can offer a high quality of life and uncrowded rural spaces with many medium-sized villages, not to mention numerous architectural treasures. Its location makes it an axis of west-to-east and north-to-south travel. (Traveling from Paris to the east, one passes through the region; traveling from the North Sea to the Mediterranean, one can pass through the region as well.) Tourism is one of the keys to the future of the region.

CULTURE

The reputation of Champagne-Ardenne derives from its most famous product—champagne. **Dom Pérignon** (1638–1715), a cellar-master monk at the Benedictine Abbey at Hautvillers near Reims, is credited with developing the champagne process. When this monk tasted the final results of his experimentation, he reportedly called out to his *confrères,* "Brothers, brothers, come quickly! I am drinking the Stars!" The champagne process, which puts the bubbles in the wine, entails a second fermentation that occurs in the bottle itself. The superior champagnes are a blend of three varieties of grapes: Pinot Noir, Pinot Meunier (red), and Chardonnay. Supposedly Dom Pérignon even invented the mushroom-shaped cork that keeps the seal under the high pressure in the bottle. Since the days of this now-famous monk, champagne has been "the king of wines and the wine of kings." Champagne production is an integral part of the culture and tradition of the region. Also produced are red wines, rosés, and white wines.

The region's fairs originated in the twelfth century, revealing that this area has long been considered a trading crossroads of Europe. For a number of centuries, two fairs were held each year at Troyes, Povins, Lézanne, and elsewhere. Merchants came to these fairs from the British Isles, Spain, Germany, Italy, and Constantinople and traded in a number of items, including luxury goods. The money changers waited on benches or "bancs"; thus the word *banque* (bank, in English) came to mean a system of money exchange and banks.

Champagne-Ardenne has also contributed to the Jewish tradition in France. During the eleventh and twelfth centuries, a relatively small Jewish community settled in Troyes under the protection of the Counts of Champagne. The best-known member of this community was **Rabbi Shlomo Yit-**

zhaki (1040–1105), known as **Rabbi Rachi** in France. He provided commentaries on both the Bible and the Talmud that have been important to Jews. His method of interpretation involved both literal and nonliteral methods. In 1475 his commentary on the Bible was the first book in France to be printed in Hebrew. Because he often explained difficult words and phrases in the vernacular, his work is also important to scholars of Old French.

North of Troyes and the champagne-producing area lies the wooded Ardennes. Through the forested area north of the main town, Charleville-Mézières, flows the Meuse River, which passes deep valleys that possess a long history of folklore and legend. The Ardennes is also a favorite spot for outdoor activities. Hunting is especially popular here, given the number of wild boar and deer that roam the forests.

Champagne-Ardenne has inspired a number of writers, the most famous being **Denis Diderot** (1713–1784) and **Arthur Rimbaud** (1854–1891). Diderot was a philosopher and the editor of the great *Encyclopédie* that was published on the eve of the Revolution of 1789. The *Encyclopédie* represented a collection of the new knowledge and thought that surfaced during the Enlightenment period in France, an era of intellectual ferment prior to the Revolution of 1789. This work helped to delegitimize the Old Regime that the Revolution would eventually overturn. The poet Rimbaud was born in the Ardennes in Charleville-Mézières on the Meuse River. His poems cover a number of subjects, from the beauty of young girls to scorn for the local bourgeoisie. At age 17 he authored a popular piece called *"Le Bateau ivre"* (The Drunken Boat). In his home town, several cafés and shops bear the name *Le Bateau ivre*. Although his close friend, the poet **Paul Verlaine** (1844–1896), was born in Metz, Verlaine had many connections with the Ardennes. He was critical of Charleville-Mézières, but he wrote lovingly of the wonders of nature in the Ardennes and surrounding area.

The Ardennes is featured, too, in some of **Emile Zola's** (1840–1902) work, such as *La Terre* and *La Débacle*. The hero of *La Terre*, Jean Macquart, joins the army to fight the Prussians and travels with his regiment to defend Sedan. *La Débacle* focuses on the French defeat by the Prussians in 1870. In this large historical, semi-documentary, and well-researched novel, Zola criticizes French leadership.

Somewhat like Zola, the contemporary novelist **Julien Gracq** (b. 1910) focuses on the cruelties of war amid a radiant and serene nature in his novel *Un Balcon en forêt* (1958). Gracq's setting is the "phony war" of September 1939 to May 1946. It deals with the innermost feelings of a young soldier who guards a blockhouse on the Maginot Line.

Also from the Ardennes is the literary critic and historian **Hippolyte Taine** (1828–1893). He was born in Vouziers. Taine represented the first republican generation of historians after the fall of the Second Empire in 1870–1871. He denounced metaphysical speculation and advocated that historians seek laws of history and human behavior.

The region's cuisine features champagne in the preparation of certain specialties, such as braised chicken and poached pike (*brochette*). Champagne is a good addition to the preparation of white meats, such as chicken, and fish. Its taste and quality are not lost in the cooking process. Among other specialties are *andouillettes* (tripe sausages) from Troyes that are normally served hot and with potatoes, fried onions, or red beans. Other popular dishes are pork and cabbage stew, breaded ham hocks from Reims, and white blood sausage and sauerkraut from Brienne. Well-known cheeses include Chaource (a rich white cheese) and Thiérache. Among the confectionery are pink biscuits from Reims, chocolate pebbles from Sedan, and almond meringues from Wassy and Bar-sur-Aube. Champagne is also readily available for the demanding gourmand. Below is a recipe made with champagne.

FRICASSÉE DE POULET AU CHAMPAGNE
(Sautéed Chicken in Champagne Cream Sauce)

1 chicken, cut into eighths	1 tbs. flour
salt and freshly ground black pepper to taste	bouquet garni composed of 1 bay leaf, 2 sprigs thyme, and 4 sprigs parsley, bound together
2 tbs. butter or oil	1 cup champagne
1 cup pearl onions	½ cup cream
2 cups mushrooms, stems removed	
1 tbs. finely chopped shallots	

Season chicken with salt and pepper.

In a large nonstick skillet, melt butter or oil over medium heat and add chicken; brown both sides. To the skillet add onions, mushrooms, and shallots. Cook for 3 minutes while stirring. Add flour, blend well, and cook for 2 minutes.

Add bouquet garni and champagne and simmer for 10 minutes, turning pieces regularly. Add cream; then bring to boil and blend. Cover skillet, remove from heat, and let sit for 5 minutes.

Remove bouquet garni and place dish on serving platter. Serve with rice. Serves 4.

ARCHITECTURE AND NOTEWORTHY SITES

Given the scarcity of adequate building stone in parts of the region and the large supply of timber and clay, one finds timber and cob construction for many rural and urban buildings. If the foundations and the roofs are watertight, these buildings can last for a long while. In fact, certain old churches built in this way are still standing, such as the churches at Nuise-ment and Lentilles. Although this form of construction is often found in the Aube region, wooden houses are common in the Ardennes. In the area known as wet Champagne, houses are normally built of fieldstone or a combination of yellow millstone grit and grey pebbles. Similar dwellings can be found in the Ardennes.

REIMS (pop. 180,620) is a city made famous by history—especially the baptism of the Frankish King Clovis in 496, which laid the foundations for French national identity; and the effort by the young heroine Joan of Arc to see Charles VII crowned here during the Hundred Years War. Also of historical importance, Napoleon won his last victory near Reims, and the Germans surrendered to Allied Commander Dwight D. Eisenhower in a small schoolroom in the city on May 8, 1945. The city has enormous squares and long, wide, tree-lined avenues. The *Cathédrale de Notre-Dame* has seen numerous royal coronations, dating back to Clovis. Con-struction of the present cathedral began in the early thirteenth century; it is the third one to occupy the site. The cathedral was planned by Jean d'Orbais, who gave the structure a sense of lightness and elegance. Inside are stained-glass windows, one set made by the famous Russian-born artist Marc Chagall (1887–1985). Close by is the *Palais du Tau,* which contains many treasures: tapestries, statuary from the cathedral, Charle-magne's ninth-century talisman, a twelfth-century chalice from which twenty kings received communion, and gold and velvet coronation vest-ments of Charles X. The *Basilique St. Remi* contains the tombs of some early French kings. Behind the altar is the tomb of St. Remi, whose bap-tism helped bring Catholicism to France. (St. Remi was the bishop who baptized King Clovis.) The *Abbaye St. Remi* is a museum displaying arti-facts of city and military history as well as archaeology. The *Porte de Mars* is a massive triumphal arch erected to honor Augustus. At the *Salle de Reddition* one can view the schoolroom where the Germans surren-dered to the Allies on May 8, 1945. In July and August, Reims hosts the *Flaneries Musicales d'Été.* Reims is also a university town with establish-ments that cater to the student clientele. The *Place Drouet-d'Erion,* a pe-destrian area with cafés, restaurants, and shops, is the hub of social activity in Reims. A number of champagne cellars, or *caves,* are found in and around Reims; some cellars provide tours.

TROYES (pop. 59,255) possesses a rich architectural heritage stretching from the Middle Ages to the Renaissance. Roughly one-third of all the stained glass in France can be seen in and around the city, much of it from the sixteenth and seventeenth centuries. There are also a number of half-timbered dwellings. Unlike Reims and Épernay, there are no champagne cellars here. Located on the Seine River, Troyes grew prosperous as a result of trade fairs dating to the twelfth and thirteenth centuries. The phrase "a troy ounce" of gold, silver, or other precious metal originated in the fairs of Troyes. Today it is the knitwear capital of France, a tradition that goes back to the sixteenth century when it produced *bonneterie* (hosiery). Much of the Old Town with its half-timbered houses dates from after 1524, when a devastating fire occurred in the city. The *Cathédrale Saint Pierre et Saint Paul* dates from 1208 but was not completed until the sixteenth century; it reflects various styles of the region's Gothic architecture. There are approximately 180 stained-glass windows from the thirteenth to the seventeenth centuries. The *Église Sainte Madeleine* is the city's oldest church. The *Musée Historique de Troyes et de Champagne* exhibits artifacts of the history of Troyes and the region. The *Musée de la Bonneterie* is an interesting hosiery and knitwear museum. The *Maison de l'Outil et de la Pensée Ouvrière* displays many hand tools and handicrafts, a number of which are from the eighteenth century. The *Musée d'Art Modern* has a superb collection, including one from roughly 1850–1950 that was donated by the hosiery magnates Pierre and Denise Lévy. On display are works by Paul Cézanne (1839–1906), Henri Matisse (1869–1954), Pablo Picasso (1881–1973), Amedeo Modigliani (1884–1920), and many more. The *Institut Universitaire Rachi* offers courses on Jewish thought and tradition.

CHÂLONS-SUR-MARNE (pop. 48,423) is the smallest regional capital in France. The city is an interesting mix of old and new architecture. *Notre-Dame-en-Vaux* is early twelfth-century Gothic, an elegant variety of Gothic architecture. It has a neo-classical facade, fifty-six bells, and wonderful stained glass. Some of the stained glass dates from the thirteenth and fourteenth centuries. The *Musée Municipal* has an archaeology collection, twelfth- through fifteenth-century sculpture, paintings, Hindu religious statuary, and a traditional Champenois interior. The *Musée Goethe-Schiller* displays the personal effects of the German poets Johann Wolfgang von Goethe (1749–1832) and Friedrich von Schiller (1759–1805). The *Ste. Croix gateway* was built in six weeks to honor the arrival of Austria's Marie Antoinette to marry Louis XVI, the last king before the Revolution of 1789.

ÉPERNAY (pop. 26,682) is the home of the great producers of champagne, such as Moët et Chandon, Mercier, and others. A tour of one of the champagne makers is a must in Épernay. The *Musée du Vin de Champagne* shows everything from the winemakers' dress over the decades to early wine bottles.

SEDAN (pop. 21,667), built early in the fifteenth century with massive ramparts and bastions, overlooks the Meuse valley. This is where Napoleon III was defeated by the Prussians in the war of 1870–1871, and where the emperor was taken prisoner. The town has a local museum of interest. Sedan is a fascinating town for those with a penchant for history and military architecture.

LANGRES (pop. 9,987) has six towers, seven gates, ramparts, and a sentry walk with a view of the countryside where the Meuse, Marne, and Aube

Rivers flow. The town is made for exploration on foot. The main square is the *Place Diderot,* named after the famous Enlightenment figure. The cathedral dates from the twelfth century; its style is Burgundian Romanesque. The *Musée St. Didier* displays artifacts of Gallo-Roman life in the region (thirteen Roman roads radiate out from Langres). The Museum of the *Breuil de St. Germain Maison* shows furniture, ceramics, and memorabilia from Diderot's life.

ROUTE DE CHAMPAGNE (CHAMPAGNE ROAD) is a major attraction around Reims and Épernay; it covers three areas that represent 80 percent of the champagne vineyards. Champagne generates more foreign currency than any other French wine, even though approximately 60 percent of French production is sold at home. Roughly 100,000 salaried workers are employed in the production and distribution of the bubbly beverage.

SELECT BIBLIOGRAPHY

Bazin, Marcel. "Champagne-Ardenne," in André Gamblin, ed., *La France dans ses régions,* vol. 1. Paris: SEDES, 1994.

Bazin, Marcel, et al. "Champagne-Ardenne," in Y. Lacoste, ed., *Géopolitiques des régions françaises,* vol. 1. Paris: Fayard, 1986.

Domingo, J., et al. *Champagne-Ardenne: une région à la recherche de son identité.* Montreuil-sous-Bois: Bréal, 1987.

Garnotel, J. *L'Ascension d'une grand agriculture. Champagne pouilleuse—Champagne crayeuse.* Paris: Economica, 1985.

Chapter 8

CORSICA
(Corse)

REGIONAL GEOGRAPHY

The island of Corsica is located 112 miles from mainland France and 51 miles from Italy. Considered one of the regions of France, this island comprises 5,358 miles, or 1.6 percent of the surface area of France. It is the fourth largest island in the Mediterranean Sea (after Sicily, Sardinia, and Cyprus). Corsica is 114 miles long and 52 miles wide; it includes two departments: Haute-Corse and Corse-du-Sud. The capital is Ajaccio.

Geographically, Corsica has an astonishingly varied landscape, which creates the impression that the island is a continent in miniature. There are snowy peaks, swaying palm trees, cool forests, burning deserts (*Désert des Agriates*), and beautiful coastlines. In reality, Corsica is a mountain in the Mediterranean. The sillon central, a lowlands section, divides the island into two geographic areas. Southwest of the sillon central is a range of approximately twenty granite mountains with peaks over 6,500 feet. The highest is Monte-Cinto, 8,876 feet above sea level. North of the depression is an upland area, too, but the mountains are younger and not as soaring. In this area the highest peak is Monte San Petrone, 5,796 feet high. Approximately two-thirds of the island is covered by *maquis*, a dense and perfumed mantle that is actually a rich undergrowth; it gives off an appealing fragrance in the spring but poses a fire hazard in the summer. Roughly one-fifth of the island is forested; the best-known trees are laricio pines, reaching heights of almost 200 feet and having a straight trunk (they have been used to make ship masts since the days of the Romans). There are also cork oaks (the source of cork) and chestnut trees (a food source on the island at one time).

CORSICA (CORSE)

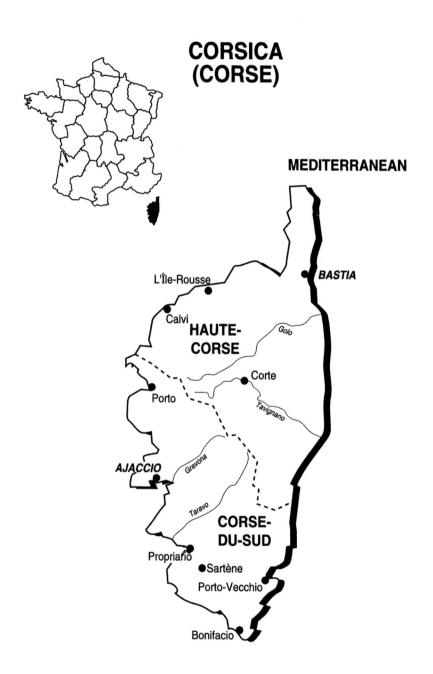

MEDITERRANEAN

BASTIA

L'Île-Rousse

Calvi

HAUTE-
CORSE

Golo

Porto

Corte

Tavignano

AJACCIO

Gravona

Taravo

CORSE-
DU-SUD

Propriano

Sartène

Porto-Vecchio

Bonifacio

Corsica's climate, although Mediterranean, varies according to elevation. Ajaccio on the western coast receives 2,900 hours of sunlight annually, more than any other area in France; yet Bastia on the northeastern coast is warmer. The climate is Alpine above 3,900 feet, with snow in the winter. Approximately 35.5 inches of rain falls on the island, with higher amounts in the north and east.

HISTORY

Human history in Corsica goes back 6,500 to 8,000 years. Yet the island's recorded history began with the Phocaeans (Greeks from Asia Minor), who founded Marseille. The Phocaeans also founded the city of Aléria and introduced wheat, olives, grapes, and mining. They established written communication and international trade as well. The Romans occupied the island in 260 B.C. and remained for two centuries. During this period the Emperor Claudius banished Seneca (4 B.C.–65 B.C.) to the island after this Roman philosopher, statesman, and orator had been charged with committing adultery with the emperor's niece. In general, the centuries of Roman rule saw Corsica's culture and language Latinized.

Following the fall of Rome in the fifth century A.D., Corsica underwent several centuries of invasions. Successive invasions by the Vandals, Ostrogoths, Byzantines, and Lombards brought anarchy to the island. During this period a native Corsican aristocracy emerged, battling with one another and forming alliances with foreign powers—such as Pisa and Genoa—that sought control over the island. Although the Franks expelled the Lombards in the eighth century, the Frankish King Pepin the Short and his son Charlemagne gave the island to the papacy. In the eighth through tenth centuries the Saracens, Muslims from North Africa, attacked Corsica and occupied parts of it.

In the eleventh century a "Pax Pisana" (a Pisa peace) occurred after Pope Gregory VII gave the island to the bishop of the city-state of Pisa. The Pax Pisana lasted until late in the thirteenth century. During this period trade increased and numerous churches were built. In 1284 Genoa defeated Pisa in the naval battle of Méloria and took over the island. During almost a 500-year occupation the Genoese founded or fortified the towns of Ajaccio, Bastia, Calvi, Porto-Vecchio, and Saint Florent. In the mid-fifteenth century, Genoa-—facing disintegrating order in Corsica owing largely to Muslim attacks on the coastal areas—gave control of the island to the *Banque de Saint Georges,* a financial power that had its own army.

Confronting the exploitation of the island by foreigners and the anarchy of continuing raids, native Corsicans revolted in an effort to win control of the island. A number of significant uprisings occurred: the *Terre de Commun* revolt of 1384, the Sampiero Corso revolt of 1564 (Corso attempted to enlist the aid of the French), and the widespread War of Independence between 1729 and 1769. One of the Corsican heroes during and after the forty-year war of independence was the patriot Pascal Paoli, who held the title of general of the Corsican nation. Paoli advocated an independent state, promulgated a constitution, made education compulsory, founded a university, and reorganized the economy. The French, who had annexed the island in 1769 after several interventions, feared Paoli. When French revolutionary leaders condemned him, he turned to the British for help. The British saw the strategic importance of the island. During 1795–1796, the British actually controlled the island. Paoli died in London in 1807 and is buried in Westminster Abbey. One of France's best-known historical figures during the revolutionary period, Napoleon Bonaparte, was born in Ajaccio on August 15, 1769, the very year that the French annexed the island.

France has ruled the island ever since annexation, with two exceptions: (1) From 1794 to 1796 during the Revolution, Corsican independence leader Paoli led a Corsican kingdom under British protection; (2) During World War II the island was occupied by Italian and German troops. In 1943 the efforts of local partisans (the *Maquis*) and Free French Forces (who arrived on the island by submarine) liberated Corsica, making it the first department to be liberated during the war.

From roughly 1830 to 1870 and the end of the Second Empire, the island thrived. A network of roads was built and more land was brought under cultivation. The population climbed from 150,000 in 1796 to 322,000 in 1936. In part, population pressure forced many to flee, especially because food resources were less than plentiful. Also, during World War I Corsica lost 5 percent (14,000) of its population, more than any other department in France.

The outward migrations continued after World War II. Corsica saw its young people migrate to more prosperous regions and failed to modernize its industry and agriculture. Because of French military conflict in Indochina and North Africa in the 1950s and 1960s, as many as 20,000 Corsicans living in these areas returned to the island. In 1974 it was divided into two departments, and in 1982 it became the first region to elect its own regional assembly. Despite French attempts to integrate the island into the French administrative structure, an independence movement still exists in Corsica; it is led by the National Liberation Front of Corsica (FLNC). This and other militant separatist organizations are proud of the language, culture, and traditions of the island. Although only a few Corsicans are active members of the FLNC, many are concerned about overdevelopment stemming from tourism and threats to the natural beauty of the coast.

RECENT POLITICS

Corsica is driven more by the division between "nationalist" and "French" parties than by a left/right division. For example, in the second round of the 1993 legislative elections the socialists in Corse-du-Sud supported, along with the bonapartists (a right-wing group supporting a strong centralized state), the eventual winner, José Rossi of the Union for French Democracy (UDF). In these elections the right won 40 to 50 percent of the vote in the first round. In recent years, hard-line nationalists have polled no more than 20 to 24 percent of the vote, as in the 1993 election. In the presidential elections of 1995 the right-wing candidates won more than 50 percent of the vote in the first round, with the left capturing 33 percent in Corse-du-Sud and 38 percent in Haute-Corse. Also in the first round, the extreme-right wing candidate Jean-Marie Le Pen of the National Front (FN) captured 10.72 percent of the vote, less than his 15 percent average for France as a whole. In the final round almost 77,000 voted for the gaullist candidate Jacques Chirac, and 53,000 for the socialist Lionel Jospin. Chirac, of course, won the presidency of France. Corse-du-Sud is more solid in its support of Chirac than is Haute-Corse. Another gaullist, Jean-Paul de Rocca Serra, has presided over the regional assembly since 1984. In the June 1995 municipal elections the diverse right maintained control in Ajaccio, but the diverse left retained control in Bastia.

In reality, political clientelism is a central part of Corsican politics. There are 360 mayors on the island with 4,000 assistants (*adjoints*) who serve a population of 253,000 people. Political patronage is important to Corsican politicians. Also, violence touches the political arena, notably with the FLNC multiplying its actions against symbols of the French state. Since 1976 there have been 5,000 armed actions associated with the FLNC. Unfortunately, violence penetrates life in general and not simply the political arena in Corsica. In 1992, for instance, there were 182 armed robberies, 154 terrorist attacks, and 40 murders. Compared to the mainland, women play a small role in Corsican politics.

When regional assemblies were first introduced by the socialist government in Paris in 1982, it was hoped that through the reversal of the long tradition of political centralization in Paris, Corsica—along with other regions with a strong independence movement—would become more integrated into a larger France. In Corsica, one wonders if this has happened and if the clannism and patronage system of its politics can be changed.

POPULATION

The population of Corsica is small, but it has grown by 9 percent since 1982. Twenty years ago the population stood at 226,000, whereas in 1993 it was 253,000—roughly 0.44 percent of the population of France. Since 1975 the birthrate has dropped; it now stands at 1.71, slightly below the national average. The population density is 29.2 inhabitants per square kilometer (47.30 per square mile), considerably below the 105.7 average for France (171.23 per square mile).

The population is highly concentrated in two areas. Almost 50 percent of the entire population lives in Ajaccio, the regional capital, and in Bastia. The interior of the island is sparsely populated.

The population is older and less educated than the national average. Those age 60 and older make up 22.9 percent of the population, whereas the national average is 19.7 percent. On the other hand, those age 19 or younger comprise 23.9 percent of the population, well below the 26.8 percent average for France. The immigrant population is considerably above the national average, with 9.9 percent of the population made up of immigrants (6.3% for France as a whole).

The urban population of Corsica is 58.6 percent, as compared to an average of 76.4 percent for the nation. Life expectancy is slightly below the national average of 77.2 years; in Corsica one can expect to live to be 76.4 years of age. Approximately 24.5 percent of all households are single-family households, below the national average of 27.1.

Educational levels are relatively low and the work force is concentrated in the agricultural and service sectors. Although 10.9 percent hold a high school degree, 41.6 percent do not possess any educational degree. Roughly 7.2 percent hold an advanced degree (11.2% is the national average). Of the work force, 10.2 percent are in agriculture, almost double the average for France. Moreover, only 17.6 percent are employed in industry (26.9% for France). However, 72.2 percent work in the service sector, above the 67.8 percent average for the country as a whole. Of course, many in the service sector are in tourism, the key activity of the Corsican economy. The unemployment rate is 12.5 percent, slightly above the average in France, with 16.4 percent of women unemployed.

ECONOMY

Tourism, the heart of the economy, has grown considerably since the 1970s. For two months during the summer (July and August) the island attracts 1,500,000 tourists. Tourists are four times more numerous today than twenty years ago. Furthermore, Corsica now ranks third in France for the creation of new businesses, especially in the service sector; but business failures are also high, ranking fifth in France overall. (Insurance costs are high in Corsica owing to the level of violence.) Since 1992 the number of jobs has risen by 6 percent. While tourism is important to the Corsican economy, roughly one-half of seasonal jobs in tourism are external to the Corsican economy.

Industry in Corsica is focused on the building trades and the food and agricultural industries. Island craftsmen produce high-quality pottery, wood sculpture, wicker work, knives, jewelry, and garments. The principal agricultural products are wine, fruits, and vegetables. However, there is no true industrial specialization and the island has a consumer economy that is highly dependent on the exterior.

The three largest towns are Ajaccio with 58,949 inhabitants, Bastia with

37,845, and Porto-Vecchio with 9,307. Approximately 24.3 percent of the work force is located in Ajaccio and 15.6 percent in Bastia. The four largest employers are the Hospital of Bastia, EDF GDF (Electricity and Gas of France), the Central General Hospital, and the Hospital Center at Castelluccio.

Economic development in Corsica will require diversification of the economy and pacification of the civil society. Driven mainly by tourism, the economy has one main focus. Moreover, tourism is seasonal and can be greatly affected by the level of internal violence. The island needs to find a way to transcend the political culture of clientelism and clannism, even though that culture is closely tied to Corsica's history and identity. The social and cultural differences—especially when they lead to violence and corruption—can do great harm to the economic livelihood of this beautiful region.

CULTURE

An important part of Corsican identity is *Corsu,* the Corsican language. Although most residents of the island speak French, in recent decades *Corsu* has become an important symbol of cultural identity. A Romance language somewhat similar to Italian, *Corsu* evolved from the colloquial Latin spoken in the Roman Empire. The development of *Corsu,* virtually an oral language, was influenced by the Italian used by Pisan and Genoese occupiers. Following France's annexation of the island, primary education in French became compulsory. Today the study of *Corsu* is optional in schools. Nationalist groups are demanding that instruction in *Corsu* be mandatory.

Language has divided Corsicans over the years, but so too have vendettas (i.e., blood feuds that sometimes last for generations). Ostensibly, vendettas originated as a form of "rough justice" and a response to decisions handed out to the Corsicans by the Genoese. Vendettas may have originated as an offense or a slight to someone's honor, or a dispute over water or pasture rights. To escape the authorities, avengers—sometimes called "bandits of honor"—often relied on the *maquis* (discussed below) as a place of refuge. Until the twentieth century, Corsica was notorious for its vendettas. The Corsicans are a very proud people with a strong sense of honor.

Corsica is known for other things as well, such as the *maquis.* Covering two-thirds of the island, it is a dense scrub up to 19.5 feet high. This scrub is made up of different mixtures of plants: cistus, arbutus, briars, asphodel, clematis, smilax, Corsican broom, and holm oak. Napoleon reportedly said that he could recognize Corsica with his eyes closed; he could just smell the *maquis.*

Corsica is also famous for its beaches, where hoards of sun worshipers descend during the summer months. Some of the most beautiful beaches with fine sand are in the Bay of Valinco around Porto-Vecchio, the beach at Palombaggia, and the cove at Ficajola. Some beaches have huge stretches of sand; Calvi has about 4.5 miles of sandy beach bordered by pine forest. The island is a haven for boaters as well, and the rocky, jagged coastline encourages exploration. Tourists can find not only beautiful beaches and coastline but also a varied landscape that can be an excellent diversion on a long, hot summer day.

Corsica is known also for its craftsmanship, related in part to the fact that the island has had to depend on its own resources in the past. During the nineteenth century, craft production declined when manufactured goods were imported from the mainland. In recent years Corsican craftsmanship has witnessed a revival, owing in large measure to the encouragement of craft associations. Pottery, wicker work, wood carving, jewelry, and the like are for sale in craft shops.

Festivals in Corsica tend to focus on religious traditions and processions. For example, the re-enactment of the Passion is held the week before Easter. In Ajaccio the largest celebration is on August 15, Assumption Day. This is also the birth date of Napoleon Bonaparte.

Napoleon Bonaparte (1769–1821) is the most famous son of Corsica. The Bonaparte family came to the island in the sixteenth century from Liguria, Italy, and settled in Ajaccio. Napoleon was one of thirteen children, five of whom did not survive infancy. He left the island at age 9 to attend the Brienne military academy on the French mainland. By age 16 he was a lieutenant in the artillery. During the French Revolution, Napoleon's decisive actions against the British during the siege of the port city of Toulon ensured him national attention and fame. In 1799 he became First Consul of the French state; in 1804 he crowned himself Emperor. As First Consul and as Emperor, Napoleon held the destiny of Europe in his hands. Moreover, as his army marched across Europe he helped to spread the ideas of the Revolution beyond the borders of France. He suffered his final defeat in 1815 at Waterloo in Belgium.

Presently in France there is another Corsican with a national reputation, **Charles Pasqua** (b. 1927). Although he was actually born on the mainland in Grasse to Corsican parents, he is thought of as a Corsican. Pasqua is a gaullist politician who served as a tough law-and-order minister of interior during the *cohabitation* government of 1986–1988 (at this time France had a socialist president, François Mitterrand, and a gaullist prime minister, Jacques Chirac). As a young man he climbed the ranks of the Ricard pastis firm, a producer of spirits, and then entered politics as a committed gaullist. He was first elected to the National Assembly in 1968. Over the years he has been a trusted lieutenant of the current president of France, Jacques Chirac; Pasqua even served as one of the principal organizers of several of Chirac's presidential campaigns.

The cuisine of Corsica features meat and fish. *Prisuttu* (Corsican prosciutto ham) is popular, as well as *lonzu* (rolled and smoked fillet of pork), *coppa, salciccie* (similar to salami), and *figatelli* (smoked pork liver sausage). Also popular are roasted leg of lamb, kid, and suckling pig. Fish dishes include mullet, bream, or bass baked over aromatic herbs, and small Mediterranean lobster called *langoustes*. There is also a local fish soup called *azima*. Equally popular are omelets flavored with *Brocciu* (a cheese), asparagus tips, and mushrooms. Brocciu cheese is often used to add flavor to soups, turnovers, fritters, and pasta dishes. Favorite cheeses are Calenzana, Niolo, Venaco, and Sartène. Chestnuts are used in many forms, such as flour for desserts, cakes, and fritters. Below is a recipe for a popular dessert made with Brocciu cheese; it is especially popular at Easter.

FIADONE
(Corsican Cheesecake with Caramel)

⅔ cup sugar

2 tbs. water

½ cup sugar

⅓ cup milk

2 tbs. vanilla extract

12 oz. Brocciu (or ricotta) cheese

grated peel of ½ lemon and ½ orange

6 eggs

In a saucepan over medium heat, mix ⅔ cup sugar and water; stir until combined. Bring to boil and simmer; when mixture turns golden brown, remove from heat and pour into 9-inch tart pan and coat the sides by swirling.

Preheat oven to 325°F. Scald ½ cup sugar and milk; cool and add vanilla. Put Brocciu (or ricotta) in bowl and stir in milk; add lemon and orange peel. Add eggs individually and beat well. Pour this mixture into prepared pan. Bake for 1 hour. Let cool for 20 minutes and then serve. Serves 6.

ARCHITECTURE AND NOTEWORTHY SITES

One of the distinctive architectural features of Corsica is the Pisan church. The island was controlled by the city-republic of Pisa from the eleventh to the thirteenth centuries. During this period the Pisans brought architects, sculptors, and stonemasons from Tuscany. Pisan builders constructed most of the Romanesque churches of Castagniccia, Nebbio, and Balagne.

Villages in Corsica tend to be small; many are perched on rocky peaks, clinging to precipitous slopes, or covering valley floors. Over time, Corsican houses came to accommodate the extended family. The shape of the house features three or four stories in a rectangular block. In the north, schist is a favorite building material; in the south, granite; around Bonifacio and Saint-Florent, limestone. Roofing can vary: in the north, schist cut into fine slabs is used; elsewhere, one finds pantiles, an s-curved roofing tile. A few houses have shingles made of chestnut wood.

AJACCIO (pop. 58,949) is a major port city on the western side of the island; it is also the birthplace of Napoleon. It is ten hours by ferry from Ajaccio to Marseille, and four hours to the Italian coast. Some of the most spectacular coastal scenery runs from Ajaccio northward to Calvi. *Place Maréchal Foch*, steps away from the car ferry dock, is the social center of the town. Ajaccio's cathedral was built in the 1500s; Napoleon was baptized here. The cathedral also has on display a Eugène Delacroix (1798–1863) painting, *Vierge au Sacré-Coeur* (Virgin of the Sacred Heart). There is a Napoleon museum, *La Maison Bonaparte*, which is the house where Napoleon was born. Here one can see memorabilia and a death mask made two days after the emperor died in 1821. The *Musée Fesch*, named after Napoleon's uncle, exhibits fourteenth- and nineteenth-century Italian primitive-style paintings. The *Salon Napoléonien* displays Napoleonic memorabilia. The *Musée d'Histoire de la Corse* shows artifacts of Corsican military history.

BASTIA (pop. 37,845), situated on the northeastern side of the island, is one of the two great cities of Corsica. It is a lively city, more active in trade and industry than its competing city on the other side of the island, Ajaccio. More ferries from France and Italy serve Bastia than any other port. It was the seat of the Genoese government beginning in the fifteenth century and gets it name from the construction of the *bastiglia*, a fortress. The Old Town has an Italian-like atmosphere. During World War II Bastia suffered damage from both U.S. bombing and German sabotage. One of the symbols of Bastia is the *Église Saint Jean Baptiste*, built in the 1600s and overlooking the old port. Not far away is the *Citadelle*, built by the Genoese between the fifteenth and seventeenth centuries. Inside the Citadelle is the *Musée Ethnographique Corse*.

CALVI (pop. 4,816) is one of the most popular seaside spots, owing in large measure to its setting. The sea, palm trees, and pine trees, and the proximity of the snow-covered *Cinto Massif* (snow until early summer), all form part of the stunning setting. A Genoese stronghold from the thirteenth to the eighteenth century, the town was known for its loyalty to Genoa. The *Citadelle* reflects the five centuries of occupation by the Genoese. Here there are rampart walls and views of the sea. British forces assisting the nationalist Pascal Paoli besieged and bombarded this citadel town in the 1790s. The *Église Saint Jean Baptiste* was originally built in the thirteenth century. Inside, near the altar, is a venerated ebony statue of Jesus known as *Christ des Miracles*. It is credited with helping to save Calvi from the Turks and the Saracens. Calvi has a famous 2.5-mile beach. There is a claim in Calvi that Christopher Columbus was born in the town—but this is highly questionable.

BONIFACIO (pop. 2,736) is situated on the southernmost point of the island. According to Homer's *Odyssey*, Ulysses sought shelter here. The marina is a popular harbor. The town itself sits on white limestone over 200 feet above the sea. It is sometimes called "Corsica's Gibraltar." The town that exists today was founded in A.D. 828. During the twelfth century the Genoese took control of Bonifacio from the Pisans and established a semi-autonomous mini-republic here. This town, like Calvi, had a reputation for its strong loyalty to Genoa. The Old Town has narrow streets and striking views. The *Église Sainte Marie Majeure* was built during the twelfth through thirteenth centuries. The *Citadelle* now serves as a base for the French Foreign Legion.

CASTAGNICCIA HEIGHTS is a garden fortress in the mountains on the eastern side of the island where resistance began against the Genoese. Pascal Paoli, the eighteenth-century Corsican independence leader, was born here.

PORTO BAY is a beautiful bay fronting Porto on the western coast of Corsica. One of the most beautiful spots is the bay of Girolata on the northern side of Porto Bay. An agreeable seaside town, Porto has a Genoese tower that affords beautiful views. There is a pebbled beach bordered by eucalyptus trees. Near Porto are *calanques,* fiords surrounded by colorful granite pinnacles.

SELECT BIBLIOGRAPHY

Antonetti, P. *Histoire de la Corse.* Paris: Robert Laffont, 1973.

Le Roy Ladurie, Emmanuel. "Français, quelles sont vos racines? Les Corses." *L'Express,* 10 août 1995.

Renucci, Janine. "Corse," in André Gamblin, ed., *La France dans ses régions,* vol. 2. Paris: SEDES, 1994.

———. *La Corse.* Paris: PUF (Que sais-je?), 1982.

Tafani, P. "Géopolitique de la Corse," in Y. Lacoste, ed., *Géopolitiques des régions françaises,* vol. 2. Paris: Fayard, 1986.

FRANCHE-COMTÉ

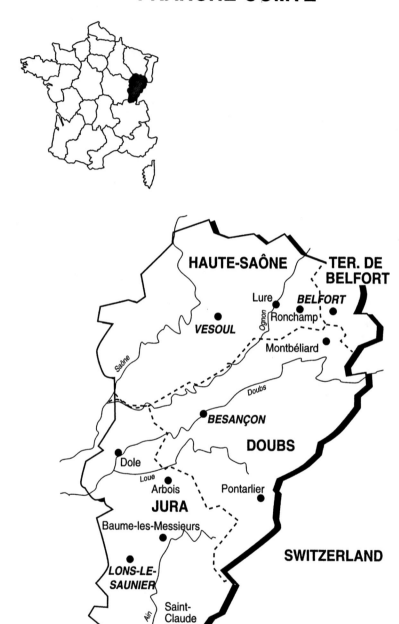

HAUTE-SAÔNE

TER. DE BELFORT

Lure

BELFORT

Ognon

Ronchamp

VESOUL

Montbéliard

Saône

Doubs

BESANÇON

DOUBS

Dole

Loue

Arbois

Pontarlier

JURA

Baume-les-Messieurs

SWITZERLAND

LONS-LE-SAUNIER

Ain

Saint-Claude

Chapter 9

FRANCHE-COMTÉ

REGIONAL GEOGRAPHY

Franche-Comté is located in eastern France on the Swiss border. The Jura mountains separate the region from Switzerland. The northern border of the region is formed by Alsace, Lorraine, and Champagne-Ardenne. On the northern border, too, are the Vosges mountains. On the western border is Burgundy; Rhône-Alpes lies to the south. The region comprises 10,001 square miles, 3 percent of the surface area of France, and includes four departments: Territoire de Belfort, Haute-Saône, Doubs, and Jura. The capital is Besançon.

Geographically, the region has a certain duality. On the one hand, the high valley of the Saône River is wide, with gentle rolling hills and a rustic character. On the other hand, the Jura mountains are untamed and wild, with considerable flowing water and forests of black spruce. The rivers that flow through the region include the Saône, Ognon, Doubs, and Ain.

The climate is usually damp and cool. There are numerous lakes and rivers but also frequent rain, especially in autumn. Nevertheless, there is adequate sunshine for vine cultivation. Winters tend to be harsh, and spring is sometimes late in arriving. The summers, however, are mild. The best season is June to September.

HISTORY

The strategic position of Franche-Comté has played a major role in its history. Even before the Christian period, the Gallic Sequanii requested outside help against Germanic invaders. When local inhabitants made an appeal to Julius Caesar, the Romans established a permanent garrison at Vesontio, which today is the city of Besançon. In an effort to expel the Roman occupiers, the Sequanii allied with the Gallic chief Vercingétorix, but they suffered defeat in A.D. 52 at Alésia. The region proved to be an important mercantile center, especially because it lay on the north-south axis of the Roman Empire.

In the second century A.D. two Greek missionaries, Ferjeux and Ferréol, introduced Christianity to the region. Despite efforts by the Romans to halt the spread of Christianity, Besançon became a bishopric. Early in the fifth century the Burgundians established a kingdom that extended from Alsace to Provence in the south and from the Jura to the Morvan in the west. During this period, the first monasteries developed locally. When Burgundy fell to the Franks early in the sixth century, the conversion of the Frankish King Clovis aided the spread of Christianity. The Irish monk Columban arrived in Franche-Comté at this time and founded monasteries at Luxeuil and Baume-les-Messieurs. Although the region experienced barbarian invasions during the ninth and tenth centuries, the abbeys remained peaceful and learning flourished in these centers, which also advanced agricultural pursuits.

When Charlemagne's empire was divided among his descendants in 843, the German emperors used this to press their claims to the territory. A division of the region occurred in the tenth century when the Jura area was linked to the county (*comté*) of Burgundy and the Saône linked to the duchy of Burgundy. In 1032 the German emperor won control of the county, but the rise of feudal warlords weakened his control. The territories were united in the late fourteenth century when Philippe the Bold received the duchy as a settlement from his father, King Jean the Good, and then married the heiress to the county. Philippe the Bold began a line of Grand Dukes of Burgundy, often more powerful than the French kings. Following the death in 1477 of the last of the Grand Dukes (Charles the Bold), King Louis XI took control of Comté.

Yet Comté later passed around the crowned head of Europe. In 1491 Charles VIII ceded the province to Emperor Maximilian of Austria, who then presented it to his son, Philip the Fair. Philip was married to Joan the Mad, the only daughter of the Spanish monarchs Ferdinand and Isabella. The son of Philip and Joan inherited Comté and Flanders from his father and ascended to the Spanish throne; he also became Charles V, emperor of the Holy Roman Empire.

France undertook initiatives beginning in 1635 to win control over Comté, finally succeeding in 1678. Local heroes who fought for independence prior to the French takeover included Jean-Claude Prost (1607–1681). The name "Franche-Comté" means "Free County" and symbolizes the long struggle to maintain the region's independence, both from foreign invaders and from French rule. When the French took control, they moved the regional capital from Dole to Besançon. The Reformation advocated by Swiss Lutherans won adherents in Montbéliard near Basel, but the region remained Catholic.

In both the nineteenth and twentieth centuries, the region has played a role in military campaigns. The key city of Belfort in the northeast, made almost impregnable by the military engineer the Marquis de Vauban (Sébastien Le Prestre, 1633–1707) who served Louis XIV, displayed heroic resistance in the sieges of 1814, 1815, and 1870. Furthermore, when Napoleon III was defeated at Sedan in 1870 by the Prussians, 85,000 French soldiers using the protection of forts in the region managed to escape to Switzerland. During World War II the geography of the Jura lent itself to resistance activity. During Liberation, heavy fighting took place along the Doubs River, owing in part to the importance of Belfort and Besançon.

In the post–World War II years the region has been known for its industrial activity. However, in recent decades numerous jobs have been eliminated in Franche-Comté because of a deep economic crisis that began in the late 1970s. This crisis has shown the need for modernization, consolidation, and diversification.

RECENT POLITICS

The right—especially the gaullist Rally for the Republic (RPR)—has made headway in the region, whereas the once strong Socialist party (PS) has lost considerable ground. In the 1992 regional elections the Socialist party lost two-thirds of its voters in the Doubs. In this election, too, the Ecologist candidate Dominique Voyney, trained as an anesthesiologist, emerged as a new political star by winning in the Jura. In the 1993 parliamentary elections the socialists continued their decline, electing only two out of thirteen deputies. The two socialist deputies elected were linked to the Citizens Movement of the dissident socialist Jean-Pierre Chevènement, leader of the pseudo–left wing of the PS. (Chevènement served as minister of state for research, technology, and industry, as well as minister of education, during socialist President François Mitterrand's first term, 1981–1988. After Mitterrand won re-election in 1988, Chevènement was appointed minister of defense, resigning in 1991 owing to anti-Iraq sentiment in France.) The RPR was the grand winner in the 1993 elections, capturing nine seats from the region. The Union for French Democracy (UDF), also a right-wing party, won two seats. Then, in the first round of the 1995 presidential election, the socialist candidate Lionel Jospin outdistanced the gaullist Jacques Chirac in all four departments. The extreme right-wing candidate Jean-Marie Le Pen of the National Front (FN) won more than 16.5 percent in the first round in the region, roughly 1.5 percent above his national average. In the second round Chirac won three out of four departments, losing only the Territoire de Belfort—Chevènement's home base—to the socialist Jospin. Chirac emerged as the new president. In the June 1995 municipal elections, the socialists retained control of Besançon.

POPULATION

Franche-Comté has a small population that numbers only slightly more than 1 million. In the 1960s and early 1970s there was a positive migration flow into the region. However, since roughly the mid-1970s the population has grown only slightly. Today, because of the lack of jobs in the region, the departures outnumber the arrivals. In 1975 the population stood at 1,060,000; in 1993 it was 1,098,000. The birthrate is 1.80, above the national average of 1.73. Population density is considerably below the average for France; in this region there are 67.7 inhabitants per square kilometer (109.67 per square mile), as compared to 105.7 per square kilometer for France as a whole (171.23 per square mile).

The age of the region's population approximates that of the nation. Those age 60 and over comprise 19.3 percent of the population (19.7% is the average for France); those age 19 and under make up 27.7 percent of the region's population (26.8 percent is the average for France). The immigrant population mirrors the national average of 6.3 percent.

In Franche-Comté 58.1 percent of the population is urban, noticeably below the 76.4 percent for the entire nation. Life expectancy is 76.8 years, slightly below the 77.2 years for France as a whole. Approximately 25.4 percent of all households are single-person households, below the national average of 27.1 percent.

Educational levels are also below the national norm, and the composition of the work force is weighted toward industry. Only 9.5 percent hold a high school degree, and 8.3 percent possess an advanced degree (10.5% and 11.2%, respectively, are the averages for France). Of the work force, 4.5 percent is employed in the agricultural sector (5.3% for all of France); and 37.2 percent work in industry, considerably above the 26.9 percent national average. The service sector is weak as compared to the national norm: 58.3 percent (as compared to 67.8% for the entire nation) work in the service sector. The unemployment rate is approximately 10 percent, below the national average, which is a bit over 12 percent. Among women the unemployment rate is 11.2 percent. Yet between 1982 and 1990 unemployment among women increased by 20 percent, a higher increase than among male workers.

ECONOMY

A certain number of products—namely, automobiles, watches, and tobacco pipes—are closely associated with Franche-Comté. Peugeot automobiles are especially associated with the region. The Peugeot family were originally weavers, but in 1810 they began to produce tools and bicycles. A Peugeot automobile factory opened in 1897, and a second factory opened in 1912 at Sochaux. Automobiles, bicycles, and tools have been the mainstays of Peugeot's success over the years.

Watches and grandfather clocks are also famous products from the region. The city of Besançon has manufactured watches since the early seventeenth century. In the nineteenth century the city annually produced 300,000 watches; in 1980 it was estimated that the region produced 15 million units. Franche-Comté is known, too, for producing the movements for tall-case clocks. The name *comtoise* was applied first to the mechanism and then to the entire clock. The latter half of the nineteenth century was the height of popularity of the grandfather clock. The town of Morez in the southeast still produces these clocks.

Tobacco pipes have been produced in Saint-Claude since 1854. When tobacco was first imported from the New World during the sixteenth century, tobacco pipes began to be used. By the eighteenth century, pipe smoking had become widely popular. The craftspeople at Saint-Claude now produce 3 million pipes per year.

Although Franche-Comté is a highly industrialized region (one of the most industrialized of all of France), it has been hard hit by the economic crisis that began in the late 1970s. During the 1980s the region lost one-fourth of its jobs in industry. Job reduction has been the price for modernization and investment in the region; the watchwords have been "re-conversion," "diversification," and "consolidation." Today the region features products such as games and toys, eyeglasses, furniture, clocks and watch-making, automobiles, and micro-electronics. Many in the region hope that micro-electronics will aid the revitalization of Franche-Comté in the future.

Ironically, even though Franche-Comté is highly industrialized, it is not overly urbanized. Even the regional capital of Besançon is relatively small, with a population of slightly more than 100,000. Many of the largest industries are located in the northeast around the urban centers of Belfort and Montbéliard.

Agriculture has been in decline in the region, as elsewhere in France. Compared to other regions, agriculture occupies an average place in the region's economic activity. Production is dominated by beef and milk.

The three largest towns are Besançon with 113,828 inhabitants, Belfort with 50,125, and Montbéliard with 29,005. Approximately 15.6 percent of the work force is centered in Besançon, 15.3 percent in Montbéliard, and 8.3 percent in Belfort. The four largest industries are Automobiles Peugeot (automobiles), GEC Alsthom (electronic products), Automobiles Peugeot (automobile equipment), and Solvay (chemical products).

CULTURE

Franche-Comté, as previously mentioned, means "Free County." The region's long struggle to maintain its sovereignty under successive waves of foreign invasion has helped to foster a strong tradition of independence. Yet this independence is combined with a community spirit. Indeed, as far back as the thirteenth century the dairy farmers and cheesemakers set up cooperatives. A motto of the wine growers of Arbois in the nineteenth century was, "We are all in charge." Independence and community characterize the culture and tradition of this region.

Franche-Comté is known also for its outdoor recreational facilities. In addition to hiking, fishing, and hunting, skiing is popular. Although there are downhill skiing facilities, the region is one of the premier cross-country ski areas in France.

One of the historical figures that exemplifies the region's spirit of independence is **Jean-Claude Prost** (1607–1681), also called **Captain Lacuzon,** who rallied local residents to resist the invading armies of the Prince de Condé and Bernard de Saxe-Weimar. A merchant from Saint-Claude (located in the southeastern portion of the region), Lacuzon rallied partisans in 1636 and continued to do so until the penetration of the region by Louis XIV.

Over the centuries Franche-Comté has produced and inspired writers, artists, and scientists. The great author **Victor Hugo** (1802–1885) was born in Besançon. **Jean-Jacques Rousseau** (1712–1778), the irreverent Enlightenment writer and philosopher, lived in Besançon for a while. The poet **Stéphane Mallarmé** (1842–1898) taught English in the local *lycée* in Besançon. However, Besançon is most often associated with **Henri Stendhal's** (1783–1842) novel *Le Rouge et le noir* (1830, The Red and the Black). In this famous work, the character Julien Sorel attends the seminary in the city and meets his mistress in the town's cathedral. Stendhal often visited the town of Dole to the west of Besançon. He called Besançon "one of the prettiest towns in France." The region's spirit of independence also influenced the vision of two noted social theorists, **Charles Fourier** (1772–1837) and **Pierre Joseph Proudhon** (1809–1865).

The painter **Gustave Courbet** (1819–1877) was born in Ornans. He gave up the study of law to take up painting, eventually switching from Romanticism to Realism. He painted scenes of daily life, rural poverty, and Comtois landscapes. In the early 1850s he became a supporter of the French utopian socialist Pierre Joseph Proudhon. Courbet was active in the Commune of Paris in 1871 and later had to flee into exile in Switzerland, where he died years later.

The famous scientist **Louis Pasteur** (1822–1895), a son of one of Napoleon's soldiers, was born in Dole. After completing his studies in Besançon and Paris he moved to Arbois, a wine-making town south of Besançon.

During his career as a scientist he studied the fermentation process and found that it was caused by the action of micro-organisms. He discovered the process of "pasteurization," a process named after him. Pasteur also studied the silkworm and made contributions to the silkworm industry. He laid the foundations for bacteriology by identifying the staphylococcus and streptococcus germs, along with developing vaccines for rabies and anthrax. Even in his own lifetime, Pasteur was considered a brilliant scientist and a benefactor of society.

Turning to the cuisine of Franche-Comté, both cheese and *charcuterie* are important. Because Franche-Comté is an important dairy region, with approximately 300,000 cows, dairy products are featured in the gastronomic tradition. The region produces a number of fine cheeses that include Comté, solid and nutty in taste; Morbier, solid with a fine black line in each slice; Vacherin, soft and uncooked; and Cancoillotte, creamlike and popular for breakfast. The smoked meats are excellent, as well as the Morteau sausage known as Jésus. Given the lakes and rivers in the region, fish— such as trout, carp, char, and pike—are abundant; they are often prepared with white or red wine. Chicken from nearby Bresse is also popular. It is often prepared with cream sauces or served *au vin jaune*. In the northeast, in and around Montbéliard, the cuisine is similar to that of southern Alsace. Wine growing in Franche-Comté goes back to the time of the Romans. Today, vineyards cover more than 1,200 acres and produce red, white, and rosé wine. The five best wine-producing areas are Arbois, Arbois-Pupillin, Côtes du Jura, Etoile, and Château-Chalon. The region also produces *kirsch* (a cherry-flavored liqueur), plum brandy, and *marc* (distilled from the skins and fruit after grape pressing). Below is a recipe from the Jura that features eggplant. Eggplant is popular throughout France and is easy to obtain, regardless of the season.

AUBERGINES FARCIES
(Stuffed Eggplant)

8 small eggplants, halved	6 oz. smoked ham, finely cubed
1 tbs. olive oil	1 cup cooked long grain rice
salt and freshly ground black pepper to taste	1¼ cups cream
6 oz. Comté cheese (or Gruyère), grated	

Place eggplants in an oiled baking dish, cut side up. Put in preheated oven (400°F) and bake for 25 minutes. Remove from oven and lower heat to 300°F.

Using a spoon, scoop out inside of cooked eggplants, being careful not to tear the skins. Reserve the skins. Place pulp in a mixing bowl; season with salt and pepper. Mash with fork and add cheese, ham, and rice; then mix.

Fill the eggplant skins with the mixture and put them in a buttered baking dish. Spread the cream over the filled skins. Place in 300°F oven and bake for 20 minutes. Serves 4.

ARCHITECTURE AND NOTEWORTHY SITES

The typical rural house in Franche-Comté is simple and built to withstand the harsh climate. Houses normally form a single, squat block and are clustered in villages on the plains or in the vineyard areas; they are scattered in the mountains. Under one roof one finds family accommodations and stables. In the mountainous Jura, the stone walls are thick and the openings are small. Many villages were destroyed by war during the eighteenth century. Following the French conquest, churches were rebuilt and modeled after the houses. Consequently, a prominent site on the landscape is the square, domed bell tower.

BESANÇON (pop. 113,828), a university town, is a clock-making center. Situated on a loop on the Doubs River, the town dates from Gallo-Roman times; the main street was once a Roman highway. The *Citadelle*, a military fortress designed by Sébastien Le Prestre de Vauban, is the home of three museums that display artifacts of local history, natural history, and the emergence of fascism and the Resistance movement. The *Musée des Beaux-Arts et d'Archéologie* is one of the oldest museums in France. It possesses a good collection of paintings, including Renaissance pieces, and also displays the history of clock-making (this display is scheduled to move to the *Musée du Temps* on the main street in town). The *Horloge Astronomique,* a large astronomical clock, is a tourist attraction in Besançon. The *Porte Noire,* or Black Gate, dates from the Roman period. Nearby is the eighteenth-century *Salines Royales* (Royal Salt Works) at Arc-et-Senans. Located 19 miles south of Besançon, this is a fascinating example of advanced town planning in the early industrial period. It was designed by Claude-Nicholas Ledoux (1736–1806). Located in the Jura is *Métabief,* a winter resort with 156 miles of cross-country ski trails and 28 miles of downhill ski trails.

BELFORT (pop. 50,125), an industrial town, is strategically located between Alsace and Burgundy and between the Jura and the Vosges mountains. It has a system of fortifications designed by Vauban that proved beneficial in the sieges of 1814, 1815, and 1870. The city's inhabitants put up such heroic resistance to the Prussians' 103 days of siege in 1870 that it was granted the right to remain French. Today the city produces rolling stock, electronic equipment, and other industrial products. The symbol of the city is a large *sandstone lion* carved by Frédéric Bartholdi (1834–1904), who is internationally known as the sculptor of the Statue of Liberty in

New York Harbor. Inside the *Citadelle* is an art and history museum that features prehistory artifacts, regional art, coins, paintings, and a relief plan of Belfort. Belfort has an Old Town as well.

DOLE (pop. 26,577) is situated on the banks of the Rhône-Rhine canal. It was the capital of Comté until it lost its title to Besançon in 1678. On December 27, 1822, Louis Pasteur was born here. The Old Town has numerous buildings from the seventeenth century. Dole also has a museum of archaeology. The *Place aux Fleurs* offers a view over the rooftops of the town. The *Froissard Museum* is a former Carmelite convent with an ornate iron gate. There is also a former Jesuit college that dates from 1582.

ARBOIS (pop. 3,900) is a picturesque town of winemakers of the Jura; there are various wine cellars here. The family home of Louis Pasteur is well maintained and open to visitors. There is also a *Musée de la Vigne et du Vin* in the cellars of the town hall. The *Musée Sarret-de-Grozon* exhibits furniture, porcelain, and silverware.

RONCHAMP (pop. 3,088) is known for its chapel, *Notre Dame du Haut de Ronchamp*. Although the chapel was dedicated to peace, it fell victim to several wars. In 1955 it was rebuilt by the noted architect Edouard Le Corbusier (1887–1965), who created a wonderful architectural treasure. The design of Le Corbusier's chapel unites elegance and function.

BAUME-LES-MESSIEURS (pop. 196), located in a deep valley, is the site of an abbey founded in the sixth century by the Irish monk St. Columban. In the tenth century, a small group from Baume-les-Messieurs founded the renowned abbey of Cluny in Burgundy. The buildings of the abbey at Baume-les-Messieurs are simple and unadorned. Jean de Watteville (1613–1702), monk, abbot, adventurer, and Mohammedan, was associated with this abbey.

GRANDE TRAVERSÉE DU JURA (Grand Jura Crossing) is a 131-mile cross-country ski trail with a summit of 4,920 feet. It is well maintained and quite popular. Each year a 47.5-mile segment of the trail is used for one of the world's largest cross-country skiing competitions. Called the *Transjurassienne* and held in February of each year, this colorful event attracts more than 4,000 skiers.

SELECT BIBLIOGRAPHY

Boichard, J. *Encyclopédie de la Franche-Comté.* Lyon: La Manufacture, 1991.
———. *La Franche-Comté.* Paris: PUF, 1985.
Mathieu, Daniel, et al. "Franche-Comté," in André Gamblin, ed., *La France dans ses régions,* vol. 1. Paris: SEDES, 1994.
———. "Franche-Comté," in Y. Lacoste, ed., *Géopolitiques des régions françaises,* vol. 3. Paris: Fayard, 1986.

ÎLE-DE-FRANCE

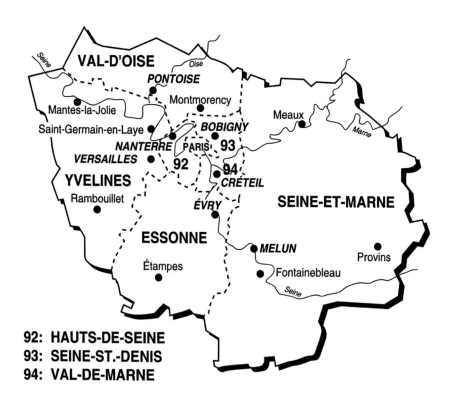

92: HAUTS-DE-SEINE
93: SEINE-ST.-DENIS
94: VAL-DE-MARNE

Chapter 10

ÎLE-DE-FRANCE

REGIONAL GEOGRAPHY

The Île-de-France, the most populous and economically dynamic region, is located in the north-central part of the nation. Its northern border is formed by the regions of Picardy and Upper Normandy. The southern border is formed by the Centre and Burgundy. The western border is contiguous with parts of Upper Normandy and the Centre; the eastern border is contiguous with Champagne-Ardenne. The region is within easy reach of the English Channel and its resorts. In fact, the new tunnel under the Channel makes it possible to travel by train from Paris to London in slightly over three hours. The Île-de-France comprises a mere 7,415 square miles, 2.2 percent of the surface area of France. The departments of the region are Paris, Seine-et-Marne, Yvelines, Essonne, Hauts-de-Seine, Seine-Saint-Denis, Val-de-Marne, and Val-d'Oise. Paris is the regional and national capital.

Geographically, this region takes its name—literally "the Island of France" from its location between the Seine, Marne, Oise, and Aisne Rivers. The region is situated at the point of convergence of three large valleys—the Seine, Marne, and Oise—that are major axes of communication. The region, too, forms part of the vast Paris Basin. The terrain is rolling and undulating, rising little over 650 feet. Along its limestone plateaux cut by winding rivers, lush valleys have formed. In other areas, such as near Beauce, Vexin, and Brie, there are large tracts of arable land. A band of greenery surrounds Paris; and there are magnificent forests nearby, such as the forests at Fontainebleau, Chantilly, and Rambouillet. Gentle hills, rivers, valleys, and forests characterize this region. It is dominated by the rapid expansion of urban Paris.

The climate of the Île-de-France is more or less continental. Weather can change relatively quickly, especially because of the region's proximity to the English Channel. Winter is generally cold, cloudy, and wet. Spring can be beautiful but wet. Summer and early fall are the best seasons, with the average high temperature in August close to 75°F.

HISTORY

In 52 B.C. the armies of Julius Caesar drove a Gaulish tribe called the Parisii from the Grenelle Plain. The Parisii moved to an island in the middle of the Seine River and founded a settlement known as Lutetia. In the fourth century A.D. this settlement became known as Paris, a name derived from its founders. At this time a Germanic people known as the Franks colonized an area between the Oise and the Marne Rivers. When the forces of Attila the Hun tried to overrun Paris, they were turned back by the statecraft of a youthful shepherdess, later known as St. Geneviève. The Frankish King Clovis chose Paris as his capital in 508.

The Île-de-France became an autonomous feudal territory in 987 when Hugues Capet became king of France. His dynasty lasted from 987 until the middle of the nineteenth century (with the exception of the period from the beginning of the Revolution in 1789 until the fall of Napoleon's empire in 1814). More or less functioning as an independent duchy, in the thirteenth century the region became identified with the French kingdom itself.

For centuries the region has been at the center of French history. As early as the twelfth century it saw the birth of Gothic art and architecture. It was the home of the northern French tongue, the *langue d'oïl,* which was adopted in 1537 as the official language. The seventeenth and eighteenth centuries saw the development of chateau architecture and garden landscapes. The Great Revolution of 1789 was to a certain degree a "Paris phenomenon" imposed on the rest of the nation. The visual revolution that drove modern art occurred in many of the region's villages: Argenteuil, Barbizon, Auvers-sur-Oise, and Bougival. Impressionism and Fauvism (an early twentieth-century movement in painting characterized by bold and often distorted forms and vivid colors) had their direct roots in this region.

The twentieth century saw the regional and national capital of Paris spared rather miraculously from destruction in both World Wars I and II. In the twentieth century, the region and its capital have attracted large numbers of people seeking economic opportunity. The Île-de-France is dynamic because of its capital. Moreover, Paris is considered one of the most beautiful cities—if not the most beautiful—of the world, adding to its attraction. Today Paris ranks as one of the leading capitals of Europe and the world.

RECENT POLITICS

The Île-de-France has been dominated in recent years by the gaullists and the UDF (Union for French Democracy), both parties of the political right. In the 1993 regional elections the right won eighty of ninety-nine possible seats in the National Assembly. The Socialist party (PS) in the 1993 elections was completely decimated in three departments: Seine-et-Marne, Yvelines, and Val-d'Oise. All in all, the PS lost eight seats in this election. The French Communist party (PCF) maintained its ground in this election and won an additional seat, bringing its total to eleven from the region. Although the extreme right-wing National Front (FN) won 12.5 percent nationwide in the 1993 elections, it captured 15 percent of the vote in the Île-de-France (11.33% in Paris). The xenophobic National Front is aided in the Île-de-France by the presence of a large number of immigrants, a key target of the FN. In the 1994 European parliamentary elections in the region, the right-wing majority obtained 25.68 percent of the vote, the PS won 14.96 percent, the PCF 7.66 percent, and the FN 11.51 percent. In the 1995 presidential contest, the socialist Lionel Jospin captured only one department—Seine-Saint-Denis—in the contest with the gaullist mayor of Paris, Jacques Chirac, who won the presidency. (In 1988 the left, symbolized by socialist president François Mitterrand, won a majority in the region.) On the other hand, the FN captured nearly 15 percent of the vote in the region in the first round of the 1995 presidential elections. In the 1995 municipal elections, President Chirac's coattails proved to be shorter than expected—especially in the capital, where the socialists won six of the twenty *arrondissements* (districts). Although Jean-Marie Le Pen won 9.8 percent in the first round of the municipal elections in Paris and higher totals elsewhere in the region, his extremist party captured the mayor's office in three towns in the south of France: Toulon, Orange, and Marignane. These elections revealed that the FN was well implanted in the region and throughout France.

Recent advances by the National Front and also by the Ecologists have made it difficult to achieve a majority in the regional council that helps to administer the region. Moreover, the relationship between the former mayor of Paris, the gaullist Jacques Chirac, and the left did not facilitate cooperation. The new mayor installed in 1995, Jean Tiberi, is also a gaullist; and the left has increased its political power on the municipal level in Paris. The struggle between the gaullists and the left will undoubtedly continue in the future.

POPULATION

In terms of population, the Île-de-France—and especially Paris—dominates France. Roughly one out of five French men and women live in the

Île-de-France. Its population is now near 11 million. Between 1850 and 1950 the region attracted people from the entire nation, with Paris serving as a national magnet. Although many parts of the country were losing population during this period, from 1850 to 1968 the population of the Île-de-France increased more than fourfold. In recent decades the growth rate has been somewhat slower. Today the birthrate is 1.83, above the national average of 1.73. Demographic growth witnessed in the present period is related not only to an increasing birthrate but also to the fact that young adults are attracted to the Île-de-France. Older people, however, tend to move out of the region. In general, young adults and foreigners have migrated to Paris. During the period 1982–1990 the region's population grew at 0.71 percent per year, as compared to 0.51 percent for the rest of France. The region's population stood at 9,879,000 in 1975 and jumped to 10,909,000 in 1993. Population density is between eight and nine times higher than the average density for France, making it the most densely populated region in the country. The density of the Île-de-France is 908 inhabitants per square kilometer (1,470.96 per square mile), whereas the national average is 105.7 per square kilometer (171.23 per square mile).

The population is relatively young. Although those age 19 and younger comprise 26.9 percent of the region's population, roughly the average for France, those age 60 and older make up only 15.2 percent of the population (19.7% is the national average). There is a considerable segment of people in the 20–50 age group, especially in the 25–35 age category. The immigrant population is more than twice the national average, with immigrants comprising 12.9 percent of the region's residents.

The urban population is considerably above the national average: in the Île-de-France it makes up 96.2 percent of the total (76.4% is the average for France). Life expectancy, 77.1 years, almost mirrors the national average of 77.2 years. Approximately one-third (31.8%) of all households are single-person households. The Île-de-France holds the distinction of having the highest percentage of single households of all the regions of France; the national average is 27.1 percent.

Educational levels are considerably above the national norm and are reflected in the composition of the work force. In the Île-de-France 12.9 percent hold only a high school degree, whereas 18.6 percent possess an advanced degree (10.5% and 11.2%, respectively, are the national averages). The number of excellent educational institutions in Paris—from the *collèges* (junior high schools) to *lycées* (high schools) to *universités* to the *grandes écoles* (specialized elite universities)—helps explain the educational levels among the region's residents. Roughly 27 percent of the nation's university-level students study in the Île-de-France. Of the work force, only 0.5 percent are in agriculture (well below the 5.3% average for France), 22.5 percent are in industry (26.9% for France), and 77 percent are in the service sector (considerably above the 67.8% national average). The unemployment rate in the Île-de-France is approximately 11.3 percent, less than the 12-percent-plus national average. Also, unemployment among women is 9.5 percent.

ECONOMY

The Île-de-France produces 30 percent of the gross domestic product (GDP) of the nation—three times the GDP of the second most productive region, Rhône-Alpes. Between 1986 and 1989 the GDP of the region grew by 13.5 percent, as compared to 10.7 percent for the remainder of metropolitan France. This growth led to a 4.6 percent expansion of employment, two times more than in the provinces, where declining agricultural employment had a large impact. More than 20 percent of the nation's work force is centered in this region. As a result of the region's economic dynamism, contiguous regions are in the orbit of the Île-de-France. Moreover, historically the region has benefited from multiple administrative districts and policies. The advantages offered by the region have made it (especially Paris and the Hauts-de-Seine) appealing for the headquarters of various companies. Correspondingly, it has seen the development of numerous companies serving businesses.

The region is productive and salaries tend to be higher than the national norm. The region's economy is far more productive than the national average. Salaries in the region are roughly 35 percent higher than in the provinces. This elevated salary level is related to the relative weakness of the agricultural sector in the region (at one time it was a major producer of wheat, corn, beets, and potatoes) as well as a large share of professions that command a high income, such as management and the liberal professions. It is estimated that 40 percent of the senior executives in business are located in the Île-de-France.

Industry here is centered around five poles of activity: printing and publishing, aeronautics, electrical engineering and electronics, automobiles, and pharmaceuticals and chemicals. In the capital, employment is weighted to a degree toward the public sectors. Traditional industries have witnessed decreasing employment, with a number of industries disappearing in recent decades—especially in the departments of Seine-Saint-Denis and Val-de-Marne. The service sector is the backbone of the economy in the region. Furthermore, unemployment and the duration of unemployment are less in the Île-de-France than in the provinces. Given the active job market and the elevated salaries, it is not surprising that many come to the Île-de-France seeking work; in 1990 alone an estimated 250,000 job seekers arrived in the region from the provinces.

The three largest cities are Paris with a population of 2,152,423 (the population of greater Paris is 9,318,821), Melun with 107,705 (Melun proper is 35,319), and Meaux with 63,006 (Meaux proper is 48,305).

Approximately 91 percent of the region's work force is located in Paris, 1 percent in Melun, and 0.5 percent in Meaux. The four largest employers are Régie Autonome des Transports Parisiens (Paris transport system), Renault Aubergenville, Air France Orly, and Automobiles Peugeot.

One problem that the region needs to overcome is the unevenness of its economic development. To the northeast of Paris is a working-class area, whereas to the southwest is middle-class. The close-in suburbs that surround Paris have traditionally been communist municipalities; today, however, the large number of office workers employed in many new offices built here in the 1980s are causing the political complexion of these areas to change. Yet the more distant suburbs tend to be more diversified. Various governments in Paris in recent years have proposed plans to make economic development more even throughout the region. However, resolution of the problem of uneven economic development will not be easy, considering the struggles between political parties on the municipal and regional levels.

For the remainder of France, one wonders if the provinces can continue to prosper given the dominant position of the Île-de-France in the national economy, not to mention its demographic advantage. With the extension of the high-speed TGV rail line, some municipalities are wondering if they will simply become suburbs of Paris. This question was raised recently when TGV service opened between Paris and Lille, making it possible to travel from Paris to this northern French city in roughly one hour.

CULTURE

The Île-de-France is the garden of kings. The destiny of France was played out to a large degree here, and those who held the reigns of royal power left their mark on this historic region. One sees the influence of royalty in a number of ways. For example, the numerous forests that surround Paris (e.g., Fontainebleau, Chantilly, and Rambouillet) are a product of the royal penchant for hunting. In past centuries, the forests were maintained as game preserves.

Another example of the presence of royalty are the region's famous chateaux. The most noted is Versailles, which was built at enormous expense by the Sun King, Louis XIV, in the seventeenth century. Located only a few minutes outside of Paris, this magnificent palace with parks and fountains played an important role in pre-revolutionary France, as well as in the nineteenth and twentieth centuries. The expense of constructing Versailles, coupled with Louis XIV's numerous and lengthy foreign wars (not to mention French support later for the American struggle for independence), helped to drive the French state into indebtedness and contributed in no small way to the outbreak of the French Revolution of 1789. In the nineteenth century Versailles was the site where Wilhelm I was proclaimed emperor of a newly united Germany following the Prussian victory in the Franco-Prussian War of 1870. In the twentieth century the Treaty of Versailles, which imposed harsh terms on Germany and ended the conflict between Germany and its neighbors, was signed in the palace of Louis XIV. The chateau at Fontainebleau is also a product of the presence of royalty. It was built originally for the kings of France who hunted in the nearby forest. Napoleon preferred Fontainebleau to Versailles. Consequently, this preference has given added importance to the smaller of the two famous chateaux near Paris.

During the Middle Ages, Gothic art and architecture emerged and flourished in this region. The desire to exalt the faith and the need to provide larger churches led to the Gothic style. Development of the ogive vault, featuring supportive diagonal ribs, was key to Gothic architecture and enabled windows and openings to be introduced more easily than in the older Romanesque churches. Beginning in the twelfth century, the architects of the Île-de-France launched a series of Gothic churches to accommodate the religious congregations of the Middle Ages. Most of the arts, from sculpture to stained glass, were involved in this architectural revolution.

Not the chateaux of royalty nor the churches of the pious, but the forests and the landscape of the Île-de-France played a part in the development of modern art. In the early nineteenth century, landscape painting was recognized as a legitimate subject matter—at least by some artists. The painter **Camille Corot** (1796–1875) moved to Barbizon in 1830 and placed his easel in the forests of Fontainebleau. Corot was interested in the way light filtered through the woods, and in the various lakes in the region. Other artists followed his lead and became known as the Barbizon School; these included **Henri Rousseau** (1844–1910), **Félix Ziem** (1821–1911), **Jean-François Millet** (1814–1875), and **Constant Troyon** (1810–1865). In 1871 **Paul Cézanne** (1839–1906) and **Camille Pissarro** (1830–1903) moved to Pointoise near Paris, while **Pierre Auguste Renoir** (1841–1919), **Alfred Sisley** (1839–1899), **Claude Monet** (1840–1926), and **Edgar Degas** (1834–1917) painted in Luveciennes and Argenteuil, also near the capital. However, ten years later Cézanne moved to Provence, Renoir to Italy and Algeria, Monet to Giverny, and Sisley to Moret. Despite this dispersion of talent, the Île-de-France must be given credit for helping give birth to the landscape movement of the nineteenth century, which played a significant role in the early development of modern art.

The landscape of the region also inspired a number of writers. During the eighteenth and nineteenth centuries, many writers who lived in the capital had country homes outside of Paris—writers such as Chateaubriand, Zola, and Rousseau. Whereas **François-René Chateaubriand** (1768–1848) found inspiration at La Vallée aux Loups to the south of the capital, where he had a beautiful mansion, **Emile Zola** (1840–1902) found inspiration at

Médan on the Seine and to the northeast of Paris, where **Guy de Maupassant** (1850–1893) was a frequent guest. Zola and Maupassant even collaborated on a collection of stories entitled *Les Soirées de Medan.* **Jean-Jacques Rousseau** (1712–1778), who possessed an intense feeling for nature, was inspired by his native Switzerland but also by Chambéry in Savoy and by the village of Montmorency just north of Paris. Residing in various houses, some lent to him by patrons, Rousseau lived in Montmorency for six years, a highly productive period in his life. During this period in this relatively rural setting, he completed three major works: *Emile, Du contrat sociale,* and *Julie ou la Nouvelle Héloise.*

Victor Hugo (1802–1885), the great recorder of the human drama, was acquainted with Montfermeil to the northeast of Paris. It is featured in his novel *Les Misérables.* Hugo lived at Port-Marly to the southwest of Paris.

Among contemporary writers, **Christiane Rochefort** (b. 1917) wrote a satiric novel about life in Sarcelles, one of the new towns that emerged outside of Paris in the late 1950s and 1960s to help relieve the housing shortage in the capital. Entitled *Les Petits Enfants du siècle* (1961), Rochefort's novel portrays life in Sarcelles as more comfortable than life in run-down parts of Paris but displaying a great potential for consumer conformism. Another who has focused on life in the French suburbs is the feminist **Marguérite Duras** (1914–1996). In her novel *Les Viaducs de la Seine-et-Oise,* an older couple commits what seems to be a motiveless murder in a town in the southern suburbs of Paris.

Turning to the cuisine of the Île-de-France, especially that of Paris, it is easy to identify a number of characteristic dishes. A highly popular dish is onion soup. Also well appreciated is *steak frites,* normally a strip steak accompanied with French fries. *Pot-au-feu,* boiled beef and vegetables, is also a favorite. The attractive and delightful *fruits de mer* is found in many restaurants; this is a bed of seafood served on a circular platter of crushed ice. A *fruits de mer* platter might include raw oysters and clams on the half shell, boiled shrimp and *langoustines,* and steamed mussels. A North African dish known as couscous is served with stewed vegetables and Merguez sausage; this has become a Parisian favorite.

Although many Parisian restaurants still serve *haute cuisine,* the style of cooking in Paris (especially restaurant cuisine) has changed over the years. For example, prior to the 1970s *haute cuisine* was fashionable. During the 1970s *la nouvelle cuisine* emerged, a cooking style that focused on freshness, presentation, and showmanship. When the economic recession hit France during the 1980s, *la nouvelle cuisine*—expensive to prepare— waned and an explosion of regional cooking occurred in the restaurants of Paris. The classical cuisine dictated by **Auguste Escoffier** (1847–1935), a noted chef and author of cookbooks, can still be found in expensive Paris restaurants; but it is inventive regional cuisine, to a large degree, that drives cooking today in the capital.

Parisian restaurants also have become internationalized, with the presence of many Chinese, Thai, North African, and other establishments. Even Mexican cooking is enjoyed in the capital today. Paris has also seen the revival of bistros, dining establishments that serve basic hearty fare. A new development—one that is frightening to restaurateurs and those who enjoy the pleasures of dining—is the emergence of "fast food restaurants." It is estimated that one out of four restaurants in Paris now serves fast food.

Food supplies for Parisian restaurants used to come from *Les Halles* in central Paris, but it was closed several decades ago to make room for urban renewal and for the Pompidou Center. A new commercial food market was established at Rungis, 30 minutes south of Paris. Rungis is now the single largest commercial food market in Europe, with approximately 3,000 trailer trucks and 15,000 individual buyers passing through each day. Paris, not to mention the rest of France, loves food.

Although the Île-de-France produces little in the way of agricultural products as compared to other regions, it is known for some excellent cheese. A soft Brie cheese made in Meaux is considered the best Brie in France. (Brie is also produced elsewhere in the region.) Fontainebleau cheese is soft, creamy, white, and quite good. Wine enjoyed in the Île-de-France comes from all over the country. This region—especially Paris—is a food and wine lover's paradise. Below is a recipe for the most famous of all French soups.

SOUPE À L'OIGNON GRATINÉE
(French Onion Soup)

3 cups finely chopped onion	6 peppercorns
3 tbs. butter	1 bay leaf
salt and freshly ground black pepper to taste	8 slices French bread, 1 inch thick
6 cups chicken or beef stock	2 tbs. melted butter
½ cup dry white wine	1 clove of garlic, cut in half
8 parsley stems tied together as a bouquet garni	1 cup Gruyère cheese, grated
¼ tsp. thyme	½ cup Parmesan cheese, grated

Using a covered saucepan, cook onions in butter with salt and pepper over medium heat, stirring occasionally, until onions are soft and golden brown. Add stock, wine, bouquet garni, thyme, peppercorns, and bay leaf; cook partially covered for 30 minutes, skimming occasionally.

Preheat oven to 350°F. Brush melted butter on bread and bake for 15 minutes, turning once. Rub garlic on the bread.

Remove bouquet garni and pour soup into four ovenproof bowls. Cover top of bowls with toasted bread. Sprinkle cheeses on toast and pour on remaining butter. Bake for 15 to 20 minutes. Place under preheated broiler until cheese is golden. Serve immediately. Serves 4.

ARCHITECTURE AND NOTEWORTHY SITES

The Île-de-France has witnessed its share of urbanization and poorly planned urban renewal. Yet the regional architecture reflects local styles and has been influenced by some of the surrounding areas, such as Normandy, Picardy, and the Beauce (Centre). The building material of farmhouses varies from stone and plaster in Yvelines and Seine-et-Marne to brick and stone in Val d'Oise. Limestone, timber frames, and millstone grit are used in other areas. A typical timber farmhouse in the region has a square courtyard that is closed by a large doorway. In previous times in the Meaux area, local straw merchants who supplied the stables of Paris lived in dwellings that had a large storage barn on one side and lodgings for cart handlers and groomers on the other side. The center of the structure was reserved for the straw merchant.

The city of Paris was rebuilt in the 1860s by Baron Georges Eugène Haussmann during the reign of Napoleon III. Haussmann's rebuilding produced a social segregation that left central Paris in the hands of the bourgeoisie, for the most part, while the proletariat was forced to move to the surrounding suburbs. Haussmann also widened the streets in order to minimize the possibility of protesters erecting barricades across the old, narrow streets of the city.

Today, the beauty of Paris is a marriage of the old and the new. Many older buildings have roofs of tin and are light grey in color, allowing the roofs to reflect the sun and giving a light quality to the large buildings. The rooftops of Paris are a favorite sight for many—some artists have even depicted them in their work. Many buildings, too, have an interior courtyard that affords residents some greenery and tranquility apart from the hustle and bustle of the city. Under President François Mitterrand (1981–1995) a number of large-scale architectural projects were undertaken that have helped to give the capital a more modern, high-tech look. These projects include the pyramid entrance and enlargement of the Louvre; the opera at the Bastille; the Musée d'Orsay; the new arch at La Défense; the science, technology, and music center at La Villette; and the Institute of the Arab World near the Seine. Mitterrand also initiated a new national library designed with a high-tech appearance.

PARIS (pop. 2,152,423; greater Paris 9,318,821), a noted French writer once said, is for humanity and not just for Parisians. The central core of the city is divided into twenty *arrondissements,* or districts. Moreover, the Seine River flows through the middle and divides the city into the Left Bank and the Right Bank. There are innumerable things to do and see in this beautiful city; below are a few of the highlights.

The *Louvre,* the great art museum of France, was built around 1200. It was first a fortress and then a residence for royalty. During the French Revolution it was turned into an art museum. Napoleon added to its collection with his European exploits. Here one can see art treasures such as the Mona Lisa, the Venus de Milo, and the Winged Victory of Samothrace. The *Musée d'Orsay,* once a train station, opened in the 1980s. Situated on the Left Bank next to the Seine, it houses many of the treasures—paintings, sculpture, and furniture—of the nineteenth century. In this relatively new and major art museum one can see the works of artists such as Claude Monet (1840–1926), Vincent Van Gogh (1853–1890), Edgar Degas (1834–1917), Paul Gaugin (1848–1903), and many others. The museum is filled with the work of the Impressionists. The *Musée Rodin* features the work of the sculptor Auguste Rodin (1840–1917), a close friend of the painter Monet. This charming and relatively small museum displays the work of the father of modern sculpture.

The *Notre Dame* cathedral was begun in 1163, but was completed two centuries later. Architecturally it is known for its Gothic styling, its stained-glass windows, and its flying buttresses. In 1804 Napoleon crowned himself emperor in the cathedral. The *Eiffel Tower* was designed by the engineer Gustave Eiffel for the 1889 World Fair, held to commemorate the one hundredth anniversary of the French Revolution. The 1,050-foot-high structure was severely criticized when it was proposed and construction began. Today, however, it is a Paris landmark and the symbol of the city.

Part of the beauty of Paris is the Seine, which divides the city and adds to the character of this urban environment. The Seine and its beautiful bridges (there are no less than thirty-three) are best seen from the *Bateaux Mouches,* or excursion boats. From the deck of these boats one can see many principal monuments of central Paris.

The *Champs-Élysées* is a grand avenue that links the *Place de la Concorde* with the *Arc de Triomphe,* a famous arch that Napoleon had constructed to celebrate his military campaigns. Recently the sidewalks bordering the Champs-Élysées were widened and more trees were planted in an effort to enhance the beauty of this busy but frequently visited avenue. On July 14, the Bastille Day (Independence Day) military parade is held on this famed avenue. The Place de la Concorde sits at the lower end of the Champs-Élysées. During the French Revolution, the guillotine functioned at the Place de la Concorde and thousands of heads rolled when its razor-sharp blade descended. The *Tuileries* is a garden next to the Louvre that was laid out by André le Porte, who designed the gardens at Versailles. For centuries it has been a place for leisurely strolls.

The *Pompidou Center* was initiated by President Georges Pompidou (1969–1974), a traditional gaullist who had a strong penchant for modern art. The center is dedicated to exhibiting aspects of modern art and culture. The building itself is a highly functional modern structure that includes gallery space as well as a library with open stacks (rare in Paris) and a music library. One of the best views of Paris is from the terrace of the roof-top café at the Pompidou Center. The center is extremely popular, especially with the young. Almost 26,000 people visit it daily. In 1994 it attracted 8 million visitors, twice as many as the Louvre. *Invalides* houses under its golden dome the tomb of Napoleon I. *Invalides* was built by Louis XIV in the 1670s to accommodate 4,000 disabled soldiers. There is a *Musée de l'Armée* on its grounds. The *Panthéon* is in the heart of the Left Bank, near the Sorbonne (the University of Paris). Dating to the 1750s, it began as an abbey church. However, during the French Revolution it was converted into a secular temple to honor the great personalities of the nation's past. Below its dome lie Voltaire (1694–1778), Rousseau, Zola, Louis Braille (1809–1852), and other famous personalities.

Parisians enjoy some delightful parks, such as the *Luxembourg Gardens* in the heart of the city or the *Woods of Boulogne* on the edge of central Paris. In the southeastern corner of the Woods of Boulogne is the Auteuil horse-racing track. There are six such tracks in the Paris area, a favorite pastime of many. In addition to parks, Parisians (and for that matter, all of France) enjoy cafés. They are particularly popular in Paris, where many residents live in cramped quarters. Many writers, such as the Existentialist Jean-Paul Sartre (1905–1980), have written books in cafés, the office away from home. In Paris and in France in general, cafés have an important social function by enhancing sociability.

VERSAILLES (pop. 87,789) is where Louis XIV built a huge chateau to symbolize his power; he once said, "I am the state." Some 30,000 workers and soldiers helped construct this gigantic palace. It was the capital and seat of government from 1682 until the Revolution of 1789. Some of the highlights of the Versailles palace include the Hall of Mirrors, a 246-foot-long ballroom paneled with mirrors on one side that allowed the king's guests to watch themselves. This is where Wilhelm I was proclaimed Emperor of Germany and where the Treaty of Versailles was signed. The *Grands Appartements* of the Sun King, the vast gardens, and the fountains are also highlights. The *Grand Trianon* was built one mile from the main chateau to allow the king to escape the restrictions of court life. The *Petit Trianon* was built mainly for Louis XV. In town, the *Cathédrale Saint Louis* has a huge pipe organ. The *Église Notre Dame* was the parish church of the king and his courtiers. The *Musée Labinet* displays furniture, paintings, and medieval religious art objects. The *Grandes* and the *Petites Écuries* are old stables that operate a carriage museum in the summer months.

SAINT-GERMAIN-EN-LAYE (pop. 39,926) is an affluent residential town. The chateau in the forest was once a royal residence. The *Antiquities Museum* has an interesting collection of artifacts from the Celtic, Gallo-

Roman, and Merovingian eras. The *Musée Prieuré* displays works of the Symbolist school and the Nabis, a group of late-nineteenth-century artists who believed that a work of art was an end product in its own right.

FONTAINEBLEAU (pop. 15,714), located 41 miles southeast of Paris, is known for its Renaissance chateau and its forest. The chateau is beautifully ornate and furnished. It served as the residence of a number of kings, as well as Napoleon. The *Musée Napoleon I* displays the personal articles of Napoleon and his relatives, including Napoleon's famed hat. A *Musée Chinois* in the chateau is filled with objects brought to France in the nineteenth century from East Asia. In town there is a *Musée Napoléonien d'Art et d'Histoire Militaire*, which has a good collection of uniforms and weapons. The *Forest of Fontainebleau* covers 150 square miles and is used for hiking, jogging, cycling, horse riding, and even training for mountain climbing.

PROVINS (pop. 11,608) is a beautiful little town that dates to the Middle Ages. The upper town has twelfth- through thirteenth-century ramparts, charming cottages, and gardens. At one time Provins was the third largest town in France, and European merchants came to the area twice yearly for regional fairs. The *Église St. Ayoul* dates to the twelfth century and was at one time a Benedictine abbey church. The *Musée des Provinois* has a collection of sculpture and ceramics.

SELECT BIBLIOGRAPHY

Beaujeu-Garnier, Jacqueline, and Jean Robert. "Île-de-France," in André Gamblin, ed., *La France dans ses régions*, vol. 1. Paris: SEDES, 1994.

Haenlin, Lydie. "Paris Region," in Wayne Northcutt, ed., *Historical Dictionary of the French Fourth and Fifth Republics, 1946–1991*. Westport, CT: Greenwood Press, 1992.

Hemingway, Ernest. *A Moveable Feast*. New York: Macmillan, 1971.

Renzo, Salvadori. *Architect's Guide to Paris*. London: Butterworth Architecture, 1990.

Robert, Jean. *Île-de-France*. Paris: PUF (Que sais-je?), 1994.

LANGUEDOC-ROUSSILLON

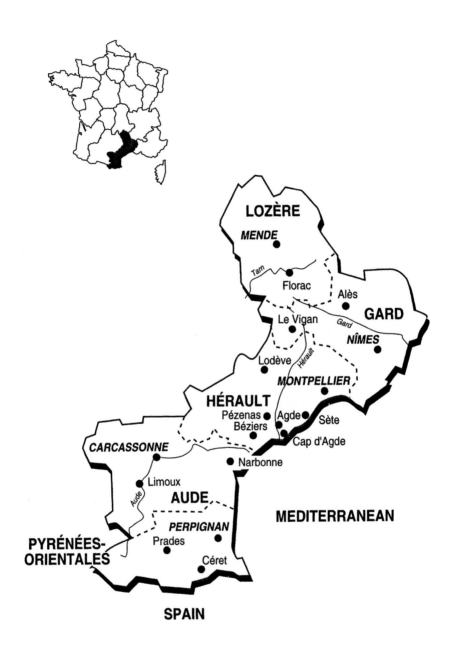

LOZÈRE

MENDE

Tarn

Florac

Alès

Le Vigan

Gard

GARD

NÎMES

Lodève

Hérault

MONTPELLIER

HÉRAULT

Pézenas
Béziers

Agde

Sète

Cap d'Agde

CARCASSONNE

Narbonne

Limoux

MEDITERRANEAN

Aude

AUDE

PERPIGNAN

PYRÉNÉES-
ORIENTALES

Prades

Céret

SPAIN

Chapter 11

LANGUEDOC-ROUSSILLON

REGIONAL GEOGRAPHY

A region of great variety, Languedoc-Roussillon stretches along the Mediterranean coast from the Rhône River to the Spanish border. On the north it borders the mountainous Massif Central. The region comprises 16,899 square miles, 5 percent of the surface area of France, and includes five departments: Hérault, Aude, Pyrénées-Orientales, Gard, and Lozère. Montpellier is the capital. This region and the south of France in general are sometimes referred to as the *Midi*.

On the Mediterranean, Languedoc-Roussillon fronts the *Golfe du Lion*, where there are numerous popular tourist beaches. On the northwestern border of the region lies the southern face of the mountainous Cévennes Massif; the southernmost portion is contiguous with the Pyrenees. Near the coast the region is relatively flat with gently rolling hills, but away from the coastal areas it is quite hilly.

The climate is exceptionally sunny and is one of the mildest in all of France. During the summer months temperatures are high along the Mediterranean coast and the Pyrenees. The town of Perpignan, near the Mediterranean and the Spanish border, is considered one of the warmest areas—excluding Corsica—in all of France. The region is noted for its warm, sunny climate and receives little rainfall. Inland, however, winters can be relatively harsh in the Cévennes and the lower Massif Central. A mountain wind, known as the *Tramontane,* sometimes blows through the region from the north. Given Languedoc-Roussillon's superb climate, it is not surprising that this region is one of the great wine-producing areas of France, accounting for roughly 40 percent of all French wine. The Hérault and the Aude are two of the largest wine-producing departments in the country. Because of its location and climate, the region has been called the "second Mediterranean"—an area like the Riviera to the west, but more authentic and less expensive for tourists seeking summer beaches, blue sky, and warm sunshine.

HISTORY

Languedoc-Roussillon, a region that may have been inhabited as early as 450,000 years ago, has a long and fascinating history. Phoenicians, Greeks, Romans, Visigoths, and Muslims dominated the region before it came under the control of the Franks. In 600 B.C. the Greeks, who had settled in Marseille, founded the town of Agde as an outpost, a perfect location because it was near the Mediterranean and the mouth of the Hérault River. One century earlier, the Gauls had begun to settle the region. Around A.D. 120 the Romans annexed the Gaulish regions in the south and in Languedoc. With the crumbling of the Roman Empire, the Visigoths took over the town of Narbonne and in time their kingdom included all of Spain and the south of France. In 720 the Muslim emir Al Samh conquered Spain and seized Narbonne. At this time the Muslim world stretched from Persia to North Africa to Spain and to the south of France. During the eighth century the Carolingian dynasty in the north of France began to penetrate the region in an effort to establish an anti-Muslim outpost. In the eleventh through twelfth centuries Languedoc came under the control of the Count of Barcelona. During the first half of the thirteenth century the French crusader Simone de Montfort launched a crusade against the Albigensians, a religious sect in southern France that the Church considered heretical. The Albigensians rejected the sacraments of Catholicism, advocated a clergy of men and women, preached asceticism, and criticized materialism. In 1209 thousands of residents of Béziers were slaughtered during one violent episode of the Albigensian crusade. This crusade led to the control of the region by the Franks by the end of the thirteenth century. The Franks suppressed the language spoken in the region, *langue d'oc* (commonly referred to as *occitan*), refortified strategic sites (*bastides*), created universities in Montpellier and in Toulouse, and introduced Northern Gothic architecture. During the Hundred Years War (1337–1453) between France and England, the region remained faithful to the French crown and was rewarded for its loyalty with a regional parliament.

Beginning in the sixteenth century the independent spirit of the region aided the development of Protestantism. Religious wars swept the region until the eighteenth century. Prior to the French Revolution of 1789, Jean-Baptiste Colbert, King Louis XIV's controller-general of finances in the latter half of the seventeenth century, initiated an anti-recession plan for the region that inspired the construction of the *Canal du Midi,* a 144-mile canal that would link the Atlantic with the Mediterranean in order to facilitate the movement of cargo vessels without having to travel around Spain. The canal would tie the region closer to the north. Generally, the French Revolution was favored in Languedoc-Roussillon. Yet the Napoleonic Wars of the early nineteenth century drained men and money from the region.

Serious economic decline struck Languedoc-Roussillon in the nineteenth century, but in the twentieth century economic forces have been more favorable. In the nineteenth century the region witnessed a serious economic decline owing to the spread of phylloxera, a vine louse that attacked the vineyards. One positive aspect of the nineteenth century was the arrival of the railroad, which helped spur the economy by opening access to many of the region's spas. Although the vineyards witnessed a recovery in the twentieth century, overproduction and fierce international competition in the wine industry have hurt Languedoc-Roussillon. After violent protests over Italian wine in the mid-1970s, the government subsidized wine producers to cut back their vineyards and encouraged them to replant with higher quality grapes. Also, underindustrialization in the interior and a rural exodus have retarded economic development. Nevertheless, in recent years the region has witnessed dynamic growth, aided both by the development of Montpellier and by tourism along the coast.

RECENT POLITICS

Languedoc-Roussillon was once known as the *Midi rouge* because of its preference for the left. However, in recent years the preference has changed somewhat, owing in part to a long recession and the inability of socialist president François Mitterrand (1981–1995) and the left to end the economic stagnation. In the 1993 parliamentary elections, the left—the Socialist party (PS) and the French Communist party (PCF)—won only three seats from this region, as compared to the fourteen that it had held prior to the election. The traditional right—comprising the gaullist Rally for the Republic (RPR) and the Union for French Democracy (UDF)—the ultra-nationalist and anti-immigrant National Front party (FN), and the Ecologists have made headway in this region since the 1992 regional elections at the expense of the socialists and communists. In the first round of the 1995 presidential elections, leftist candidates outpolled right-wing candidates in all departments except for Lozère. However, the extremist Jean-Marie Le Pen of the FN won more than 16 percent of the vote in the region (15% for all of France), polling close to 20 percent in the departments of Hérault, Gard, and Pyrénées-Orientales. In the second round when the socialist Lionel Jospin and the gaullist Jacques Chirac squared off against one another, the socialist won only the Aude. Chirac emerged as the new president of France. In the June 1995 municipal elections the socialists maintained control over the city hall in Montpellier, but the UDF captured Béziers and Perpignan, and the communists—owing to a division on the right—won Nîmes.

Languedoc-Roussillon is marked by fierce competition between its cities and towns and their political stars. Montpellier is led by its socialist mayor Georges Frèche; Nîmes is under the leadership of the communist Alain Clary; and Perpignan is under the mayorship of the UDF's Paul Alduy. Regional politics is a closely watched sport in this region.

POPULATION

Over the past two decades Languedoc-Roussillon has experienced a small but steady population increase. In 1975 the population was 1,789,000; in 1993 it stood at 2,188,000, approximately 3.8 percent of the national population. Moreover, between 1982 and 1990 the population grew at roughly 1.2 percent per year, making the region the fastest-growing area in France. The birthrate is currently 1.69, slightly below the 1.73 national average. The population density, 79.1 inhabitants per square kilometer (128.14 per square mile), is well below the national average (105.7 inhabitants per square kilometer/171.23 per square mile).

Some areas of the region, however, are experiencing an exodus—such as the rural department of the Aude. With 33 percent of its *communes* (municipalities) having a population of under 100 and offering little in terms of public services or conveniences, it is difficult for the Aude to retain those living in small villages and to attract new inhabitants.

Although in general Languedoc-Roussillon has experienced demographic growth, due principally to migrations from other regions, it has an elderly population as compared to the national norm. Those 60 years of age and over make up 24 percent of the population, as compared to 19.7 percent for France as a whole. Young people, those 19 years of age and under, comprise 24.5 percent of the region's population, as compared to a national norm of 26.8 percent. Immigrants, on the other hand, make up 6.3 percent of the population, the national average for immigrants.

The urban population of Languedoc-Roussillon is 73.1 percent of the total, slightly less than the 76.4 percent average for all of France. Life expectancy in the region is 77.3 years, above the national norm (77.2 years). Roughly 26.2 percent of all households in the region are single-person households.

The educational level and the composition of the work force are telling aspects of Languedoc-Roussillon. The educational level is as follows: 10.9 percent possess only a high school diploma, and 9.8 percent have advanced degrees. Of the work force, 6.7 percent are in agriculture, 28.8 percent in industry, and 72.5 percent in the service sector. The unemployment rate is one of the highest in France at this date, with 17 percent out of work (more than 12% for France as a whole). Unemployment among women is 16.4 percent.

ECONOMY

Although employment has grown by 1.2 percent since 1982 (owing mainly to the impact of population increases), unemployment has also grown and today is considerably above the national average. In terms of economic development, the region faces two handicaps: the age of its population and the low birthrate.

Agricultural production is focused on wine, vegetables, and fruit. The wine industry here is one of the largest in the world and is in the process of restructuring, with an emphasis on producing better quality wines. Both overproduction and foreign competition in the wine industry have motivated a diversification of crops, namely, vegetables and fruit.

The industrial sector is somewhat weak; it offers less than 100,000 jobs, mainly in agro-food production, textiles, the wood industry, electronics, and construction materials. Only approximately twenty industries employ more than 500 people. Given the increasing population, the building industry and related services are growing in this region.

Research—namely, public research—is especially important in Languedoc-Roussillon, placing the region in an advantageous position. Principal research is being undertaken in the fields of agriculture, food, and water, as well as biomedical and medical fields. This work is supported by a large university at Montpellier that enrolls approximately 60,000 students.

The three largest towns are Montpellier with 207,996 inhabitants, Nîmes with 128,471, and Perpignan with 105,983. Roughly 16.3 percent of the work force is centered in Montpellier, 9 percent in Perpignan, and 9.3 percent in Nîmes. Although 16 percent of the work force in Montpellier is out of work, it is estimated that one out of two new jobs in the region is centered in Montpellier. The four largest employers in the region are the regional hospitals in both Montpellier and Nîmes, IBM France, and Perrier.

The economy of this region is fragile. Development of the coastal tourist trade has aided the area. Along the Mediterranean coast a number of modern resorts have been constructed, such as *La Grande Motte,* which is known for its futuristic architecture. This and similar resorts were built, in part, to attract tourists from the overcrowded beaches of the *Côte d'Azur* between Marseille and the Italian border. The coastal areas of Languedoc-Roussillon boast numerous sandy beaches, including several well-known nudist beaches, which attract sun worshippers from all over France and Europe. Nevertheless, tourists remain for short periods of time and spend relatively little. The sun attracts people, but not necessarily capital for extensive development. In recent years the interior region has attempted to develop a tourist industry by featuring festivals, sightseeing tours, gastronomic tours, and exhibitions by artists and artisans. Although the economic growth of the region is currently a robust 3 percent per year, the number of new jobs has not kept pace with the growing population.

CULTURE

As the name of the region implies, two cultures have dominated here. Languedoc dominated much of southern France from the ninth to the thirteenth centuries. During this era the people spoke *langue d'oc (occitan)* as opposed to *langue d'oïl* of northern France, which developed into modern French. The name of the region, therefore, is taken from the ancient language spoken here. Today students can still study *occitan* in school. The *occitan* banner, which is still displayed in the region, has yellow and red vertical stripes and a black cross. An *occitan* independence movement has existed in the region for decades and draws the attention of officials in Paris from time to time.

The area of Roussillon lies at the eastern edge of the Pyrenees, close to Spain. Roussillon was once part of Catalonia, an area in the northeast of present-day Spain. In 1659 under the terms of the Treaty of the Pyrenees, Roussillon was taken over by the French. The region is often referred to as the French Catalonia. Perpignan is the principal city here, in many ways more Catalan than France. In Perpignan and Roussillon in general, the Catalan language is widely spoken. In other ways, too, Roussillon has preserved some resemblance of Catalan unity—the *sardane,* a dance expressing the twin themes of peace and revolt, is still performed in local festivals. Spanish culture has left its mark on the region as a whole as well. Bullfights are popular throughout the region. In Béziers in Languedoc, for instance, there is even a running of the bulls. Two other notable sports include rugby—especially around Béziers—and water jousting, a sport that dates back 300 years and involves two teams on large oar-powered boats with mounted lancers who try to knock each other in the water as the boats pass alongside each other. One can watch this unusual and interesting sport in towns such as Sète and Agde. Soccer, of course, is the French national sport and is followed closely in the region.

Situated on the ancient trade routes between Italy and Spain, Languedoc-Roussillon has been open to the larger world for centuries; thus it is not surprising that the region has long been a refuge for minorities and immigrants. After the Reformation, Protestantism flourished in parts of the region. At the beginning of the twentieth century Italians and Spaniards settled in Languedoc-Roussillon. In the 1960s many *Harkis* (repatriated French from Algeria who supported a French Algeria during the Algerian struggle for independence, 1954–1962) migrated to the region. In the 1970s *Maghrébins* (immigrants from former French colonies in Algeria, Morocco, and Tunisia) sought refuge in the region. Thus over the centuries an interesting mix of peoples and cultures have given Languedoc-Roussillon an intriguing identity.

Historically the region possesses a strong heretical tradition, both religious and political. Well known, for instance, are the Albigensians from the twelfth and thirteenth centuries who resided in this area of southern France. (In the 1970s, the contemporary French social historian Emmanuel Le Roy Ladurie wrote a best-selling work entitled *Montaillou* on this subject.) In addition to its religious "heretics," the region witnessed in the nineteenth and twentieth centuries a strong attachment to socialism, somewhat unusual for a rural area. Yet embracing socialism was one way that the region could display its independence and opposition to northern France, especially Paris.

The climate, beauty, and history of this region have ensured it a place in the history of twentieth-century art and culture. A number of well-known artists painted in Languedoc-Roussillon, such as **Henri Matisse (1869– 1954)**, **André Derain (1880–1954)**, **Pablo Picasso (1881–1973)**, and **Georges Braque (1882–1963)**. Fauvism, a style of painting that features bold colors and often distorted forms, was born in the seaside village of Collioure near Perpignan in 1905 when both Matisse and Derain developed this new artistic style while residing there. The region also gave birth to another major development in art, cubism. During the summers of 1911–1913, Picasso resided in the village of Céret near the Spanish border; here he and Braque developed cubism as a new and revolutionary style of art. Céret is sometimes referred to as "the mecca of cubism." Céret also attracted other notable artists, such as **Juan Gris (1887–1927)**, **Marc Chagall (1887–1985)**, **Raoul Dufy (1877–1953)**, and **Joan Miró (1893–1983)**. This particular corner of the region attracted so many artists who were seeking inspiration that the famous surrealist painter Salvador Dali (1904–1989) once said that the train station at Perpignan was at the "center of the world."

A number of notable artists and writers were born in this region. **Aristide Maillol (1861–1944)**, born in Banyuls near Spain, revolutionized classical sculpture at the turn of the century. He is often considered the father of modern sculpture. The painter **Paul Gauguin (1848–1903)** was among the first to discover and to support Maillol. (A large collection of Gauguin's work is found in the town of Béziers.) The poet **Paul Valéry (1871–1945)** as well as the popular songwriter and singer **Georges Brassens (1921–1981)** were from the port town of Sète.

The contemporary French novelist **Jean Carrière** was born into a Catholic family in Nîmes in 1928. Carrière is known for his story of life in an isolated hamlet in the Cévennes. His best-known book, *L'Epervier de malheux* (The Sparrowhawk of Misfortune), sold several million copies and won him the coveted *Prix Goncourt* in 1972. In this novel he tells the story of a savagely beautiful landscape that is cruel to those who live there. The Cévennes is also the subject of the work of the novelist **André Chamson**

(1900–1983), a Protestant born in Nîmes. His novel *Les Hommes de la route* (Men of the Road) tells the story of peasants applying the Protestant ethic to their difficult lives.

Another art in the region, cooking, is provençal and is characterized by the use of olive oil and garlic, enhanced with aromatic herbs. The cuisine ranges from seafood dishes along the coast (large quantities of oysters and mussels are cultivated in the Thau Lagoon near Agde) to delicious sausage and hams, *foie gras,* and truffles. *Cassoulet,* a hearty stew of white beans, sausage, and other ingredients, is one of the more popular regional dishes. Mutton and lamb are common meat dishes on the plateaus and valleys of the Causse. Specialties include *foie gras* and turkey *pâtés* flavored with truffles. Languedoc-Roussillon also produces delightful pastries and sweet breads made from almond paste and flavored with aniseed, pistachio, and orange flower water. Although relatively few cheeses come from the region, two of the more popular are Roquefort and Bleu des Causses. Full-bodied red wines, such as Minervois and Corbières, are readily available and inexpensive. Below is a typical recipe from the region.

OMELETTE AU ROQUEFORT
(Roquefort Omelette)

10 large eggs	salt and freshly ground black pepper to taste
7 oz. Roquefort cheese	2 tbs. butter or olive oil

Beat the eggs in a large bowl and then crumble in the Roquefort. Add salt and pepper (because the cheese is salty, little salt is needed).

Heat 1 tablespoon butter or oil in a 10- or 12-inch nonstick skillet over medium heat. When the skillet sizzles, pour in mixture. Shake skillet gently and turn. Reduce heat to medium low. Shake skillet and lift sides of omelette periodically to let mixture run underneath. Cook approximately 10 minutes. Light broiler. Put the additional tablespoon of butter on top of the omelette, or drizzle on remaining olive oil. Brown omelette for 1 to 2 minutes. Serve hot. Serves 4.

ARCHITECTURE AND NOTEWORTHY SITES

The architecture of Languedoc-Roussillon is Mediterranean in form and adapted to fit local conditions. The houses normally have gently sloping tile roofs. Construction materials range from limestone in the coastal regions, to sandstone and schist in the Corbières, to granite in upper Languedoc (especially in the Montagne Noire), to drystone in the Cévennes and Pyrenees valleys. During times of war in centuries past, houses were densely clustered in defensive villages on hilltops.

MONTPELLIER (pop. 207,996), situated a mere 7 miles from the sea, began as a trading port on the spice route from the East prior to the silting up of the city's waterway to the sea. Today it is known for its university (founded in the thirteenth century) and medical school (founded in the year 1000), which enroll nearly 60,000 students. The medical faculty of Montpellier is considered, along with its counterpart in Paris, to be the leading medical body in France. The humanist François Rabelais (1494–1553) attended the university here in the sixteenth century. In recent years Montpellier has became a dynamic regional capital. The socialist mayor Georges Frèche is credited with much of its urban renewal and recent renaissance. Some consider it the "Paris of the south" because of its rich cultural resources. The *Musée Fabre* possesses an impressive collection of French, Italian, Flemish, and Dutch works since the sixteenth century, plus a collection of the works of the nineteenth-century realist Gustave Courbet (1819–1877). Other museums in Montpellier feature local and regional history and a collection of French and Italian drawings.

NÎMES (pop. 128,471), once a showplace of the Roman Empire, is filled with Roman monuments, including an exquisite amphitheater built in the first century A.D. that now hosts concerts and bullfights. Centuries ago under the Romans, Nîmes was situated at the crossroads of the Domitian Way between Narbonne and Arles and the Régordane Way leading to the mountains. Other important Roman monuments include the *Maison Carée,* a beautiful and well-preserved temple; and the 160-foot-high *Pont du Gard,* an aqueduct that once supplied Nîmes with water. The chief town in the department of the Gard, Nîmes is a center for the wine and spirits trade and the clothing industry. In 1860 the Austrian Lévi-Strauss began to export a heavy cloth from Nîmes to serve as tent cloth for gold diggers in California, giving birth to the denim industry and jeans. Nîmes is also the home of France's most notable bullfighting school, *l'École Française de Tauromachie.* The city's *Musée d'Art Contemporain* features the works of Picasso, Braque, René Magritte (1898–1967), Marcel Duchamp (1887–1968), Man Ray (1890–1976), Jasper Johns (b. 1930), and Andy Warhol (1928–1987). The *Musée des Beaux-Arts* houses a collection of fifteenth-through nineteenth-century art that covers French, Italian, Flemish, and Dutch schools of painting.

PERPIGNAN (pop. 105,983), near the Mediterranean Sea and the Spanish border, is the capital of French Catalan and Roussillon. Numerous festivals keep alive the Catalan spirit of the town, which is also known for its beautiful flowers. Perpignan is not a museum town; the wine, vegetable, and fruit trade generate prosperity for its residents. Nearby is the *Côte Vermeille,* which attracts tens of thousands of sun worshippers during the summer months.

NARBONNE (pop. 45,849) began as a Roman town in 118 B.C. and became Rome's first colony outside of Italy. Over the centuries Narbonne became a Visigoth and an Arab town. In the past it had an active export trade, but the silting up of the waterway to the sea changed its fortunes. Until the nineteenth century the town and the region in general prospered from the wine trade, but in the nineteenth century phylloxera devastated the vineyards. In the mid-twentieth century the region began to recover from the devastation. In Narbonne itself, the huge *Cathédrale St. Just* dominates the skyline. Begun in the thirteenth century, the cathedral is one of the three largest in France and is an excellent example of Gothic architecture. The *Archbishop's Palace,* which housed the former Archbishop of Narbonne, reveals the importance of this ancient Mediterranean town. Today the town is divided by the romantic Robine canal that links the Aude River to the sea.

CARCASSONNE (pop. 43,470) is known for its walled city whose origins date to the Romans and the Visigoths. In the eighth century A.D., Charlemagne, who attempted to conquer the region, attacked this walled fortress over a five-year period. Owing to the thirteenth-century Wars of Religion, the fortress fell into a state of disrepair. In 1844 the architect Eugène Viollet-le-Duc was charged with the task of restoring it. Today it is a popular tourist attraction, and the walled city is an example of medieval fortifications.

AGDE (pop. 17,583), situated on the Hérault River near the coast, is sometimes called the "black pearl" of the region because its buildings are constructed from black volcanic rock. It was founded as an outpost for the Greek colony of Marseille. Agde is known for its picturesque narrow streets and its proximity to the sea.

PÉZENAS (pop. 7,613), a small town located 27 miles to the west of Montpellier, served as the seat of Languedoc regional government between the fifteenth and seventeenth centuries. During this period the town became a cultural haven that attracted the famous playwright Jean-Baptiste Molière (1622–1673), who spent time there. The Old Town has splendid architecture from the fifteenth through seventeenth centuries and earlier. Pézenas is now famous for its summer arts festival, which features cultural and theatrical activities.

CAP D'AGDE is a totally planned summer resort community on the Mediterranean and close to Agde. With beautiful walkways along the sea, a huge marina, cafés, restaurants, recreational activities, and small beaches (including a famous nudist beach), Cap d'Agde is a favorite vacation spot not just for the French but for Europeans in general—especially northern Europeans. In the winter months the population of Cap d'Agde is only a few hundred, but in the summer it swells into the tens of thousands.

SAINT-GUILHEM-LE-DÉSERT is a beautiful village of only a few hundred people in the Hérault valley, situated in the narrow Verdus Gorge.

SELECT BIBLIOGRAPHY

Berger, Alain, and Jacques Rouzier. *Vivre et produire en Languedoc-Roussillon: approche économique et humain.* Toulouse: Privat, 1981.

Ferras, R. "Languedoc-Roussillon," in Y. Lacoste, *Géopolitiques des régions françaises,* vol. 3. Paris: Fayard, 1986.

Le Roy Ladurie, Emmanuel. *Montaillou: The Promised Land of Error,* trans. Barbara Brayl. New York: G. Braziller, 1978.

———. *The Peasants of Languedoc,* trans. John Day. Urbana: University of Illinois Press, 1974.

Loubere, Leo. *Radicalism in Mediterranean France: Its Rise and Decline, 1848–1914.* Albany: State University of New York Press, 1974.

Madaule, Jacques. *The Albigensian Crusade: An Historical Essay,* trans. Barbara Wall. New York: Fordham University Press, 1967.

Verlaque, Christian. "Languedoc-Roussillon," in André Gamblin, ed., *La France dans ses régions,* vol. 2. Paris: SEDES, 1994.

LIMOUSIN

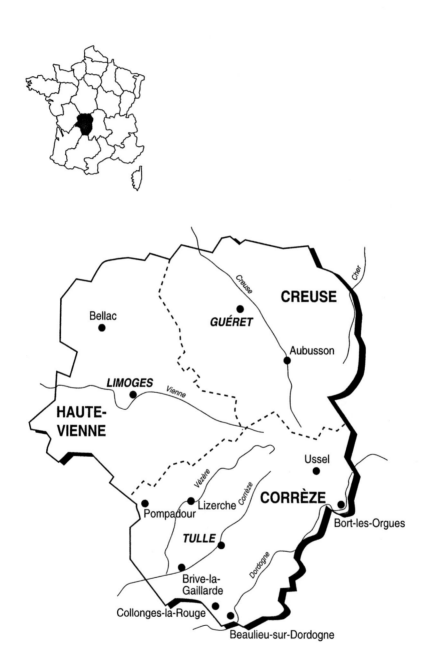

Chapter 12

LIMOUSIN

REGIONAL GEOGRAPHY

Limousin is located in the heart of France between the mountainous area known as the Massif Central and the Atlantic Ocean. Its southern boundary is formed by the regions of Aquitaine, Midi-Pyrénées, and Auvergne. A small region, it comprises a total of 10,483 square miles, 3 percent of the surface area of France. Limousin is made up of three departments: Haute-Vienne, Creuse, and Corrèze. The regional capital is Limoges.

The region's geography is characterized by lakes and trees; the colors blue and green dominate the landscape. Chestnut, oak, and beech trees can be seen from the roadways. It is a region of hills that are inconsistent in size. The highest point is Mont Bessou, which rises to almost 3,280 feet; in the western portion the altitude does not exceed 1,148 feet. There are several spectacular gorges, especially in Corrèze.

The climate is influenced by the Atlantic, with west and southwest winds. It is relatively mild except in the east in an area known as the Plateau de Millevaches, which tends to be more continental. However, the temperatures are often slightly lower than those in surrounding regions. Limousin has a reputation for precipitation, although it is not exceedingly heavy as compared to other regions and localities. In the towns of Limoges, Tulle, and Guéret, the average annual rainfall is more than 36 inches.

HISTORY

Although Limousin's history goes back to prehistoric times, it is not as well known as that of the neighboring Dordogne area. Neanderthal people lived in the southern portion. The region itself is named after the Lemovici, a gallic tribe that fell to Roman domination around 49 B.C. In 27 B.C. it became part of Aquitainia, which later became Aquitaine. During the Middle Ages the region was the route of pilgrimages to Santiago de Compostela in Spain, and many churches were built along the pilgrims' way. England also influenced the development of the region. When Eleanor of Aquitaine married Henry Plantagenet, who later became Henry II of England, Aquitaine (including Limousin) came under English control. Although France won back control of Limousin in the first part of the 1200s, during the Hundred Years War (1337–1453) Aquitaine and Calais fell again to the English. In the 1370s the French regained control of the region. The French king Henry IV united the region with France in 1607. Nevertheless, it remained a frontier region between northern France (the *langue d'oïl,* or the culture and language of the north with its written laws) and southern France (the *langue d'oc,* or the culture and language of the south with its laws based on custom). When Cardinal Richelieu, a religious prelate and statesman under Louis XIII, began a centralization policy, a number of revolts occurred in 1636 and 1637. During the eighteenth century royal administrators known as *intendants* pursued more flexible policies and began to pay attention to the economic development of Limousin, stressing road building, improving agriculture (introducing the potato), developing the porcelain industry, and encouraging the making of tapestries. The twentieth century has witnessed a serious depopulation of the region. With less than a million people residing in Limousin, the region's population was higher 100 years ago than it is today.

RECENT POLITICS

Limousin has been a long-standing bastion of the left; that is, until the 1993 legislative elections. Prior to the 1993 elections, only one deputy sent to the National Assembly in Paris came from the right; the others were all socialists. The only right-wing deputy representing Limousin prior to 1993 was the gaullist Jacques Chirac, who was born in Limousin and who was the mayor of Paris (1977–1995) and is now president of France. In the 1993 legislative elections, only one out of nine deputies elected was a socialist. The remaining deputies elected came from the right. In the 1995 presidential election, the region's native son won a majority in Limousin; however, in the first and second round of the voting, the left (namely, the socialist Lionel Jospin) won the department of Haute-Vienne. In the first round, too, the extremist Jean-Marie Le Pen of the National Front (FN) won only 6.3 percent of the vote in the region, well below his 15 percent national average. Chirac's department, the Corrèze, gave a large majority of its vote to its native son in the final round of the contest. In the June 1995 municipal elections, the Socialist party (PS) retained control over Limoges, whereas the gaullist Rally for the Republic (RPR) maintained control over Brive-la-Gaillarde. In the Corrèze the RPR candidate Jean-Pierre Dupont easily won the mayorship of Bort-les-Orgues and continues the gaullist hold on its Corrèze fiefdom.

POPULATION

During the twentieth century there has been an exodus of people out of Limousin. In 1975 the region had a population of 739,000; by 1993 it had fallen to 717,000. The region's birthrate is a low 1.44, as compared to the national average of 1.73. In general the population is grouped around two dominant poles, Limoges and Brive-Tulle, making up half the region's population. The density is a mere 42.3 inhabitants per square kilometer (68.52 per square mile), considerably below the national average of 105.7 per square kilometer (171.23 per square mile). Limousin is the least dense region in France. In certain areas of the region, the population density is less than 10 inhabitants per square kilometer (16 per square mile).

Limousin also has an elderly population. Those age 60 and over make up 28 percent of the population (the national average is 19.7%); yet those age 19 and under represent 21.5 percent of all inhabitants (26.8% is the average for France as a whole). The immigrant population, as might be expected, is low, 2.9 percent, and considerably less than one-half the national average.

Although the urban population is markedly less than the average for France, life expectancy is high. Limousin's urban population is 51.4 percent of the total population, well below the 76.4 percent average for France. Nevertheless, life expectancy in Limousin is 77.2 years, exactly the national average. Approximately 27.9 percent of all households are single-person households, slightly above the 27.1 percent average for all of France.

Educational levels, as might be expected in this rural region, are below the national norm: 9.3 percent possess only a high school diploma, and 7.9 percent hold some form of an advanced degree (10.5% and 11.2%, respectively, are the national averages).

The composition of the work force reflects the rural character of the region. In industry one finds 22.3 percent of the work force, below the 26.9 percent national average. Almost 11 percent work in agriculture, a high percentage as compared to other regions. Those working in the service sector represent 67 percent of the work force, roughly the same as the average for the nation as a whole. The unemployment rate is 10.3 percent; the national rate is more than 12 percent. Unemployment among women is approximately 10.4 percent in the region.

ECONOMY

In terms of economic opportunity, Limoges and Brive-Tulle are dominant centers. The most agricultural and most aged areas are found in the north: Creuse and the Plateau de Millevaches. The western and southwestern areas of the region, where one finds Limoges and Brive-Tulle, are more industrial. Agriculture, representing 10.7 percent of the work force, occupies a place two times more important than the average for France as a whole. Moreover, 57 percent of all agricultural areas in the region raise cattle for beef, and 26 percent raise sheep for both meat and milk. All in all, animal husbandry comprises 90 percent of all agricultural production. Yet the income generated by agriculture was 32 percent of the national average for this sector in 1991. The agricultural work force is characterized as well by a relatively aged population. Moreover, over the past decade Limousin lost 15,000 full-time jobs in the agricultural sector. Today less than one out of seven live on a farm; in 1970 the figure was one out of four.

Industry is relatively diversified and is dominated by medium-size to small firms. Of the 3,000 industrial establishments in the region, only eight employ more than 500 people. Thus it is not surprising that per capita income is 20 percent less than the national average. The industrial structure inherited from the nineteenth century has been stressed in the region, with continued production of porcelain, leather, shoes, paper products, and furniture. Production of porcelain, paper products, and even uranium is found mainly in Haute-Vienne, which also produces textiles (mainly clothing), leather, and shoes.

Limousin may appear underdeveloped to the outsider, but one must consider several facts about the region. From the Middle Ages to the Industrial Revolution, it looked as if Limousin would become one of the primary industrial areas of France. It produced wool and leather and also had potential for mining. In the fourteenth century Aubusson became a center for the production of tapestries. In the seventeenth century Tulle became the manufacturer of royal arms; in the eighteenth century it began to produce porcelain. However, the acceleration of the Industrial Revolution at the end of the nineteenth century, with the beginning of the railroad and improved transportation, left Limousin behind. The indigenous "revolution" in Limousin could not keep pace with the highly competitive Industrial Revolution that transformed other parts of France, especially areas with an adequate transportation system.

The three largest towns in the region are Limoges with 133,464 inhabitants, Brive with 49,765, and Tulle with 17,164. Approximately 30.5 percent of the work force is centered in Limoges, 10.9 percent in Brive, and 4.6 percent in Tulle. Although there is a relatively large number of women in the work force, unemployment affects them more frequently, especially those between 25 and 49 years of age. Furthermore, those unemployed, both men and women, are staying out of work for longer periods than national averages. The four largest employers in the region are Centre Dupuytren (Limoges), Legrand (electrical equipment), the city of Limoges, and SNCF-Limoges (railroad).

Although Limousin is becoming more and more a region of passage between north and south, the transportation system has developed slowly. Today Limousin is the only region of metropolitan France not to be crossed by an autoroute or a TGV high-speed rail line. However, the idea of a Paris-Limoges-Toulouse autoroute was accepted by Parisian authorities in 1988, and the project is expected to be completed in 1996; plans for a TGV line were accepted in principle in 1991. The principal airport at Limoges-Bellegard was constructed only in the 1970s. Moreover, the region's higher education structure has only been recently developed. For instance, the university at Limoges dates only to 1968.

In recent years regional authorities have launched a program to attract young European agricultural workers. The region has invested more recently in culture as well, seeing this as a way to aid economic development. According to French specialists on the region, Limousin may be well positioned for a number of new technologies in various fields: ceramics, hydroelectric energy, uranium, optics, electrical engineering, and biotechnology. The region is beginning to view itself as an experimental laboratory for regional development.

CULTURE

The name of the region reflects its rural character. While to much of the world it calls to mind a luxury automobile, in the local dialect, the word *limousine* refers to a rough woolen cloak worn by a shepherd. Over the centuries Limousin has often been depicted as a backwater. Such notable writers as **François Rabelais** (1494–1553), **Jean-Baptiste Molière** (1622–1673), **François-Marie Voltaire** (1694–1778), **Jean de La Fontaine** (1621–1695), and **Jean-Paul Sartre** (1905–1980) portrayed Limousin as an archetype of backwardness and ignorance. To counter this negative image, residents of the region like to recall that a number of its native sons have been innovators and pioneers. For example, **Jean Dorat** (1508–1588), the master of *La Pléiade* (The Pleiad); **Tristan l'Hermite** (1601–1655); **Jean-François Marmontel** (1723–1799), the writer and philosopher; **André Antoine** (1857–1943), the director; and **Auguste Renoir** (1841–1919), the painter, came from this region. **President Jacques Chirac** also comes from Limousin.

However, for the most part, the illustrious people born in Limousin left the region to make their mark. One of the twentieth-century writers born just north of Limoges and who wrote on the region was **Jean Giraudoux** (1882–1944). Yet he too left the region, traveled abroad as a diplomat, and then took up residence in Paris. Two of his novels, *Suzanne et la pa-*

cifique and *Siegfried et la Limousin,* describe the region. *Siegfried et la Limousin* centers on a man from Limousin who falls victim to amnesia and accidentally becomes German. The novel is a satire of sorts on the differences between French and German mentalities.

Limousin has a long tradition of producing quality porcelain, tapestries, and enamels. Limoges has long been associated with porcelain. The fine art of enamel is also found in this region, notably at Limoges, where an international competition is held every two years. Even though the region is rural, it is known for its fine craftsmanship. Long overlooked by tourists, its lakes, trees, and green landscapes make it a superb location for outdoor enthusiasts who enjoy sailing, canoeing, fishing, kayaking, and hiking. Given the low population density of Limousin, one can rest assured that this tranquil vacation spot will not be overrun with tourists.

The cuisine of Limousin features vegetables and meat. A traditional soup called *bréjaude* is thick with cabbage and other vegetables and is eaten with rye bread. *Charcuterie,* or pork products, are popular here, such as *andouille* (chitterling sausage) and *boudin* (blood sausage) with chestnuts. Traditional dishes include stews and sauce dishes served with chestnuts and rye pancakes. The cabbage stew and *cassoulet* are delectable. The region's beef is both tender and flavorful. Because cattle in the region are raised mainly for breeding, there are few local cheeses except for Brach, somewhat similar to Roquefort. Homemade cakes are often served as dessert. Some cakes are made with cherries or apples. There is also a *galette Corrézienne* and an almond cake that are made in Creuse. Below is a recipe for *clafoutis,* a popular dessert.

CLAFOUTIS LIMOUSIN
(Baked Cherry Flan)

1½ lbs. fresh, pitted cherries (or canned tart cherries)	2½ ozs. butter, melted
	⅔ cup all-purpose flour
2 eggs	1 cup milk
1 egg yolk	confectioners' sugar
½ cup sugar	

Preheat oven to 400°F. Butter an ovenproof china or earthenware dish, and add cherries to it in a single layer. In a mixing bowl combine eggs and yolk, add sugar, and whisk until mixture is smooth and creamy. Whisk in the butter. Sift in the flour and mix well, then add milk and whisk. Continue beating until the batter is smooth, then pour mixture over the cherries. Bake for 40 minutes or until browned. Remove *clafoutis* from oven and sprinkle with confectioners' sugar. Serve lukewarm. Serves 6.

ARCHITECTURE AND NOTEWORTHY SITES

The architecture of Limousin is not known for its originality; yet over the generations numerous masons have come from Limousin. Although there is little ornamentation on the houses, weathervanes became popular after the seventeenth century and still can be viewed on the houses in the region. In the northern part of Limousin, Mediterranean-style roofs with gentle slopes are common. In other areas, roofs are steep and are covered with slate, stone, or flat tiles. In the eastern section of Limousin the architecture resembles that of Auvergne, whereas in the southern section the architecture shares common features with that of the Dordogne. In the department of Creuse in the north, granite is the building material for walls; river stone is used in the Dordogne; and sandstone, ochre or red in color, is used in the Brive valley in the south. In the south, too, wood is used for balconies and porches.

LIMOGES (pop. 133,464) is not only the capital of the region but also a major center for the French porcelain and ceramics industry. An attractive town surrounded by pleasant countryside, it was founded in Roman times and is situated on the Vienne River. In the eleventh century it became (and still is) a stopping point on the pilgrimage route to Santiago de Compostela in Spain. St. Martial's Abbey is in Limoges. He came to the town in the third century and converted it to Christianity; he also became bishop here. The Chateau quarter has many half-timbered houses and the *Rue de la Bucherie*, which runs through the heart of the picturesque area of the town. In the Middle Ages, Rue de la Bucherie was lined with butcher shops. The oldest church in Limoges is the *Église Saint Pierre du Queyroix*. The *Église Saint Michel des Lions,* built between the fourteenth and fifteenth centuries, has a number of handsome fifteenth-century stained-glass windows. The *Musée Municipal du Palais de l'Église* displays Gallo-Roman and Egyptian artifacts, enamel pieces from the twelfth to the twentieth centuries, and paintings by Renoir, who was born in Limoges in 1841. The *Musée de la Résistance* honors local resistance combatants from World War I. The *Musée National Adrien Dubouché* has—along with a collection in Sèvres near Paris—one of the best displays of porcelain in France. The Limoges collection contains nearly 12,000 pieces, including local works and pieces from countries such as Iran and China. One can view porcelain being made at *Le Pavillon de la Porcelaine,* just outside the town. For enamels, there are small galleries in town where examples of this fine art may be viewed. Every two years Limoges hosts an international enamel exhibition. What gives the local enamels their brilliant color is the local soil: in and around Limoges the soil is rich in metallic oxides. Given the presence of metallic oxides and the abundance of firewood, the art of enamel making became highly developed here as early as the twelfth through the fourteenth centuries.

TULLE (pop. 17,164) is the principal town in the department of Corrèze. There is a handsome twelfth-century cathedral with a 246-foot-high bell tower. One can also view a conservatory of regional crafts and old tools. The *André-Mazeyrie Museum* has displays of archaeology and art. One can also view an impressive collection of weapons at the *Manufacture Nationale d'Armes*.

AUBUSSON (pop. 5,097) is famous for its tapestry, which dates to the sixteenth century. One can view the local tapestries at many places: *École National d'Art Décoratif*, the *Centre Cultural et Artistique Jean Lurçat*, and the *Maison du Vieux Tapissier*. In the summer months the *Hôtel de Ville* has art and other exhibits.

BORT-LES-ORGUES (pop. 4,208), located near the boundary with Auvergne, is a small town once known for its tanneries and now a popular holiday resort. The surrounding countryside is appealing. Nearby are enormous phonolitic columns (formed from prehistoric lava) standing 262–318 feet high. Also nearby is a 394-foot-high dam that forms a large lake on the Dordogne; boating is popular here.

UZERCHE (pop. 2,813) is a picturesque little town built on a loop in the Vézère River. Here one can find a number of turreted and elegant fifteenth- and sixteenth-century houses. The *Cathédrale St. Pierre* is a twelfth-century Romanesque building with an attractive Limousin bell tower.

POMPADOUR (pop. 1,474) is famous for its close ties to history and political power. Louis XV gave the Marquise de Pompadour a chateau here when she received her title in 1745. After she died, the king repurchased the chateau and created a stud farm, which is known today by the Marquise's name. The stud farm breeds Anglo-Arab horses. Both the chateau and the stud farm can be visited. In the summer there are horse shows and races.

BEAULIEU-SUR-DORDOGNE (pop. 1,265) is located on the banks of one of the most beautiful rivers in France. The small town is known for its twelfth-century abbey church, which is a superb example of Limousin Romanesque art. A number of charming old houses surround the church, including one built during the Renaissance.

COLLONGES-LA-ROUGE (pop. 381) is considered one of the prettiest, if not the prettiest, villages in Limousin. The name of the village is derived from the fact that the fifteenth- through seventeenth-century houses are built of red sandstone. There is a charming covered market with a communal oven. The village also has a church that dates to the eleventh century.

SELECT BIBLIOGRAPHY

Balabanian, Olivier, and Guy Bouet. *Le Guide du Limousin.* Paris: La Manufacture, 1994.

Barbey, Adélaide. "Limousin," in André Gamblin, ed., *La France dans ses régions,* vol. 2. Paris: SEDES, 1994.

Mauratille, G. *Le Limousin.* Paris: Arthaud, 1987.

Robert, M., ed. *Limousin et Limousins, image régionale et identité culturelle.* Limoges: Lucien Souny, 1988.

LORRAINE

BELGIUM

LUXEMBOURG

GERMANY

MEUSE   Briey   Thionville   Forbach

Verdun   **METZ**   Sarreguemines

MOSELLE

Aisne

Meuse

Moselle

Château-Salins

BAR-LE-DUC   Sarrebourg

Commercy   **NANCY**

Toul   Lunéville

Meuse   **MEURTHE-ET-MOSELLE**

Saint-Dié

Neufchâteau   Moselle

ÉPINAL

Meurthe

Saône

VOSGES

Chapter 13

LORRAINE

REGIONAL GEOGRAPHY

Located in the northeastern corner of France between the Paris Basin and the Vosges mountains, Lorraine borders Alsace to the east and Belgium, Luxembourg, and Germany to the north. The region comprises 14,535 square miles, roughly 4.3 percent of the surface area of France, and is divided into four departments: Meuse, Meurthe-et-Moselle, Moselle, and Vosges. The capital is Metz.

Geographically, the region occupies the sprawling Lorraine plateau, an extension of the Paris Basin, and is known for its wooded areas. In general the region is hilly. Its physical geography makes it an excellent passageway linking northern and southern Europe. Lorraine's grand lines of relief run in a north-south direction, including its valleys. Practically all the rivers are tributaries of the Meuse and the Moselle, both of which flow into the North Sea. In the southeastern corner of Lorraine, the Vosges mountains separate the region from Alsace.

The continental climate is similar to that of other regions in eastern France. Lorraine has a reputation for being rainy; the benefit, of course, is a lush green landscape.

HISTORY

Centuries ago when the Romans invaded Lorraine they found it inhabited by two Celtic peoples located around what is today Metz and Toul. The Romans also found that iron was already being smelted, salt mines were in production (Lorraine is France's largest producer of salt), and travel was developing between this region and what would later be known as Belgium and Burgundy. Roman roads and city planning spurred economic development.

In A.D. 843 Lorraine entered history. In this year, the Treaty of Verdun divided the Frankish holdings of the Carolingian emperor Louis I among his three sons. One son, Lothair, received the area that would later become Lorraine. The region's name is derived from Lothair.

Lorraine also gained historical importance with the birth of a peasant girl who became known as Joan of Arc, France's national heroine in the Hundred Years War (1337–1453). Born in the small village of Domrémy near Nancy, she left home at age 16 to support the dauphin Charles. Owing in part to her exploits, the dauphin was crowned Charles VII in 1422. Joan's fate was different—she was burned at the stake by the English at Rouen.

Lorraine became part of France only in 1766. Prior to this the region was controlled by Stanislaw I, the former king of Poland and father of Louis XV, who had received Lorraine in 1738 under the terms of the treaties ending the War of Polish Succession (1733–1738).

In the late nineteenth and twentieth centuries, Germany figured prominently in the region's history. Lorraine was annexed by Germany in 1871 following the Franco-Prussian War, which led to the unification of Germany. Long known for its important coal and iron industries, Lorraine continued to develop as an industrial region. During World War I, Verdun was the site of one of the major battles in this prolonged and bloody struggle; approximately 800,000 perished in the Battle of Verdun (1916–1917). At the end of World War I the defeated Germans had to relinquish control over Lorraine, as well as Alsace. During the interwar period the French constructed the Maginot Line, a defensive fortification that stretched from Alsace to Lorraine. During World War II the region came under German control once again following the fall of France to Hitler's war machine at the start of the conflict. In the post–World War II years Lorraine has had to confront the decline of its heavy industries, owing to its failure to modernize and the economic recession that hit France and the western world in the 1970s and 1980s.

RECENT POLITICS

Although a majority of the electorate in Lorraine voted for the socialist presidential candidate François Mitterrand in the 1981 elections, the region is now anchored on the right. This political change is due in part to the long economic crisis that has persisted since the early 1980s. Given Lorraine's frontier position close to the contested German border, its strong Catholic tradition, and its numerous national and paternalistic industries, it has often supported conservatives. Christian democracy, represented by the Popular Republican Movement (MRP), has been strong in the region. So, too, have been the non-socialist and non-communist unions, the French Confederation of Christian Labor (CFTC) and the French Confederation of Democratic Labor (CFDT). The 1992 regional elections and the 1993 parliamentary elections confirmed the region's conservative bent. Voters in the 1992 regional contest elected a majority of representatives from diverse political parties of the right, whereas the Ecologists won 16 percent of the vote. In the 1993 parliamentary elections twenty of the twenty-three deputies elected represented right-wing parties, with all the elected deputies from the Vosges and Meuse coming from right-wing parties. In the 1995 presidential contest right-wing candidates swept all departments in the region except for Meurthe-et-Moselle, where the left made the best showing. The extreme right-wing candidate representing the National Front (FN), Jean-Marie Le Pen, captured 20.42 percent of the vote in the first round, 5 percent more than his national average. Le Pen captured 23.82 percent in the department of Moselle. In the second round of the presidential contest the gaullist candidate Jacques Chirac (the eventual winner), representing the Rally for the Republic (RPR), won all departments in Lorraine except for Meurthe-et-Moselle, which the socialist Lionel Jospin captured. Jospin lost the contest with Chirac on the national level as well. In the June 1995 municipal elections the RPR won control over Thionville and Vandoeuvre and retained control over Épinal; the center-right Union for French Democracy (UDF) retained control over Nancy. The diverse right retained its dominance over the city hall in Metz.

POPULATION

In recent years Lorraine has witnessed a steep population decline. Although the population stood at 2,331,000 in 1975, it had fallen to 2,304,000 in 1991. Between 1982 and 1990 Lorraine saw a population decline of more than 14,000 people; this meant that 37 people left the region daily. The principal reason for this decline has been the economic crisis in the industrial sector. The region's birthrate, 1.76, is slightly above the national average. Today the population density is 97.5 inhabitants per square kilometer (157.95 per square mile), slightly below the national average of 105.7 per square kilometer (171.23 per square mile).

The region's population is slightly younger than the national average. Only 18.7 percent of the region's inhabitants are age 60 or over (19.7% is the national average). On the other hand, those age 19 or younger make up 27.7 percent of the population, slightly above the national average of 26.8 percent. The immigrant population is 6.6 percent, slightly more than the national average.

In Lorraine the urban population is 72 percent, less than the 76.4 percent for all of France. Life expectancy is 75.8 years, more than one year below the national average. Roughly 24.3 percent of all households are single-person households, below the 27.1 percent average for the nation.

The educational levels of this industrial and working-class region are below the national averages. Only 8.7 percent possess a high school diploma, and 8.1 percent hold advanced degrees (the national average is 10.5 percent and 11.2 percent, respectively). Of the work force, 3.4 percent are employed in agriculture, 34.3 percent in industry, and 62.3 percent in the service sector. Whereas the percentages of those in agriculture and the service sector are below national averages, the percentage in industry is more than 7 percent higher than the national average. The unemployment rate, 11.5 percent, is less than the national average of more than 12 percent, despite the region's deep industrial crisis. Although one might expect the unemployment in Lorraine to be higher, migration out of the region helps keep unemployment below the national average. Unemployment among women is 12.3 percent, approximately the national average for joblessness among women.

ECONOMY

Long a steel producing area, Lorraine has been especially hard hit by the worldwide crisis in the steel industry. Today, only 2 percent of the work force is found in the steel industry; fifteen years ago this figure was 10 percent. The four pillars of the industrial economy in Lorraine have been steel, coal, salt, and cotton. The industrial crisis has hit the mining industry related to steel and coal production the hardest. Nevertheless, all pillars of the economy have felt the impact of the recent economic crisis. In fact, Lorraine is often viewed as the archetype of an industrial region in crisis.

Since the mid-1980s there have been national and regional efforts to restructure and diversify industry in Lorraine. In the past, its industry has been dominated by large national firms and foreign concerns, such as Usinor-Sacilor (steel), Renault, Peugeot, Daewoo (electronics), and Grundig (electronics). Situated slightly more than two hours from Paris by train and relatively close to the Rhine River, its crossroads location makes it favorable to welcoming foreign capital and tourists. Today the region is attempting to promote itself as a "green" region to attract tourists who enjoy the out-of-doors, tourists who might enjoy the Vosges mountains and the thermal stations such as Vittel. Lorraine also has improved its road system and its international links, opening a new airport, Louvigny, to service the region. Efforts to retrain the work force, coupled with a new emphasis on job training in general and education, have contributed to increased university enrollment (figures climbed from 48,000 in 1986–1987 to 62,000 in 1990–91). It is hoped that Nancy and Metz will become centers for the creation of new technologies, thereby strengthening the region's economy. There have also been attempts to transform the cultural image of Lorraine by attracting international-class exhibits, such as "The Warriors of Eternity," a rare Chinese collection of ancient military statues.

The three largest towns in the region are Nancy with 99,351 (greater Nancy 329,447) inhabitants, Metz with 119,594, and Thionville with 39,712. Approximately 15 percent of the work force is centered in Nancy, 9 percent in Metz, and 6 percent in Thionville. The four largest employers are Houillères des Bassins de Lorraine (coal mining), SOLLAC (metallurgy), Uni Etal Rombas, and Sté Mécanique Automobile de l'Est.

Lorraine's agricultural sector, although quite small, is highly modernized. In the west and the center of the region, cereals are the principal crops. Today, retail services (*service marchands*) represent 32.4 percent of the economy, followed by industry (30.2%), nonretail services (*service non-marchand*) (19.3%), commerce (9.4%), construction (5.3%), and agriculture and fishing (3.4%). It is estimated that the economy must create 10,000 jobs per year to absorb those seeking work and new additions to the work force.

CULTURE

This frontier region, often invaded and disputed between France and Germany, has inspired the patriotism of many in France, both inside and outside of Lorraine. **General Charles de Gaulle** used the double cross of Lorraine as his symbol of resistance in wartime France. The region has inspired literature on themes such as wartime suffering and patriotic loyalty. Verdun, the battleground where hundreds of thousands of soldiers perished during World War I, has inspired numerous books—such as the novels of one survivor of Verdun, **Jules Romains** (1885–1972), whose *Prélude à Verdun* and *Verdun* are well known. The region, too, is known for Domrémy, home of **Joan of Arc** (1412–1431), a military leader and national heroine who led a crusade to expel the English from France. The well-known story of Joan of Arc has inspired a large volume of literature, from the French writers **Voltaire** (1694–1778), **Paul Claudel** (1868–1955), and **Jean Anouilh** (1910–1987) to the (Irish-born) British playwright **George Bernard Shaw** (1856–1950).

Lorraine is the home, too, of **Maurice Barrès** (1862–1923), a nationalistic writer and politician who attended school in Nancy. Barrès campaigned against Alfred Dreyfus, a Jewish French army captain unjustly charged with high treason in the 1890s; championed the cause of Charles Maurras and the extreme right-wing group known as *Action Française;* and even supported General Georges Boulanger's attempt in the late 1880s to overthrow the Third Republic.

Unlike Barrès, some native sons have had a strong attachment to the Republic. Three such figures include Jules Ferry, Raymond Poincaré, and Albert Lebrun. **Jules Ferry** (1832–1893) was a politician who played a key role in educational reform that strengthened the public school system; he also promoted the extension of the French Empire. **Raymond Poincaré** (1860–1934) served as prime minister before and after World War I as well as president from 1913 to 1920. Before World War I he was clearly identified with the policy of national preparedness. **Albert Lebrun** (1871–1950) served as the last president of the Third Republic; it was Lebrun who sealed the fate of the Third Republic (1870–1946) when he asked Marshal Philippe Pétain on June 16, 1940, to form a government and seek an armistice with a Germany that had humiliated France with a quick victory at the start of World War II.

Besides being a region of strong patriotism that has inspired writers and politicians, Lorraine possesses Mont Sion, a site 20 miles south of Nancy that has been attributed for over 2,000 years with sacred and magical qualities. Barrès once referred to Mont Sion and other sites in France as "open-air temples."

Because of Lorraine's military importance, from Joan of Arc to World Wars I and II, many tourists visit the region to see the famous military fortifications, the military cemeteries, and the town of Verdun, site of one of the bloodiest battles in human history. In Lorraine one senses the history and patriotism that have inspired many of France's public figures, from writers to politicians to statesmen.

Regarding the region's cuisine, it is said that what it lacks in sophistication it makes up for in heartiness. Residents of Lorraine are fond of bacon, cream, butter, and eggs. This is where quiche was invented; it is still referred to as quiche lorraine. The famous tart can include mushrooms, chives, onions, and many other ingredients. Another regional specialty is *tourte,* a pie enclosing a mixture of minced pork veal marinated with red wine, onions, parsley, and other seasonings. Also popular is a hearty stew called *potée Lorraine* that includes bacon. Other favorites are pike, perch, trout, freshwater crayfish, and frogs. Poultry and game are also popular. Although Lorraine produces more cheese than any other region, its cheeses are not outstanding. Other regional favorites are yellow and sweet *mirabelle* plums and a plum brandy also known as *mirabelle.* Two of France's most widely consumed mineral waters come from Lorraine, namely, Vittel and Contrexéville. Below is a recipe for the region's best-known dish.

QUICHE LORRAINE

pastry shell for 9-inch pie	3 eggs (large or extra large)
6 bacon strips	2 cups cream
1 thinly sliced onion	¼ tsp. nutmeg
1 cup Gruyère cheese, cubed	½ tsp. salt
¼ cup grated Parmesan cheese	¼ tsp. white pepper

Preheat oven to 450°F. Bake pastry shell in pie plate for 5 minutes.

Cook bacon in skillet and remove. Pour out all but 1 tsp. of fat from skillet and cook onion until transparent.

Crumble bacon; then sprinkle bacon, onion, and cheeses into pastry shell. Combine eggs, cream, nutmeg, salt, and pepper; pour into pastry shell. Bake for 15 minutes, then reduce heat to 350°F and bake for approximately 10 minutes. Serves 4–6.

ARCHITECTURE AND NOTEWORTHY SITES

Architecture in Lorraine tends to be uniform, especially in villages. Here the houses are alike except for minor details; they are also roughly the same height. The walls are often built of fieldstone or limestone. At one time the roofs were covered with grooved terra-cotta tiles, but now industrial tiles are the norm. Isolated houses are relatively uncommon in Lorraine.

NANCY (pop. 99,351; greater Nancy 329,447), once the capital of the Dukes of Lorraine, still retains an air of refinement in this industrial region. Today it is an important university town. At the heart of the city is the beautifully proportioned eighteenth-century *Place Stanislaw*. The buildings around the Place are considered the best example of eighteenth-century architecture in France. The turn-of-the-century Art Nouveau movement was centered in Nancy; many notable examples of this art form are found in the *Musée de l'École de Nancy*. There is also a *Musée des Beaux-Arts* that contains—in addition to Italian, French classical, and contemporary paintings—a fine display of glass and crystal. Regional art and folklore dating to Gallo-Roman days is found at the *Musée Historique Lorrain.*

METZ (pop. 119,594) is a junction for many international rail lines. Since Roman times it has been considered a crossroads of Europe. Many of the city's public buildings date to the late nineteenth and early twentieth centuries, when Metz was part of the German Empire. The primary tourist attraction is the enormous *Cathédrale Saint Étienne*. Constructed in the thirteenth century, it is known for its stained-glass windows; one panel was done by the twentieth-century Russian-born artist Marc Chagall (1887–1985). The *Musée d'Art et Histoire* has an important archaeological and medieval collection. Nineteen miles northeast of Metz near the village of Veckring, one can see the largest section of the Maginot Line in the region.

VERDUN (pop. 20,753) is known for the World War I battle that took place here in 1916–1917. Almost 800,000 soldiers perished in this bloody battle, including 400,000 Frenchmen. The British statesman Winston Churchill once called Verdun "the anvil upon which French manhood . . . was hammered to death." In 1920 an unidentified corpse was taken from the battlefield here and placed beneath the *Arc de Triomphe* in Paris to mark the nation's tribute to the "Unknown Soldier." Verdun recently adopted the title of "World Capital of Peace," hoping that the violence that occurred here will never be repeated.

LUNÉVILLE (pop. 20,711) was called "the Versailles of Lorraine" by the eighteenth-century philosopher Voltaire, mainly because of the brilliant evenings at the court of Duke Leopold and Stanislaw Leszczynski. Also, the chateau, built in 1702, was laid out to resemble Versailles.

SELECT BIBLIOGRAPHY

Gehring, J. M., and C. Saint-Dizier. "Géopolitiques de la Lorraine," in Y. Lacoste, ed., *Géopolitiques des régions françaises,* vol. 1. Paris: Fayard, 1986.

Reitel, F. *La Lorraine.* Paris: PUF (Que sais-je?), 1982.

———. "Lorraine," in André Gamblin, ed., *La France dans ses régions,* vol. 1. Paris: SEDES, 1994.

Agde

Bastille Day parade, Aix-en-Provence

St.-Nazaire Cathedral, Béziers

The countryside near the Burgundy-Centre border

Cahors

The *Canal du Midi*

The walled city of Carcassonne

The Mediterranean resort of Cap d'Agde

The cathedral at Capestang

Market day in Cassis

The medieval village of Lagrasse

A market day in town, Montpellier

The *Comédie* (theater) in Montpellier

The *Cathédrale St.-Just*, Narbonne

The village of Nézignan l'Evêque in the South of France

The *Rue St.-Dominique* and the Eiffel Tower, Paris

An artist at work, Paris

Notre Dame, Paris

The glass pyramid entrance to the Louvre, Paris

The Pompidou Center, Paris

An amusing fountain, Paris

A serious game of *pétanque*, Pézenas

The small and beautiful village of St.-Cirq-Lapopie

Sancerre

Sète

Chapter 14

MIDI-PYRÉNÉES

REGIONAL GEOGRAPHY

With its southern boundary being the Spanish border, the Midi-Pyrénées is situated between Languedoc-Roussillon and the Aquitaine, essentially between the Mediterranean Sea and the Atlantic Ocean. It comprises 27,993 square miles, 8.3 percent of the surface area of France, making it the largest region in the nation. The Midi-Pyrénées includes eight departments: Ariège, Aveyron, Haute-Garonne, Gers, Lot, Hautes-Pyrénées, Tarn, and Tarn-et-Garonne. The regional capital is Toulouse.

Given its size and location, the Midi-Pyrénées encompasses a varied geography. The southern border next to the Pyrenees and the northwestern border next to the Massif Central are mountainous, whereas the interior has hills, valleys, and flatlands. Numerous rivers flow through the region: Dordogne, Lot, Aveyron, Tarn, Baise, Gers, Save, Garonne, and Ariège.

Although the hilly and mountainous areas can be cold in winter, the region is generally known for its warm climate during the summer and its relatively mild winters; but it is rainy in some departments, such as Aveyron and the Tarn. A variety of microclimates are due, in part, to the numerous valleys with differing degrees of sunshine and wind conditions. A wind known as the *Autan* sweeps the middle valleys of the Garonne.

HISTORY

As far back as 300,000 to 400,000 years ago, humans inhabited this region. Their traces have been discovered in caves in Haute-Garonne and Ariège, where there are paintings by Paleolithic hunters. Much of the his-

MIDI-PYRÉNÉES

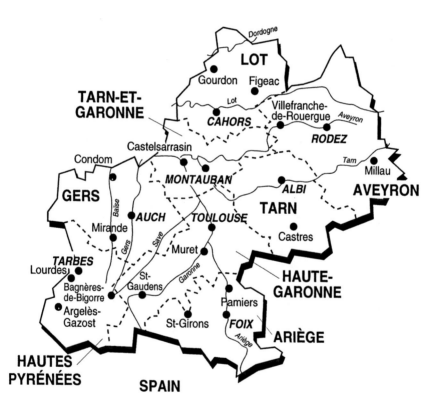

tory of the Midi-Pyrénées revolves around the regional capital and largest urban center, Toulouse. When the Romans occupied this area of France, the city was known as Tolosa. During much of the fifth century and the first part of the sixth century A.D., Toulouse served as the Visigoth capital. The Visigoths had invaded the Roman Empire during the fourth century A.D. and settled in France and Spain, establishing a monarchy that endured until the early part of the eighth century. In 721 the city successfully defended itself against a Muslim attack. By the beginning of the twelfth century, Toulouse controlled much of southern France. During the height of the Albigensian heresy, which was based on a dualistic view of the material world as evil and the spiritual world as good, the Counts of Toulouse supported the Cathars (Albigensians); three centuries later the city supported the Church, due in part to the suppression of the Albigensians. The University of Toulouse was founded in 1229 to promote orthodox thought and to combat the Albigensian heresy. During the sixteenth and seventeenth centuries, Toulouse was an important center for the woad pastel dye trade; this lasted until the Portuguese began importing indigo from India. The powerful Parliament of Toulouse governed Languedoc from the fifteenth century until the Revolution of 1789.

For centuries the region has had a rebellious and a leftist tradition. The rebellious tradition can be traced to the Albigensians. The leftist tradition emerged clearly in the nineteenth and twentieth centuries, during which time the Midi-Pyrénées firmly supported the Republic, public education, and Parliament. The leftist tradition aided the development of Radicalism at the turn of the twentieth century, and subsequently the development of socialism. In the past the region rejected both communism and gaullism. Yet this moderate left tradition is now changing, partially because of urbanization, exodus from rural areas, and economic recession. Politically, the region now conforms more to national norms. This is clearly seen in Toulouse.

RECENT POLITICS

Once referred to as *la ville rose* (the pink city) because of the color of its buildings, as well as the long hold of the socialists on city government, politically the city of Toulouse and the region are changing. Dominique Baudis, from the center-right *Centre des Démocrates Sociaux* (CDS), has been the mayor of Toulouse since 1986 and a deputy in the Parliament in Paris. He possesses solid support in the region. The 1993 parliamentary elections revealed the swing away from the Socialist party (PS). In these elections the left retained only seven seats, as compared to the twenty-two it had previously held. On the other hand, the traditional right-wing parties saw their representation jump from four to nineteen, ensuring complete control over Aveyron as well as two departments that normally support the left: Gers and Tarn-et-Garonne. However, in the 1995 presidential contest the left emerged victorious in the first round. The right-wing extremist Jean-Marie Le Pen of the National Front (FN) captured 10.85 percent of the vote in the first round, well below his 15 percent national average. In the second round the socialist candidate Lionel Jospin won all departments except for Aveyron and Tarn-et-Garonne, which voted for the gaullist candidate Jacques Chirac (the eventual winner in the presidential elections). The June 1995 municipal elections saw Baudis, representing a CDS and UDF (Union for French Democracy) alliance, maintain his mayorship in Toulouse; the socialists held on to Montauban, and the communists retained Tarbes. The gaullist Rally for the Republic (RPR) captured Albi, and the socialists won in Castres.

POPULATION

The population of the Midi-Pyrénées has increased slightly, growing from 2,268,000 in 1975 to 2,475,000 in 1993. Today the region represents 4.3 percent of the national population. The birthrate, 1.55, is below the national average of 1.73. The population density, 54.6 per square kilometer (88.45 per square mile), is considerably below the national average of 105.7 (171.23 per square mile).

Between 1851 and 1954, the area around Toulouse experienced a rural exodus and a fall in the birthrate, a twin phenomenon that led to a 20 percent decline in population outside of the Toulouse metropolitan region. Today, although a rural exodus continues in some parts of the region, Toulouse itself is a dynamic and growing city owing in part to the aerospace and high-tech industries located there. Over the past twelve years Toulouse has grown by roughly 100,000.

Compared to the national average, the region's inhabitants are rather elderly. Those age 60 and older comprise 23.7 percent of the population in the Midi-Pyrénées (19.7% is the national average), whereas 23.4 percent are 19 years old or less (26.8% is the national average). The immigrant population is two percentage points below the national average, with only 4.3 percent of the population of the Midi-Pyrénées made up of immigrants.

The urban population is 60.9 percent, considerably below the national average of 76.4 percent. Life expectancy in the region is 78 years, about one year above the national average. Approximately 26.3 percent of all households are single-person households, below the 27.1 percent average for France.

Although educational levels almost approximate national averages, the composition of the work force differs from the average profile of France. Those possessing high school diplomas represent 11 percent of the population; those with advanced degrees comprise 10.9 percent (10.5% and 11.2%, respectively, are the national averages). Of the work force, 11.2

percent are in agriculture, 24 percent in industry, and 64.8 percent in the service sector. The agricultural work force is almost twice the national average; the industrial work force is approximately 3 percent smaller than the national average. The percentage of the work force in the service sector is only slightly below the national average. The unemployment rate iş 12 percent, slightly less than the national average. Unemployment among women is 11.3 percent.

ECONOMY

The economy of the Midi-Pyrénées is a study in contrasts. On the one hand, there is the dynamic urban economy of Toulouse with aerospace and high-tech industries. On the other hand, vast rural areas comprise the remainder of the region. As noted previously, almost twice the percentage of the region's work force is in agriculture as compared to France overall. Yet the agro-food industry is relatively modest, and agriculture is primarily linked to local production of beef and milk. The region also has a large number of artisans, particularly in the rural departments of Aveyron, Gers, and Lot. Given the advancement of aerospace and high-tech in and around Toulouse, many traditional activities are slowly declining—such as textile production (especially clothing), leather goods, and furniture making. Nevertheless, the Midi-Pyrénées ranks second in France for wool production and first for production of chard and wool cloth. In the Tarn the textile industry is important; yet since 1986 unemployment has run high in this industry.

In many ways, the twentieth century has been kind to Toulouse. During World War I the French government in Paris decided to make Toulouse the center for arms, chemicals, and aircraft manufacturing. The city was chosen in part because it was so far away from Germany, a traditional enemy of France. Following World War II the central government in Paris chose Toulouse to become the national center for the aerospace industry. Since then, the aerospace industry here has produced a number of famous passenger planes, such as the Concorde and the Airbus. Toulouse also makes the highly successful *Ariane* rocket used for both French and European space ventures, such as the launching of satellites. Another factor that has aided the economic development of Toulouse—and the Midi-Pyrénées in general—has been the entry of Spain into the Common Market (1986). This has facilitated trade between the region and Spain.

The service sector, the strongest in the region's work force, has expanded slightly faster than the national average over the past few years. Of course, this sector is linked to the development of Toulouse as a vital center for technology.

Toulouse is also an important university center. With approximately 80,000 students, its university is the third largest in France. The presence of a large university means that the city offers great potential for both public and private research.

The three largest towns in the region are Toulouse with 358,688 (greater Toulouse 650,336) inhabitants, Tarbes with 47,566, and Albi with 46,579. Approximately 33.6 percent of the work force is employed in Toulouse, 3.8 percent in Tarbes, and 3.2 percent in Albi. The four largest employers are the regional hospital, SNI Aérospatiale (aeronautics), the City of Toulouse, and GIAT Industry (arms and munition makers).

In examining the economy of Toulouse and the region, there are two ways of viewing the regional capital. One can see Toulouse as a dynamic and growing city with international standing in aerospace and high-tech industries. Yet one can also see it as an oasis in the middle of a desert, a city surrounded by a region that lacks the brilliance and potential of the regional capital. For example, whereas Toulouse is a key university town in France, one out of three municipalities in the region lacks primary schools. Nevertheless, some towns in the region (e.g., Rodez, Decazeville, and Millau) are relatively thriving population centers. As in other parts of France, the cities and towns are witnessing a rural exodus. One authority of the Midi-Pyrénées has suggested that in the future fully one-half of the region's rural population will be centered around urban areas.

CULTURE

For centuries the area now known as the Midi-Pyrénées has had a reputation for opposing authority. The region's Cathar (Albigensian) heretics, found principally between Toulouse and the Mediterranean, caught the attention of Western Christendom in the thirteenth and fourteenth centuries. Pope Innocent III (reigned 1198–1216) even felt compelled to launch an Albigensian Crusade, which wiped out members of the Cathar sect who had gathered in the town of Albi and also led to the annihilation of others in various towns and villages. In 1244 at Montségur, southeast of Foix, 200 Cathar *parfaits,* or "perfect ones," were burned alive by armies sent from Paris to help crush the heresy. One legend suggested that a Cathar treasure was smuggled out of Montségur before it fell and was buried in the area. Some even suggested that the secret treasure was the Holy Grail. This legend inspired writers and others, especially Germans. The composer Richard Wagner, who was interested in the legend, visited Montségur when he was preparing his opera *Parsifal.* Later, the Nazis tried to incorporate elements of Catharism into their own ideology. In the 1970s the French social historian Emmanuel Le Roy Ladurie published a best-selling book, *Montaillou,* about medieval village life as practiced by the Cathars. In addition, during the mid-sixteenth century thousands of Huguenots (French Protestants) perished in the area in the Wars of Religion.

Other challenges to authority have been more political. The Midi-

Pyrénées is known for its opposition to Parisian authority. At the turn of the century it supported Radicalism, republicanism, and secularism. In the twentieth century it has lent its support to socialism, the moderate left in France, while shunning both communism and gaullism, as previously noted. Until the mid-1980s it was a long-time socialist bastion. Now, however, the politics are shifting to the right.

Given the political culture of the region and its long tradition of opposing authority, it is not surprising that one of France's greatest socialist leaders, Jean Jaurès (1859–1914), was a native of the Midi-Pyrénées. Born in Castres, Jaurès became one of the key founders of the Socialist party in 1905. He was an ardent pacifist on the eve of World War I and was assassinated for his political beliefs and pacifism on the brink of 1914. Many streets throughout France are named after Jaurès.

The region also has had a long tradition as a pioneer in aviation. During the 1920s the writer Antoine de Saint-Exupéry (1900–1944); (author of Le Petit Prince) and others began mail service from Toulouse to Africa and South America. Today, Aérospatiale, a key center for European aeronautical research, is located in Toulouse. Moreover, the rocket that has launched most of the world's satellites, the Ariane, is produced in the Toulouse region, as well as the supersonic Concorde and the jumbo jet Airbus.

Even though the region is known for its rebellious spirit in terms of religion and politics, throughout the centuries Toulouse has been a Catholic stronghold. Consequently the city possesses important architectural and historical monuments. The Basilique St.-Sernin is the largest Romanesque structure in the world. Another treasure, Les Jacobins, is an example of southern Gothic architecture. (Later, during the French Revolution, the radicals—known as Jacobins—who led the upheaval took their name from a Jacobin monastery where they first met.)

The most noted artist from the region is Henri de Toulouse Lautrec (1864–1901), who was born in Albi. Born into a staunchly aristocratic family, he became a painter, draftsman, lithographer, and designer of posters. He is well known for his portrayals of cabarets, dance halls, circuses, theaters, and race tracks at the turn of the century. Deformed from the waist down, he dedicated his life to drawing and painting. In the mid-1880s he moved to Paris and captured life in the French capital during the gay 90s.

The cuisine of the Toulouse region is typical of the Midi-Pyrénées. The traditional dish is cassoulet, made with white beans, sausage, and other ingredients. There are a number of different recipes for this dish. A particular type of sausage, saucisse de Toulouse, is also popular in the region; it is made from coarse-cut saddle of pork. Various forms of goose are popular, such as foie gras (liver), magrets (breast of goose or duck), and confits (meat cooked and preserved in its own fat). In addition, duck and truffles are featured in the Midi-Pyrénées, as well as thrush, partridge, pigeon, and rabbit. An assortment of delicatessens, but especially pork *charcuterie* of all kinds, are popular. Ewe cheese, made from sheep's milk, is considered excellent. Of the numerous regional wines, particularly noteworthy are the reds, rosés, and dry white wines from the Tarn. A well-known dish from the region is *cassoulet;* a recipe appears below.

CASSOULET
(Casserole)

Beans:

1½ lbs. dried white beans

8 oz. fresh pork rind with fat, cut into strips

8 oz. salt pork, diced

1 large onion studded with 6 cloves

4 large cloves of garlic, finely chopped

2 carrots, sliced

bouquet garni composed of 2 bay leaves, 1 stick celery, 3 sprigs thyme, and 3 sprigs parsley, bound together

salt and freshly ground black pepper to taste

Cassoulet:

1½ lbs. boned shoulder of lamb, cut into 2-inch cubes

1½ lbs. pork loin, cut into 2-inch cubes

6 cloves of garlic, finely chopped

2 onions, finely chopped

1 lb. fresh garlic sausage, or kielbasa, halved lengthwise and cut into 3-inch pieces

2 large tomatoes, chopped

8 oz. dried spicy garlic sausage

salt and freshly ground black pepper to taste

3 tbs. bread crumbs

For beans: Rinse, then soak at least 6 hours in cold water (or overnight); drain. Put pork rind in saucepan, cover with water and simmer for 10 minutes, then remove from heat. Put rind under cold water and cool; roll up and tie with a string.

Combine beans with pork rind and rest of ingredients and put in a saucepan. Cover with 2 inches of water and bring to a boil. Skim off any scum that rises. Reduce heat, cover, and cook for 1 hour. Remove from heat; discard onion and bouquet garni. Remove pork rind; untie and cut into large pieces. Strain off liquid from beans and retain.

For cassoulet: In a large saucepan, render a piece of the fat from the pork loin to obtain 3 to 4 tablespoons of melted fat. Brown the lamb cubes in the fat. Remove from pan and set aside. Add pork cubes and half the garlic, and brown. Remove from pan and set aside. Fry onions with remaining garlic until golden. Remove from heat and pour off remaining fat into a bowl.

Brown fresh sausage on outside in small portion of fat. Remove from heat. Preheat oven to 275°F.

Lay pork rind in large earthenware casserole, fat side down. Place ⅓ of beans in a layer over pork rind. Layer half the meat; then half the onions, garlic, and tomatoes; and top off with half the dried sausage. Layer another third of the beans over the meat; then layer the remaining meats, vegetables, and sausage over the beans. The top layer should be the final third of the beans. Pour cooking liquid (from the beans) over the beans. Add salt and pepper to taste. Sprinkle bread crumbs and drizzle 2 tablespoons of fat poured off from the meat over the top. Bake for 1½ to 2 hours. Add a small portion of boiling water or stock if the cassoulet dries out during baking. The cassoulet should have a crust at the end of the baking period. Serves 10.

ARCHITECTURE AND NOTEWORTHY SITES

In many parts of the Midi-Pyrénées the typical southern roof constructed with hollow tiles can be found. Stone construction is not commonly found in Gers or in Toulouse, where brick (rosé in color) is the main building material. The style of architecture changes near the Pyrenees and the high mountain valleys: in these areas houses are grouped in villages or hamlets and the building material is normally sandstone, schist, granite, or stones from riverbeds. Roofs in these areas are steeply sloped and made of granite or stone.

TOULOUSE (pop. 358,688; greater Toulouse 650,336) is France's fourth largest city (after Paris, Lyon, and Marseille). In this high-tech center and university town, the city center is constructed of rosé-red brick and most buildings have tiled roofs. The *Église Notre Dame du Taur* was constructed in a southern Gothic style in the fourteenth century and was named after a local evangelist. The largest Romanesque structure in the world, the *Basilique St. Sernin,* is in Toulouse. The vigilant Cathar hunter St. Dominique led an inquisition from this church. *Les Jacobins* is another southern Gothic structure begun early in the thirteenth century after the founding of the Dominican Order to combat the Cathars. Some relics of St. Thomas Aquinas, an early leader of the Dominicans, are located here. The *Musée des Augustins* has a superb collection of Romanesque and Gothic sculpture and Romanesque capitals. The *Musée St. Raymond* has an excellent collection of archaeological finds dating from prehistory to A.D. 1000. There is also a *Musée de Vieux Toulouse,* which contains exhibits of Toulouse's history and popular culture. The *Musée d'Art Moderne et Contemporain* houses the works of well-known and younger artists.

TARBES (pop. 47,566) is the main agricultural market of the Hautes-Pyrénées, as well as an industrial center. The *Massey Garden* is considered one of the most beautiful parks in southwestern France; there are vestiges of medieval architecture here. Tarbes is the birthplace of the World War I army commander and hero Marshal Ferdinand Foch (1851–1929).

ALBI (pop. 46,579) was named after the Albigensians, who resided here in the twelfth and thirteenth centuries. Many buildings in the center of town are constructed of a reddish clay from the Tarn River. The interior of the huge *Cathédrale St. Cécile,* begun in the late thirteenth century, was decorated by Italian artists in the early sixteenth century. Also located in Albi is the *Musée Toulouse-Lautrec,* with over 500 works on exhibit.

CASTRES (pop. 44,812) straddles the Agout River. Religion, politics, and art attract visitors to this town. In the eleventh century, Castres acquired the revered remains of St. Vincent de Paul and subsequently became a stopping point for pilgrims. There is also a museum dedicated to the socialist politician Jean Jaurès, the town's most famous resident. The *Musée Goya* possesses the second largest collection of Spanish art in France.

LOUDRES (pop. 16,300) is the world's most visited pilgrimage site. In the nineteenth century a young peasant girl saw the Virgin Mary in a series of visions here. The Vatican confirmed that this was a bona fide miracle; the young girl was later canonized as St. Bernadette.

FOIX (pop. 9,964) is the former capital of the Count of Foix; above the town is his medieval chateau. In the summer months, medieval festivals are held in Foix. There is also the *Musée de l'Ariège,* which features geological, paleontological, and prehistory collections. Foix is a popular stopping place for many en route to Andorra and Spain.

MONTSÉGUR, a former fortress, was the last stronghold of the Cathar movement. After a month-long siege, the Cathars were captured here in 1244. The 200 Cathars taken prisoner refused to renounce their beliefs and were burned alive.

SELECT BIBLIOGRAPHY

Collectif Pambenel. "Midi-Pyrénées," in Y. Lacoste, ed., *Géopolitiques des régions françaises,* vol. 2. Paris: Fayard, 1986.

Marconis, Robert. "Midi-Pyrénées," in André Gamblin, ed., *La France dans ses régions,* vol 2. Paris: SEDES, 1994.

Thompson, Richard, et al. *Toulouse-Lautrec.* New Haven: Yale University Press, 1991.

Wolff, Philippe. *Histoire de Toulouse.* Toulouse: Privat, 1970.

Chapter 15

NORD-PAS-DE-CALAIS

REGIONAL GEOGRAPHY

Nord-Pas-de-Calais is the northernmost region in France, located above Picardy and fronting the English Channel. The north/northeastern border of this region is contiguous with Belgium. Nord-Pas-de-Calais comprises 7,663 square miles, 2.3 percent of the territory of France. There are two departments: Nord and Pas-de-Calais. The region is well positioned for the planned full integration of the European Economic Community (EEC, Common Market); Lille, capital of the region, is within approximately 160 miles of six European capitals.

Contrary to popular impression, the region is not flat and without relief. The southern section possesses plateaus that rise from 394 to 656 feet above sea level. The northern and lower section rises from 0 to roughly 164 feet above sea level. It is in Nord-Pas-de-Calais that the Paris Basin meets the North Sea Basin. For a long while the region has been a coal-producing area. This resource, coupled with the region's location and geography, helped to make the area a highly productive industrial zone in France. The geography has contributed to making it a highly productive agricultural zone as well. The narrowest stretch of the English Channel lies between Calais and the white cliffs of Dover in the southeastern part of England. It is not surprising that the recently opened tunnel under the English Channel (a project envisioned by Napoleon and others over the centuries) surfaces just south of Calais, making the journey by train from Paris to London slightly more than three hours in duration. Furthermore, several busy commercial and passenger ports dot the coastline—Calais, Dun-

NORD-PAS-DE-CALAIS

kerque, and Boulogne-sur-Mer (commonly referred to as Boulogne). The location and geography give this region easy access to Belgium.

The climate is similar to that of Picardy—temperate. Winter and spring are often wet. Yet despite the cloudy periods, summer is a pleasant season, with an average maximum temperature around 70°F. The weather is changeable in autumn, but the temperature is mild.

HISTORY

At the beginning of the first century B.C., the regions known today as Nord-Pas-de-Calais and Picardy were inhabited by Celtic tribes living in numerous villages. The Romans called this area Belgium. Christianity began to spread throughout the region in the fourth century A.D. At the same time the Franks and other Germanic groups continued their westward expansion, forming large communities in unpopulated northern areas. The limits of their expansion would later define the linguistic divide between the French-speaking groups and the Flemish, who spoke a language very close to Dutch.

By the seventh century, numerous abbeys had been founded. These served as centers of both learning and trade and attracted local inhabitants. In the eighth century Charlemagne subdivided his kingdom into domains administered by counts. The aftermath of the Norman invasion in the ninth century increased the power of the counts, whereas royal power suffered. These developments prepared the way for early feudalism.

In the tenth century, as security increased, an active urban upper class emerged. Concurrently, towns won liberties and in the large cities a stunning artistic life developed, symbolized to a large degree by the spread of Gothic art. In 1191 King Philippe Auguste united Artois (one of the ancient regions that is now part of Nord-Pas-de-Calais) with France. At the Battle of Bouvines (1214) the same king stopped the southward expansion of the Count of Flanders. French influence spread to Flanders itself with advances in 1304 by Philippe le Bel (Philip the Fair). However, the English gained control of the Calais and Ponthieu areas at the start of the Hundred Years War (1337–1453) under the Treaty of Brétigny. The King of England also gained Boulogne and Picardy in 1420 under the Treaty of Troyes. With the military reconquest led by Joan of Arc (1412–1431), the French crown gave sovereignty over the two northern provinces to the Duchy of Burgundy in 1435 under the Treaty of Arras; this gift of sovereignty was a reward for the Burgundians' loyalty. Under the Burgundians, artistic achievement flourished in certain towns. When the last Grand Duke of Burgundy died in 1477 his only daughter married Maximilian of Austria, giving him all the Burgundian states in her dowry. However, during the sixteenth century the northern provinces of France passed from the Austrian Hapsburgs to the Spanish Hapsburgs. Yet in 1536 François I of France captured Calais from the English.

In the seventeenth and eighteenth centuries Louis XIV pursued an expansionist policy in northern France, firmly establishing the northern frontiers of the nation. Under Louis XIV, France regained Artois, southern Flanders (including Lille), and Hainaut (another ancient region). The Treaty of Utrecht, concluded in 1713 following a French military victory over the English, fixed the northern frontiers of France.

The nineteenth and twentieth centuries saw the industrialization of the region, and the twentieth century witnessed the horrors of world war. The discovery of coal deposits in the late eighteenth century and nineteenth century attracted heavy industry. Today, Nord-Pas-de-Calais is heavily industrialized and is one of the key industrial zones of France. The two world wars of the twentieth century had a significant impact, with numerous casualties and with a number of urban areas destroyed. In recent years this region has struggled under the weight of deep recession and the globalization of the French and European economy—as well as the Europeanization of the French economy as a result of the integration policies of the EEC.

RECENT POLITICS

Regarding the politics of Nord-Pas-de-Calais, two facts should be noted. First, although the socialist government in Paris in the late 1980s and early 1990s hailed the region as the first "Euroregion" as EEC integration marched forward, the inhabitants of Nord-Pas-de-Calais voted against a September 1992 referendum on accelerating European integration. With a high voter turnout of 72.5 percent in the referendum, 55.7 percent rejected the Maastricht Treaty accords calling for additional integration. For a decade the socialists in power had talked about the region as the crossroads of Europe. The "no" vote expressed the extent to which the region had been traumatized by a long economic crisis with European and world dimensions.

Second, Lille, the capital and dynamic center of Nord-Pas-de-Calais, is the fiefdom of the socialist Pierre Mauroy. He has been a close associate of former president François Mitterrand (1981–1995), mayor of Lille since 1973, deputy in the National Assembly since 1973, prime minister under Mitterrand from 1981 to 1984, and first secretary of the Socialist party (PS) beginning in 1988, following Mitterrand's re-election. He represents a social democratic tendency in the PS. Mauroy, born in Cartignies in 1928, has played a major role in the region and on the national scene as well.

The region at one time was a bastion for the left. However, given the economic downturn of the 1980s, the right has emerged as a leading political force. The 1993 legislative elections confirmed trends that were foreshadowed in the 1992 regional elections. The socialists, who had won 35.8 percent of the vote in the 1988 parliamentary elections, garnered 21 percent in the 1992 regional elections and only 18.5 percent in the 1993 parliamentary contest. In the 1993 elections, in the Nord the gaullist Rally for the Republic (RPR) won eleven seats out of the seventeen captured by the right. In contrast, the Socialist party retained only three deputies out of the fourteen that the left had held previously. The PS did slightly better in Pas-de-Calais, retaining five of its twelve seats. The French Communist party (PCF) remained a force in the region, taking four seats from Pas-de-Calais, with especially strong showing in the mining areas. The extremist right-wing National Front (FN) continued to progress in the region, faring better in the Nord than in Pas-de-Calais. In the 1993 elections the FN won 15 percent of the vote in the Nord, as compared to 10 percent in Pas-de-Calais. In Roubaix and Tourcoing the FN did better than the PS in the first round in 1993, winning 22 percent and 27 percent, respectively, in these towns.

The regional council represents an uneasy alliance of Ecologists, socialists, and communists who have attempted to govern the region. This alliance came into being in 1992 when the Ecologists won the presidency of the regional council. Future regional elections may well change this balance.

In the 1995 presidential elections the leftist candidates won the first round, whereas the extreme right-wing candidate Jean-Marie Le Pen of the National Front won 16.7 percent of the vote, above his 15 percent national average. In the second round of the presidential elections the socialist Lionel Jospin triumphed over the gaullist Jacques Chirac, who eventually emerged as the new president of France. The June 1995 municipal elections saw the socialists emerge victorious again in Lille under the banner of mayor Pierre Mauroy; yet the long-time socialist town of Arras, Robespierre's hometown, fell to the center-right Union for French Democracy.

POPULATION

The population of Nord-Pas-de-Calais is both large and dense. Over the past twenty years it has grown slightly; in 1975 it stood at 3,914,000 and in 1993 at 3,986,000, roughly 7 percent of the national total. Moreover, the birthrate, 2.01, is above the national average of 1.73. The population density is a high 321 inhabitants per square kilometer (520.02 per square mile), more than three times the average density for France (105.7 per square kilometer/171.23 per square mile). The population is highly concentrated, with eight towns having a population of more than 100,000 inhabitants.

Although the dynamic metropolitan area of Lille has witnessed an increase in population, especially between 1982 and 1990, towns such as Valenciennes and Avesnes have lost population. With 20,000 people leaving the region each year, Nord-Pas-de-Calais has the highest external migration rate of all regions of France.

Another distinctive characteristic of the region is that its population is the youngest in France. Those 60 years of age and over comprise 17.4 percent of the population (19.7% is the national average); those age 19 and under make up 30.8 percent of the population (above the national average of 26.8%). Immigrants comprise 4.2 percent of the region's inhabitants, below the 6.3 percent national average.

The urban population of Nord-Pas-de-Calais is considerably higher than the average for France, but life expectancy is lower. Approximately 86.2 percent of the region's population is urban (76.4% for France as a whole). Life expectancy is 74.3 years, almost three years less than the average for the nation. Approximately 23.3 percent of all households are single-person households, below the 27.1 percent average for France.

The industrial and agricultural character of the region may explain the relatively low educational levels. Approximately 8.7 percent of the inhabitants possess only a high school degree, and 8.1 percent hold advanced degrees (10.5% and 11.2%, respectively, are the national averages). Of the work force, 2.9 percent are in agriculture—in 1975 the figure was 5.1 percent—a highly mechanized component of the work force focused on the agro-food business. Roughly 31.9 percent of the work force is in industry, above the 26.9 percent national average; 65.2 percent are in the service sector. The unemployment rate is a high 16.3 percent, above the 12 percent national average. Almost 16 percent of women are out of work in Nord-Pas-de-Calais.

ECONOMY

The communications network in the region is exceptional. Not only are there autoroutes connecting Calais, Lille, and other cities with Paris, but the opening of a new high-speed TGV rail line has put Lille at the doorstep of Paris, now one hour away by the new line. Moreover, the new Channel Tunnel that connects France to Britain emerges near Calais. The region's excellent location (given the integration of the EEC) and its communications system reinforce the image of Nord-Pas-de-Calais as an area in the midst of change.

This change is reflected in a number of ways. Over the past twenty years, for example, there has been a transfer of jobs from industry to the service sector—a transfer of roughly 230,000 positions. The region also has witnessed a large number of women entering the work force, with the unemployment rate among women being almost 4 percentage points higher than the national average. Two industries hit hard by unemployment are mining and steel, especially near the cities of Valenciennes, Lens, Sambre-Avesnois, and Béthune. Along the coast the situation has been slightly more favorable, especially around Dunkerque, the third largest port in France, and around Boulogne, the chief fishing port for the nation.

Until the 1970s single-focus industries predominated in the region—such as coal and textiles, including 95 percent of spun linen and 80 percent of combed wool. Today the region possesses a number of integrated industries, many connected to a network of small and medium-sized firms. Tourcoing is the world capital for the wool trade business. Usinor-Sacilor is the largest steel producer in Europe and the second largest worldwide. The region is Europe's leading producer of equipment for thermal power stations. It also produces factory equipment and refines 12 percent of the nation's gasoline. The glassware firm Arques is the world's leading producer of household glassware. Alsthon produces 50 percent of French railway trains. The region also is the second largest producer of electricity in France.

In terms of agriculture, the region ranks second or third for all of France depending on the criteria used. Within the agricultural sector, production is focused on plants and animals. The region is the world's leading producer of chicory and endive. It also produces one-fourth of all French hops and linen. Fishing, too, is an important part of the economy. With its 87.5-mile coastline, 25 percent of French fishing is found here; 75 percent of frozen fish for French consumption comes from Nord-Pas-de-Calais. The agrofood industry here is the third largest in France, making up 8 percent of the nation's total.

The three largest towns are Lille with 172,142 inhabitants (greater Lille 959,234), Valenciennes with 38,441 (greater Valenciennes 338,392), and Lens with 35,017 (greater Lens 323,174). A large percentage of the work force is centered in Lille, where 31.3 percent of all jobs are located. Valenciennes comprises 7.3 percent of the work force, and Lens 6.2 percent. The four largest employers are Verrerie Cristallerie d'Arques (glassware), CHR Hôpital Swynghedauw de Lille, Renault, and SOLLAC (steel).

Although its location within the EEC and its superior communications network give Nord-Pas-de-Calais advantages over many other regions, there is concern that the new transportation links may erode regional identity. For instance, when the new high-speed TGV rail line recently opened, observers in both cities wondered if Lille would simply become a suburb of Paris. In the past and in the present, the region has been a highly productive area. The economic crisis that first surfaced in the 1970s and the 1980s has changed the composition of the work force, but so has the integration of the EEC. Today Nord-Pas-de-Calais is a region undergoing change, trying to maintain its identity and hoping to capitalize on its location in the heart of the European Community.

CULTURE

The region is known for its ties with the medieval principality of Flanders, its industrial zone, and its wartime battlefields. Before the emergence of nation-states, part of this region nearest the Belgian border—along with much of Belgium and part of Holland—constituted an area known as Flanders. Near the border with Belgium the traditional Flemish language is still spoken in some towns and villages. This part of Pas-de-Calais is fond of beer, as is much of northern Europe. This section, too, holds carnivals or annual fairs called *braderies* in which huge wicker statues called *géants* (giants) make an appearance and join in the festivities. These giants, some nearly 30 feet in height, are normally based on personalities from legends or from local history. They can be seen at pre-Lent festivals, Easter, and summer festivals. This tradition is celebrated only in the north of France, a tradition that dates to the sixteenth century. The modern-day spirit of Flanders is captured in the poems and songs of the late popular performing artist **Jacques Brel** (1929–1978), who was born in nearby Brussels. The local writer **Germaine Acramant** (b. 1889), a native of the region, provides a positive view of life in Flanders in her books *Ces dames aux chapeaux verts* and *Le Carnaval d'été*.

Flanders claims the writer **Marguerite Yourcenar** (1903–1988) as one of its own. Yourcenar was born in Brussels; her mother was Belgian, and her father was French Flemish. As a young girl she spent part of her youth in a townhouse in Lille. Many of her summers were spent at the family's chateau in the region, where she learned to love nature and animals. She discussed the region to some extent in one book of memoirs entitled *Souvenirs pieux*. Her work *Archives du nord* traces, in part, her family history in Flanders since the Middle Ages. In later life Yourcenar moved to the United States, where she lived on the coast of Maine. Much of her writing is imbued with a love of nature and animals, something that she learned in Nord-Pas-de-Calais. In 1980 she was the first woman to be elected to the *Académie Française,* a learned society founded in the seventeenth century to safeguard the purity of the French language.

The industrial character of the region and its hard-working people have attracted writers from outside the region seeking to capture for their readers the harsh realities of industrialization. The two best-known writers who attempted to portray the misery and poverty of the industrial working class were **Victor Hugo** (1802–1885) and **Emile Zola** (1840–1902). In *Lettres à Adèle,* Hugo recounts the appalling misery and overcrowding of the slum cellars of Lille in the 1850s. Of course, the most famous portrayal of the harshness of industrial life in this region is Zola's *Germinal,* which is set among struggling mining families in this region.

Other native writers have also attempted to capture the essence of the area. For example, **Abbé Prévost** (1697–1763) wrote a book entitled

Manon Lescaut. The critic **Charles-Augustin Sainte-Beuve** (1804–1869) also published material on this northern region. Better known is the Catholic writer **Georges Bernanos** (1888–1948). Although he was born in Paris, he spent part of his youth in the village of Fressin. The heroes in his best-known works are priests, most likely drawn from the country priests in the region.

The horrors of war are well known in Nord-Pas-de-Calais and have inspired the work of many writers. **Henri Barbusse's** (1873–1935) *Le Feu* (1916, Under Fire) is a powerful novel about the conflict of 1914–1918. Barbusse himself fought in World War I and was wounded. *Le Feu* is based on his own trench experiences during this horrible encounter. Barbusse was a man of the left who became active in the French Communist party (PCF).

A number of battlefields, monuments, and war cemeteries in the region serve as a constant reminder of the horrors of war. One of the most famous battles that occurred in the region took place at Vimy Ridge on April 9, 1917. On this date, soldiers of the Canadian Corps launched an assault on a fortified German position at Vimy Ridge, 6 miles north of Arras. After heavy fighting and heavy losses, German resistance broke. Following the war the French government gave the site to Canada in 1922; it was subsequently made into a memorial to honor the 60,000 Canadians who died in World War I. In 1936 the Canadian government built the *Mémorial Canadien,* a twin tower memorial where the names of 11,000 Canadians whose bodies were never recovered are inscribed. Near Arras there are a number of military cemeteries.

Nord-Pas-de-Calais often appears in the works of a number of British travel writers, owing in part to the fact that it is the first stopping point in France after crossing the English Channel. **Tobias Smollett's** (1721–1771) *Travels through France and Italy* describes the author's culture shock when he landed in Boulogne. Others, such as **Arthur Young** (1741–1820), wrote glowingly of the neat houses with gardens on the sand dunes near Dunkerque. Young traveled in France just before the early phase of the Revolution of 1789.

The cuisine of Nord-Pas-de-Calais is often dominated by seafood, and sometimes beer is the preferred beverage instead of wine. A standard favorite in the north of France, but served in various localities (especially near the sea), are steamed mussels and *pommes frites* (French fries). The mussels can be prepared with a number of different sauces. A variety of fresh fish is served, including salted and pickled. Shrimp, oysters, and eel are also plentiful. A freshwater fish or chicken stew called *waterzoï* is popular. *Andouillettes* (chitterling sausages) is another favorite. *Carbonnade flammande* (beef and onions cooked in beer) is a typical regional dish in Flanders. Galettes (a form of *crêpes*), too, are served here. Endive used in salads and chicory blended with coffee are characteristic of the northern cuisine. Below is a recipe for a favorite lunch or dinner dish.

MOULES MARINIÈRES
(Steamed Mussels)

4 dozen mussels	1 bay leaf
6 tbs. butter	1¼ cup dry white wine
1 clove of garlic, chopped	4 tsp. flour
½ cup finely chopped onion or shallot	½ cup cream
	2 egg yolks
2 leeks, chopped	salt and freshly ground black
½ cup finely chopped parsley	pepper to taste

Clean and de-beard the mussels.

In a large, deep kettle, heat 3 tablespoons of butter and add garlic and onions or shallots; cook over low heat for 1 minute. Next, add leeks, most of parsley, and bay leaf; cook for an additional 2 minutes.

Add mussels, salt and pepper, and wine. Cover and simmer gently for 10 minutes or until mussels open.

Remove the mussels. Strain the liquid and bring to a boil. Cream the remaining butter with the flour, and add to kettle to thicken the mixture. Remove kettle from heat and add cream mixed with egg yolks. Heat the sauce, not letting it boil, and pour over the mussels. Sprinkle with more parsley and serve immediately. Serves 4 to 6.

ARCHITECTURE AND NOTEWORTHY SITES

In the north of France, protection from the wind is a prime architectural consideration. Usually rectangular, many houses are only one storey high. Some houses are built on hillsides and are protected by a windbreak of trees, or grouped around a small courtyard. Common roofing materials are wood, tile, and slate shingles. Brick is a common building material; yet cob and wood facings can be found in some buildings. Stone is often used in the Avesnois area. In the ancient area known as Flanders, brick of various colors—such as red and yellow—is used to make geometrical patterns.

LILLE (pop. 172,142; greater Lille 959,234), situated between two arms of the Deûle River, was referred to as L'Île (The Island) until the eighteenth century. The city is located 70 miles from Brussels. During the Middle Ages it was a center of wool and cloth production. After Louis XIV captured the city in 1667, it became the capital of French Flanders. In the nineteenth century it became a symbol of the misery of the working class during the Industrial Revolution, especially in the work of the writer Emile Zola. Today

Lille has been refurbished, especially the central core, and is an interesting city to visit. Charles de Gaulle (1890–1970), Resistance leader and founder of the Fifth Republic and its first president, was born in Lille. The *Musée Charles de Gaulle* occupies the house where this important French leader and statesman was born. The *Musée des Beaux-Arts* is a superior arts museum, displaying works from the fifteenth to the twentieth centuries. The museum includes paintings by Peter Rubens (1577–1640), Jacques-Louis David (1748–1825), Eugène Delacroix (1798–1863), Vincent Van Gogh (1853–1890), Claude Monet (1840–1926), Pablo Picasso (1881–1973), and others. There is also a collection of archaeology, medieval sculpture, coins, and ceramics. The *Musée d'Art Moderne du Nord* is a highly respected museum just outside of Lille in the city of Villeneuve-d'Ascq. It exhibits numerous pieces, especially from 1900 to 1940, with such artists represented as Fernand Léger (1881–1955), Amedeo Modigliani (1884–1920), and Pablo Picasso (1881–1973). The ancient *Bourse* is the ornate and old stock exchange built in 1652 that reflects Flemish Renaissance style. Just north of the stock exchange is the pleasant quarter known as the Old Town (*Vieille Ville*) of Lille. The *Citadelle* is a star-shaped fortress built by Sébastien le Prestre de Vauban (1633–1707), a towering seventeenth-century military engineer. The Citadelle still functions as a military base. The Germans executed many people here during World Wars I and II.

CALAIS (pop. 75,309), just 21 miles from Dover, England, is the main travel port between France and Great Britain. Because it is a gateway to Europe, roughly 10 million people pass through Calais each year. The new Channel Tunnel surfaces 7.5 miles southwest of Calais. The main cultural attraction is the sculptor Auguste Rodin's (1840–1917) *The Burghers of Calais*. Rodin's work shows six citizens of Calais who in 1343, after eight months of resisting English forces, surrendered the keys of the city to Edward III to save the city's population from being massacred. The English king spared the population and the six leaders. This famous sculpture stands before the City Hall; there are also castings in Paris, London, and Washington, D.C. The *Musée des Beaux-Arts et de la Dentelle* displays nineteenth- and twentieth-century art, local history, and lace samples. The *Musée de la Guerre* focuses on local events during World War II.

BOULOGNE-SUR-MER (pop. 43,678), a pleasant town, is the most important fishing port in France. The town is situated on three parts or levels: the walled hilltop upper town (completely rebuilt after World War II), the lower town, and the port itself. The *Château-Musée* is a thirteenth-century castle with an eclectic collection. The *Basilique Notre Dame* was built in the nineteenth century; its construction and architecture were influenced by St. Paul's in London and St. Peter's in Rome. *Nausicaa* is the largest marine aquarium in France, an ultra-modern complex that opened in 1990.

ARRAS (pop. 38,983) is considered one of the most beautiful towns of the region. In the Middle Ages it was an important center for weaving and the cloth trade. The city center is known for its seventeenth- and eighteenth-century Flemish-style buildings. The Revolutionary leader who led France into the Reign of Terror, Maximilien Robespierre (1758–1794), was born in Arras. The *Musée des Beaux-Arts* shows Gallo-Roman artifacts, medieval sculpture, fifteenth-century Arras tapestries, and French and Flemish paintings from the sixteenth to nineteenth centuries.

CASSEL (pop. 2,177) is a picturesque hill town with narrow streets and flights of stairs. In 1914–1915 General Ferdinand Foch, the French forces commander, made his headquarters here. The massive *Église Notre-Dame* is a building of Flemish-style architecture. The local museum possesses a collection of early Flemish paintings, Italian Renaissance works, seventeenth-century Flemish and Dutch canvases, and other seventeenth- through nineteenth-century works. Mont Cassel rises to 574 feet, offering a sweeping view of the flat plain of Flanders. An equestrian statue of Foch sits at the top of Mont Cassel.

ST.-OMER (pop. 14,434), situated on the edge of Flanders and Artois, is a quiet country town. It developed around a Benedictine monastery founded by Omer, who helped to drain, canalize, and cultivate the marshes of the area. The *Basilique Notre Dame* dates from the thirteenth century and has an imposing tower. The *Musée des Beaux-Arts* exhibits eighteenth-century woodworks and furnishings, medieval art, Dutch and regional ceramics, and seventeenth-century Flemish and Dutch paintings.

SELECT BIBLIOGRAPHY

Gamblin, André. "Nord-Pas-de-Calais," in André Gamblin, ed., *La France dans ses régions,* vol 1. Paris: SEDES, 1994.

Giblin-Delvallet, B. *La Région, territoires politiques. Le cas du Nord-Pas-de-Calais.* Paris: Fayard, 1990.

Grand atlas de la France: Région Nord-Pas-de-Calais. Paris: Éditions Alpha S.A., 1987.

Hilaire, Y.-M., ed. *Histoire du Nord-Pas-de-Calais de 1900 à nos jours.* Toulouse: Privat, 1982.

Paris, D., ed. *Nord-Pas-de-Calais: une région d'Europe en mouvement.* Paris: La Documentation Française, 1989.

Chapter 16

LOWER NORMANDY
(Basse-Normandie)

REGIONAL GEOGRAPHY

Lower Normandy extends from the western edge of the Paris Basin to the Breton peninsula. Its long, 294-mile coastline stretches from the beautiful port town of Honfleur in the northern part of the region to the historic site of Mont St.-Michel in the western corner of the region. Its southern boundary is adjacent to the Pays de la Loire region. Lower Normandy comprises 10,857 square miles, 3.2 percent of the surface area of France. There are three departments: Calvados, Manche, and Orne. The capital is Caen.

The region's geography is dominated by the colors blue and green—the blue waters of the English Channel and the verdant green farmlands and fields of the interior. The geography of both Lower and Upper Normandy may remind many people of southern England because of the lush pastoral countryside. Lower Normanady is known as the land of the *bocage,* farmland subdivided by hedges and trees. There are two bands of hills, rising to roughly 1,000 feet, stretching from the east to the west. The Cotentin peninsula, where Cherbourg is located, rises to roughly 588 feet and divides the Bay of the Seine from the Gulf of Saint-Malo, which is known for its extraordinary tides. Several miles off the Cotentin peninsula are the Channel Islands. Because Norman beaches are relatively close to Paris, much of the coastline is dotted with seaside resorts.

The climate of Lower Normandy is moist and temperate. Frequent rains promote lush vegetation. In some parts of the region—namely, in localized parts of the Cotentin peninsula and to the south near the Vire Basin—annual rainfall is more than 36 inches. Along the coast, summer and winter

LOWER NORMANDY
(BASSE-NORMANDIE)

ENGLISH CHANNEL

Cherbourg

MANCHE

D-Day Beaches

Honfleur

Cabourg

Deauville

ST-LÔ

Bayeux

CAEN

Lisieux

Coutances

Vire

CALVADOS

Granville

Orne

Vire

Avranches

Argentan

Risle

Mont St.-
Michel

ORNE

Mayenne

ALENÇON

Sarthe

Mortagne-
au-Perche

climates differ only slightly. Although winter is seldom cold, the swimming season is normally June–September.

HISTORY

This section describes the history of both Lower and Upper Normandy.

The region takes its name from the Norsemen, the Vikings, who invaded the area during the ninth century. However, the history of the region predates the Vikings. Inhabitants were found in Normandy in the pre-Stone Age. During the Bronze Age the region established trade relations with the British Isles. Celtic Gauls entered the region in the Iron Age; in 56 B.C. the Unelli tribe was defeated by Caesar's armies. At the beginning of the Christian era a "Pax Romana," or Roman peace, fostered the emergence of relatively prosperous Gallo-Roman cities. The Romans created a separate northwestern province in the third century A.D. that included present-day Normandy. Rouen, in Upper Normandy, was the capital of this Roman province.

Beginning in 820 Vikings from Denmark and Norway began raiding the region, eventually establishing settlements and adopting Christianity. In 911 the Viking chief Rollo and the Frankish king Charles the Simple agreed that the area around Rouen would be the Viking center. (Many place names in the region reflect the Viking past. For instance, one can find the words *bec* [stream], *beuf* [home], *cirque* [church], *fleur* [bay], *mare* [lake or pond], etc.)

In 1066 William, Duke of Normandy, asserted his claim to the English throne, crossing the English Channel with 6,000 troops and crushing the English in the Battle of Hastings. William the Conqueror, as the Norman duke was called, brought with him French culture and language. This is one reason why many English words are of French origin, especially in relation to law, education, and the church. The conquest eventually led to the establishment of the Plantagenet dynasty in France.

During the Hundred Years War (1337–1453) Normandy passed back and forth between French and English rule. Only in 1449, with the resurgence of French power under Joan of Arc, was Charles VII able to consolidate his hold on Normandy. At the end of this war Normandy saw increased urbanization, coupled with the rise of the middle class. Port towns began to prosper, and Normans took a new interest in overseas exploration.

With the start of the Protestant Reformation in the sixteenth century, Normandy became a Protestant stronghold. When Louis XIV revoked the Edict of Nantes (which had allowed some measure of religious tolerance) in 1685, many Protestants went into exile.

In the eighteenth century agriculture increased in order to feed the growing population of Paris. Normandy quickly became one of the "breadbaskets" of France. The region also became known for its cotton and lace. During the French Revolution, Normandy remained rather aloof, providing little support for either the revolutionaries or the royalists.

In the nineteenth century, rail lines and oceanic shipping breathed new life into the region. In 1843 the Paris-Rouen railway opened, followed in 1858 by the Paris-Cherbourg line. These new rail lines spurred the development of coastal restort towns such as Dieppe, Deauville, Étretat, and Le Tréport. Many writers and artists were attracted to these towns.

In the twentieth century, the two world wars took their toll on the region. In World War I it paid a heavy price in terms of loss of life, but the region and its towns were little marked by physical destruction. However, World War II caused serious physical damage. The German Occupation saw the bombardment of many towns, some partially or totally destroyed, such as Caen, Rouen, Le Havre, Saint-Lô, Lisieux, Falaine, Argentan, and Évreux. On June 6, 1944—D-Day—tens of thousands of Allied troops landed on Normandy beaches near Bayeux. The engagement that followed, the Battle of Normandy, involved massive casualties. However, the battle led to the final defeat of Hitler's war machine and the liberation of France and Europe. The extensive physical destruction in the region necessitated postwar reconstruction that entailed industrial modernization and the introduction of new technologies in electronics and the petrochemical industries, together with the development of nuclear power stations.

RECENT POLITICS

Normandy in general is conservative. The typical Norman is conservative not so much because of ideological convictions but because of a profound respect for the established order. Elected officials in Normandy are usually well-known but not often highly visible leaders. The parliamentary elections of 1993 echoed the results, generally speaking, of the 1992 regional elections. The 1993 elections saw only one socialist voted into power; in this election the socialists lost one seat in each of the three departments. The Socialist party (PS) won approximately 18 percent of the vote in 1993, whereas the French Communist party (PCF) garnered a mere 5 percent. On the right, the gaullist Rally for the Republic (RPR) won five seats and the Union for French Democracy (UDF) captured six. Together these two parties won 45 percent of the vote in the final round of the 1993 elections. The extreme right, the National Front (FN), polled roughly 10 percent of the vote. In the final round of the election the Ecologists received roughly 12 percent of the vote. During the 1995 presidential contest, right-wing candidates triumphed in the first round. The National Front's Jean-Marie Le Pen captured 12.77 percent of the vote, below his 15 percent national average. In the second round of the contest the gaullist Jacques Chirac won all departments in the region as he opposed the socialist candidate Lionel

Jospin. Chirac succeeded the socialist François Mitterrand as the president of France. In the 1995 municipal elections, the center-right Union for French Democracy retained control of the city hall in the regional capital of Caen.

POPULATION

Since 1975 the population of Lower Normandy has grown, but only slightly. In 1975 it stood at 1,306,000; in 1993 it was 1,402,000, approximately 2.5 percent of France's total population. The birthrate, 1.83, is slightly higher than the national average (1.73). The population density is 79.7 inhabitants per square kilometer (129.11 per square mile), well below the national average of 105.7 per square kilometer (171.23 per square mile).

The region's population is relatively young. In 1991 those 19 years of age or younger made up 27.9 percent of the total population, higher than the 26.8 percent national average. Several decades earlier, those under age 19 comprised an even larger percentage—33.9 percent in 1975. (It has been difficult to keep the young in the region as the nation has experienced economic recession.) Those age 60 and older comprise 20.5 percent of the region's population, about the national average. There are relatively few immigrants in Lower Normandy; only 1.6 percent of the inhabitants are immigrants. This is far below the 6.3 percent average for all of France.

The urban population of Lower Normandy is 53.2 percent, considerably below the national average of 76.4 percent. Life expectancy is 76.5 years, whereas the average for France is 77.2 years. Roughly 25.8 percent of all households are single-person households, below the 27.1 percent national average.

Educational levels reveal the agricultural tradition of the region, as does the composition of the work force. Only 8.5 percent of the inhabitants possess a high school diploma (10.5% for all of France), and only 7.9 percent possess an advanced degree (11.2% for the entire nation). Of the work force, 10.2 percent are in agriculture (almost double the 5.3% national average), 26.3 percent in industry, and 63.5 percent in the service sector. Although the percentage of those in agriculture is higher than the national average, the percentages of those in industry and the service sector correspond roughly to the national averages. Unemployment in Lower Normandy is 11.7 percent, less than the 12 percent plus national average. Unemployment among women is 11 percent in Lower Normandy.

ECONOMY

The region is characterized not just by its green landscape but by a strong agricultural sector. In certain areas, up to 30 percent of the employment is in agriculture. In general, there are four principal industries that employ workers: meat and milk, electronics, automobile manufacture, and metallurgy.

In recent years industries revolving around research and development have emerged in Lower Normandy, a development that may strengthen the regional economy. For example, there is a nuclear industry in Cherbourg, a plastics industry in Alençon, a computer industry, *télématique,* and a nuclear physics industry in the university town of Caen.

The three largest towns are Caen with 112,846 inhabitants (greater Caen 191,490), Cherbourg with 27,121 (greater Cherbourg 92,045), and Alençon with 29,988. Roughly 18.5 percent of the work force is centered in Caen, 7.1 percent in Cherbourg, and 4.1 percent in Alençon. The four largest employers are the regional hospital, Direction de la Construction d'Armes Navales, Renault Véhicules Industriels, and the municipal government of Caen.

In terms of long-term economic development, Lower Normandy has four key strengths. First, its long coastline offers a great potential for tourism. Moreover, although fishing is already an important industry, there are possibilities for developing the shellfish industry and a coastal truck-farming industry as well. Second, the region's geographical position is a great advantage: on one side is the densely populated Paris Basin, and on the other side is Brittany, a favorite vacation area for many in France. Furthermore, the link with Great Britain is important for the region; there is regular ferry service from Cherbourg and near Caen to the south of England. The recent opening of the long-awaited tunnel that connects London and Paris makes the region even more accessible. Third, the quality of the environment, which has not been damaged by new industries, makes the region attractive to many. Fourth, even though Lower Normandy has attracted a number of retirees, its youthful population could be an advantage. Of course, the pull of nearby Paris has attracted many young people, and job opportunities in Lower Normandy have not been able to keep them from the attractions of the capital. Nevertheless, these four factors give the region trump cards to play in the future.

CULTURE

The sea has played a major role in the life of both Lower and Upper Normandy over the centuries. Because of its accessibility, Normandy has been invaded many times in the past, from the Vikings to the English to the Germans to the Allies who helped end World War II in Europe. It has also been "invaded" by tourists attracted to its seaside resorts, beaches, and cliffs.

A number of fashionable seaside resorts, such as Cabourg and Deauville, attracted writers as well. **Marcel Proust** (1871–1922) visited Cabourg many times between 1881 and 1914; he stayed at the Grand Hotel, observed the social life, and collected material for his books.

Western Normandy has produced a regional writer of some note. **Jules-Amédée Barbey d'Aurévilly** (1808–1889), a royalist and lover of the macabre, was born on the Cotentin peninsula south of Cherbourg. His best works, such as *L'Ensorcelée* (Bewitched), deal with local traditions and the people in western Normandy. He is considered a true regional writer.

Painters, too, have found inspiration in Normandy—especially forerunners of the Impressionists such as **Eugène-Louis Boudin** (1824–1898), the Impressionists themselves, and those that followed. (See Chapter 17, "Upper Normandy," for additional details.)

The same coast inspired other painters as well, such as **Camille Corot** (1796–1875), **Camille Pissarro** (1830–1903), and **Johann Barthold Jongkind** (1819–1891). **Jean-François Millet** (1814–1875), who was born near Cherbourg, made a reputation painting men and women toiling in the fields, often offering a powerful social commentary on his own industrial era.

Normandy is also known for its horses and race tracks. Horse breeding in the region dates back as far as the fourteenth century; today it is particularly widespread in Orne and Calvados. There is horse racing at Caen, Lisieux, Rouen, Argentan, Saint-Lô, Graignes, and elsewhere. The highlight of the racing season is the Grand Prix at Deauville.

The cuisine of both Lower and Upper Normandy is based on the region's ample agricultural resources and its access to the sea. To a large degree, cooking revolves around the use of Norman butter and *crème fraiche* (clotted butter). The region produces a large number of cheeses—thirty-two to be exact—including Pont l'Eveque, Camembert, and Livarot (the skin of this cheese is washed in Calvados, an apple brandy). Local beef and lamb are also available. A large variety of fish, especially sole, are found in coastal waters; near Honfleur, small gray shrimp are found. Norman-style cooking often features the use of cream, or cream blended with Calvados or cider. Regional specialties are *andouilles de Vire* (chitterlings sausage), *tripe à la mode de Caen* (tripe braised in cider), *poulet Vallée d'Auge* (chicken cooked with mushrooms, cream, and either cider or Calvados), Mont St.-Michel's *omelette de la Mère Poulard* (soufflé omelette), and *canard à la Rouennaire* (duck cooked in its own juices). Typical desserts are *pommes Bourdalouse* (poached apples baked with an almond cream and crumbled macaroons), and *douillon Normande* (baked apples or pears wrapped in a sweet pastry crust). Normandy has no vineyards, yet the region produces cider and Calvados. The region grows the best and widest variety of apples in France; below is a recipe for this delicious fruit that can be served as a simple dessert.

SAUTÉ DE POMMES
(Sauteed Apples)

4 green apples   2 tbs. sugar
4 tbs. butter

Peel, core, and quarter the apples. Place the cut apples into a
nonstick skillet over medium heat with the butter and sugar.
Cook for approximately 10 minutes; stir occasionally until
juices begin to caramelize and apples are tender. Serve immediately, or keep warm and serve later. Serves 4.

ARCHITECTURE AND NOTEWORTHY SITES

In the eleventh and twelfth centuries A.D., Norman Romanesque architecture emerged in both Normandy and England. During this period, especially from the start of the twelfth century through 1346, Normandy saw
the emergence of Gothic architecture; it is from this period that much of
Mont St.-Michel and the cathedral at Rouen (in Upper Normandy) dates.
    Today in the Norman countryside, one sees many apple orchards as well
as half-timbered houses. In the western section of Lower Normandy, houses
are one or two stories with gabled walls to the side. Door and window
openings are more symmetrical than in other parts of Lower and Upper
Normandy. Pink granite is used for walls north of Cotentin; further south,
grey granite is used. Schist is found around Thury-Harcourt. In Caen, plain
houses are normally clustered together and Caen limestone is used for construction. In the Caux area (a limestone plateau around Le Havre, Rouen,
and Dieppe), houses have a foundation of black flint, an oak framework,
colombes (small planks) placed diagonally or vertically in the framework,
and asymmetrical window and door openings.
    CAEN (pop. 112,846; greater Caen 191,490) was rebuilt after approxi-
mately two-thirds of the city was destroyed in World War II. Today Caen
is a thriving industrial and university town. The Orne canal provides the
city with access to the English Channel. Caen is both a ferry and a rail
hub. The city was the seat of William the Conqueror's duchy from 1035
to 1087. The ruins of the king's beautiful castle, known as the *Château de
Caen,* are still visible. The grounds of the chateau contain a medieval garden of aromatic herbs as well as the *Musée de Normandie,* which displays
artifacts of the history of Normandy. There are two Romanesque abbeys—
Abbaye aux Hommes and *Abbaye aux Dames*—built by William the Conqueror after the Church "forgave" him for marrying a distant cousin. There
is also a *Musée des Beaux-Arts.* The city's best-known museum is the *Mémorial—un musée pour la paix,* which is dedicated to memorializing World
War II and promoting world peace.

ALENÇON (pop. 29,988) is a commercial center and lace-making town that is known today for the manufacture of household appliances. Formerly a duchy, it retains an aristocratic air to some degree. Alençon was the birthplace of Thérèse Martin (1873–1897), who was canonized in 1927 at St. Thérèse. Besides the lace-making school, *École Dentellière,* there is a flamboyant Gothic church, a *Musée des Beaux-Arts et de la Dentelle,* and a fourteenth- through fifteenth-century ducal castle.

BAYEUX (pop. 14,704) is situated to the west of Caen and 6 miles from the coast. It possesses the famous *Bayeux Tapestry,* which depicts in fifty-eight panels the conquest of England by William the Conqueror in 1066. Bayeux is also famous for another Channel invasion—the D-Day landings of June 6, 1944, that eventually led to the liberation of Nazi-occupied France. Bayeux was the first town liberated by Allied forces. The *Bayeux War Cemetery* is located here; it is the largest Commonwealth military cemetery in Normandy, containing 4,648 gravesites of soldiers from the United Kingdom and other nations. There is also a municipal war museum that contains material relating to D-Day and the Battle of Normandy. The cathedral in Bayeux dates from the thirteenth century and is an excellent example of Norman Gothic architecture. There is also a lace conservatory, *Conservatoire de la Dentelle,* where visitors can watch lacemakers create intricate lace designs. It is the only place in France where the practice of this ancient art can be seen.

HONFLEUR (pop. 8,272) is a beautiful port town on the Norman coast; it is a popular tourist attraction, especially because it is located only 120 miles from Paris. During the Hundred Years War it served as an important military port. Several significant voyages of discovery began here in the sixteenth and seventeenth centuries; the most important was that of Samuel de Champlain, who set sail in 1608 and proceeded to found Quebec City. In the nineteenth century numerous painters were drawn to Honfleur, notably Eugène Boudin and Ferme St. Siméon. Today tourists flock to Honfleur to visit the *Musée Eugène Boudin,* which displays the work of Boudin and his contemporaries. There is also a *Musée d'Art Populaire.* During Pentecost there is a *Fêtes des Maison* where the town's boats are blessed and where mariners have been giving thanks for centuries.

DEAUVILLE (pop. 4,261) is a fashionable coastal town just 10 miles south of Honfleur. Like neighboring Trouville, it attracts an international crowd to its wide beaches, long boardwalk along the sea, famed casinos, and popular horse-racing track. Its proximity to Paris makes Deauville a popular get-away for Parisians. An American film festival is held here annually.

MONT ST.-MICHEL, lying just off the coast and seen from miles around, is a stunning tourist site that seems to rise from the sea. It is one of the most popular tourist sites in all of France. Resembling a fortified island connected to the mainland only by a causeway and surrounded by ever-changing tides, it is a dazzling structure that is difficult to forget once it has been viewed. The history of this world-famous site dates to the seventh century A.D., when a monastery was first constructed here. This was followed in the eighth century by construction of a place of worship. In 966 the Benedictine monks, inspired by the beauty of the spot, began the construction of a larger church. During the Hundred Years War, French kings utilized Mont St.-Michel as a fortress. During the French Revolution of 1789, the island became a state prison. It became a national monument in 1874. After passing the thick walls at the entrance of the site and then climbing the only street on this tiny island, *La Grande Rue,* one sees (in addition to souvenir vendors) a succession of buildings in Romanesque and Gothic architecture. Eventually one reaches the magnificent abbey at the highest point on the island. In the late 1960s, priests and nuns returned to Mont St.-Michel.

D-DAY BEACHES will forever be a part of Normandy's history and the history of Europe. On June 6, 1944, a huge flotilla of ships and boats dropped more than 100,000 Allied troops on the beaches of Normandy; more than 20,000 Allied troops were parachuted onto Norman soil. This massive war effort represented an attempt by the Allies to liberate France and Europe from the Nazis and end World War II. Operation Overlord, the code name for this war effort, was the largest single military operation in history. The Allied troops landed along 50 miles of beaches given the code names Utah, Omaha, Gold, Juno, and Sword. With almost one-half million Allied and German casualties, the 76-day Battle of Normandy will never be forgotten. Today one can visit the battle sites and see the scars of this horrible twentieth-century war. Caen's *Musée Mémorial* offers the visitor a good introduction to what happened and why it happened on the Normandy coast in June 1944.

SELECT BIBLIOGRAPHY

Brunet, Pierre. "Basse Normandie," in André Gamblin, ed., *La France dans ses régions,* vol 1. Paris: SEDES, 1994.

Clary, D. *La Normandie.* Paris: PUF (Que sais-je?), 1987.

Frémont, A. "Basse Normandie," in Y. Lacoste, ed., *Géopolitiques des régions françaises,* vol. 2. Paris: Fayard, 1986.

Chapter 17

UPPER NORMANDY
(Haute-Normandie)

REGIONAL GEOGRAPHY

Situated between the greater Paris region and the English Channel, Upper Normandy is one of the smallest regions in France. In terms of size, only Alsace and the Île-de-France are smaller. Upper Normandy comprises 7,603 square miles, 2.3 percent of the surface area of France. The region is bordered to the west by Lower Normandy and to the east by Picardy and the Île-de-France. Upper Normandy has only two departments: Eure and Seine-Maritime. Rouen is the regional capital.

Besides its coastline, the other dominating feature of this region is the winding Seine that flows through it. The presence of the English Channel and the Seine, coupled with the region's close proximity to Paris, have made Le Havre and Rouen two of the most important ports in France. To a large degree, the region is organized around the valley of the Seine, with most of the population grouped between the two poles of Le Havre and Rouen. Of the numerous valleys, the one formed by the Seine is by far the most important. The region ranges in altitude between 400 and 650 feet above sea level, with a slightly higher elevation to the west. Upper Normandy has a variety of landscapes but lacks geographical unity.

The climate is similar to that of Lower Normandy: moist and temperate. Rain is frequent. Along some parts of the coast, the summer and winter climates differ relatively little.

HISTORY

The history of Upper Normandy is covered in Chapter 16, "Lower Normandy."

UPPER NORMANDY
(HAUTE-NORMANDIE)

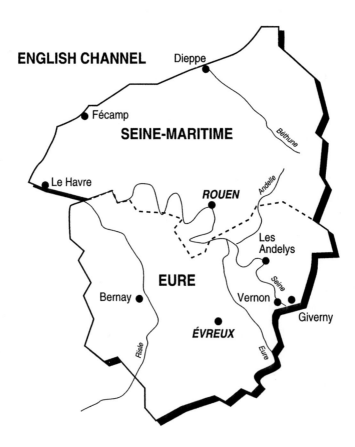

RECENT POLITICS

Upper Normandy has witnessed the consolidation of the right and the strengthening appeal of the extreme right. In the 1993 parliamentary elections the right-wing coalition of the gaullist Rally for the Republic (RPR) and the Union for French Democracy (UDF) won 38.2 percent of the vote, as compared to 34.7 percent in 1988. The 1993 results gave to the right twelve of the seventeen available seats in Parliament from this region. The Socialist party (PS) won 21.3 percent of the vote, as compared to 40.1 percent in 1988. Consequently the PS saved only three of its thirteen seats, one being held by the former prime minister Laurent Fabius (1984–1988), who represents a suburb of Rouen. The French Communist party (PCF) saw its electoral decline continue, winning 11 percent in 1993 (in 1988 it captured 15 percent of the vote in Upper Normandy). The Ecologists received only 7.7 percent of the vote in 1993. The extremist National Front (FN), however, made impressive gains in the 1993 legislative elections, jumping from 8.1 percent of the vote in 1988 to 13.1 percent in 1993. These inroads by the FN drew the attention of many political observers in France.

The 1995 elections echoed some of the trends noted above. In the first round of the 1995 presidential elections, the right-wing candidates won Eure and the left won Seine-Maritime. The National Front candidate Jean-Marie Le Pen captured 17.08 percent of the vote, a better score than his 15 percent national average. In the second round of the contest, the gaullist Jacques Chirac won Eure and the socialist Lionel Jospin won Seine-Maritime. Chirac, of course, won the presidential election. However, in the June 1995 municipal elections the socialists made some gains, as well as the RPR. The socialists won the traditionally conservative city of Rouen; the RPR won Le Havre from the communists, the last historical stronghold of the PCF. Nevertheless, the communists retained control of Dieppe and Évreux.

Over the decades, the region's political slant has paralleled the parties in power in Paris. For example, the region gave strong support to the Radical party in the 1930s, to the gaullists in the 1960s, to the socialists in the 1980s, and to the right (at least to some extent) in the 1990s.

For decades Upper Normandy has been the home of Jean Lecanuet, a politician of national stature. Born in Rouen in 1920, Lecanuet served in various governments under both the Fourth (1946–1958) and Fifth (1958–   ) Republics, ran for the presidency in 1965 to challenge Charles de Gaulle, served in the National Assembly and Senate, and reigned as mayor of Rouen from 1968 until his death in 1993. One of his political goals was to construct a centrist party as an alternative to gaullism and any type of alliance with the Communist party. During his career he pursued this goal through involvement in the Christian Democratic party known as the

Mouvement Républicain Populaire (MRP), the Democratic Center, and the Reformers' Movement. He consistently advocated the construction of the European Community and was considered an effective mayor of Rouen.

POPULATION

The population of Upper Normandy has shown strong growth, jumping from 1,596,000 in 1975 to 1,763,000 in 1993. The birthrate, 1.90, is above the national average (1.73). Between 1982 and 1990 the region witnessed a large population increase of 81,885 inhabitants. Eure saw an increase of 11 percent during this period, pushing it over the 500,000-inhabitant mark. Seine-Maritime, on the other hand, grew 2.7 percent during the same period. The varying growth rates are products of migratory trends in this region. Relatively high population density characterizes Upper Normandy, with 143.2 inhabitants per square kilometer (231.98 per square mile), considerably above the 105.7 (171.23 per square mile) average for France. Three-fourths of the population is located in the valley of the Seine.

The age of the population, similar to Lower Normandy, is considerably younger than that of France as a whole. Fully 29.3 percent of the population of Upper Normandy is 19 years of age or younger (26.8% for the nation); those age 60 and over comprise 17.6 percent (19.7% is the national average). The immigrant population is roughly one-half the national average; it stands at 3.3 percent.

The urban population is 68.8 percent, as compared to 76.4 percent for all of France. Life expectancy is 76.4 years, below the average of 77.2 for France as a whole. Roughly 23.9 percent of households are single-person households, less than the 27.1 percent national average.

Educational levels in Upper Normandy are slightly below the national averages, whereas the work force more or less approximates the figures for the entire nation. In Upper Normandy 8.7 percent of the inhabitants possess only a high school diploma (10.5% for France) and 8.2 percent have advanced degrees (11.2% for France). Of the work force, 4.8 percent are in agriculture, 32.4 percent in industry (26.9% for the nation), and 62.8 percent in the service sector. The unemployment rate is 14.6 percent, more than two percentage points above the average for the nation. The high concentration of industry explains, in part, the high unemployment figure in the region. The unemployment rate among women is 14.7 percent.

ECONOMY

Much of the economic base of Upper Normandy is located in the valley of the Seine. Here one finds ancient industries producing textiles and paper, but also newer industries producing automobiles, electronics, pharmaceuticals, and perfumes. Roughly 80 percent of all jobs in the region are located here. The presence of an important river provides the region with a valuable corridor between the capital city of Paris and the sea. It is not surprising, therefore, that the region's two major ports, Le Havre and Rouen, are the second and fourth busiest, respectively, in France in terms of sea-going traffic. These two ports have helped foster the development of a highly internationalized petrochemical industry. In the 1980s two nuclear energy facilities began operation in the region at Paluel and Penly.

Industrial activity is paramount in Upper Normandy. More than 32 percent of the work force is in industry and roughly 40 percent of the region's economy is produced by the industrial sector (29.8% is the national average). The largest industrial concerns are petroleum and petrochemicals. Although over 60 percent of the work force is employed in the service sector, it represents only 54 percent of the regional economy. In fact, it is the weakest service sector in all of France—perhaps because of the close proximity of Paris and the strong industrial base of the Upper Normandy region. Employment in agriculture has fallen in the region, as it has throughout France. Agriculture in Upper Normandy is focused on cattle breeding and the production of cereals. The declining number of jobs in the region and the increasing population explain the high and persistent levels of unemployment in Upper Normandy.

The three largest towns are Rouen with 102,723 inhabitants (greater Rouen 380,161), Le Havre with 195,854, and Évreux with 49,103. Roughly 27.1 percent of the work force is located in Rouen, 14.4 percent in Le Havre, and 5.7 percent in Évreux. The four largest employers are Renault, Renault Automobile Equipment, Société Européenne de Propulsion (aerospace), and Saint-Gobain (glass, electronics).

In many ways Upper Normandy lives in the shadow of Paris. This is one reason why the service sector has developed so slowly. Nevertheless, the port at Le Havre opens the region to the world; and with two major nuclear installations, the region has become one of the nuclear power centers in France. A long-standing problem has been the region's neglect of training and educational advancement for its population. The university at Rouen was officially created only in 1964 and the university at Le Havre only in 1984. The region is truly a corridor between Paris and the English Channel that is overshadowed by Paris; this overshadowing is enhanced, according to some, by the traditional reserve of the Normans. However, the long-term hope is to maximize Upper Normandy's geographical position and transform the region into one with an international role. The opening of a new autoroute in Upper Normandy and a Paris-Normandy high-speed TGV train (not scheduled until after the year 2,000) will undoubtedly enhance the region's development, especially tourism.

CULTURE

Many literary figures have been inspired by the triangle of land between Rouen, Le Havre, and Dieppe. According to one authority, this small part of Normandy has more literary connections than practically any other area of the same size. From this area have come the great Norman writers **Gustave Flaubert** (1821–1880) and his devoted friend and disciple **Guy de Maupassant** (1850–1893), as well as **Pierre Corneille** (1606–1684), **Raymond Queneau** (1903–1976), **Armand Salacrou** (1899–   ), **André Maurois** (1885–1967), and **André Gide** (1869–1951). Other notable authors came to the area from the outside, such as **Victor Hugo** (1802–1885) and **Jean-Paul Sartre** (1905–1980). Hugo not only spent time here but lost his youngest daughter in a boating accident in the area. The Existentialist philosopher Sartre taught high school for five years in Le Havre, a city that became the setting for his first novel, *La Nausée* (1938, Nausea). The town of Rouen has nurtured a number of literary figures, more than many towns much larger. For example, the dramatist Corneille was born in Rouen. Flaubert was born here as well. Rouen, which had 200 factories and was the third largest city in France in his time, was featured in the urban area of Flaubert's novel *Madame Bovary* (1857). Flaubert, like Maupassant, loved the Norman coast. Some of Maupassant's best-known stories, however, such as *Boule de suif* (The Sphere of Tallow), are set in and around Rouen. Maupassant's *Pierre et Jean* deals with a middle-class family in Le Havre. This same city produced the playwright Salacrou and the author Queneau. The famous writer Gide and his wife are buried in the village churchyard of Cuverville near Le Havre. One of Gide's best novels, *La Porte étroite* (1909, Strait Is the Gate), is set in Cuverville.

The beauty of the Normandy coastline has inspired a number of painters, from the precursors of Impressionism to Impressionists and others. **Claude Monet** (1840–1926), a leading Impressionist and one of the important figures in modern art, lived and died in Giverny between Paris and Rouen. Monet is famous for his study of light on subjects and for his painting of water lilies and the cathedral at Rouen. He also painted coastal towns such as Honfleur, Le Havre, and Dieppe. (For additional information on the culture and traditions of Normandy, including the cuisine, see Chapter 16, "Lower Normandy.")

ARCHITECTURE AND NOTEWORTHY SITES

The architecture of Normandy in general is discussed in Chapter 16, "Lower Normandy."

ROUEN (pop. 102,723; greater Rouen 380,161) is the fourth largest port in France; it is also a beautifully restored city that suffered heavy bombing during World War II. Located on the Seine River, it is slightly more than an hour by train from Paris. In addition to its many spires and church towers dotting the skyline, the city has numerous historical monuments. Many important people have been associated with Rouen, including William the Conqueror, Joan of Arc (who was burned at the stake in Rouen by the English in 1431), the dramatist Pierre Corneille (1606–1684), and the writer Gustave Flaubert (1821–1880). In Rouen is the *Cathédrale Notre Dame,* built between 1201 and 1514 and considered a gem of French Gothic architecture. The Impressionist Claude Monet (1840–1926) painted the cathedral many times. The *Musée des Beaux-Arts* features paintings from the sixteenth to the twentieth centuries. The *Musée Le Secq des Tournelles* displays the blacksmith's craft and has instruments from the third through the nineteenth centuries. The *Église Saint Maclou* is a flamboyant Gothic church in which much of the decoration dates to the Renaissance. The *Église Saint-Ouen* dates to the fourteenth century and exemplifies High Gothic architecture. The *Monument Juif* is a building used by the Jewish community as long ago as 1100; it was discovered only in 1976 during restoration work on the *Palais de Justice.*

LE HAVRE (pop. 195,854), the nation's second largest port, is used as a gateway for ferries to Britain and Ireland. Although the city is not on the tourist map, it does have an excellent *Musée des Beaux-Arts* that includes a collection of Monet's paintings and works of other Impressionists. Paintings by Raoul Dufy (1877–1953) can also be viewed here; Dufy was originally from Le Havre.

ÉVREUX (pop. 49,103) is built on the Iton River; like a number of cities in Normandy, it was rebuilt after World War II. Today it manufactures electrical equipment and automobile accessories. The *Cathédrale Notre-Dame* has a superb collection of stained glass dating from the thirteenth through the sixteenth centuries. Besides a municipal museum, there is a fifteenth-century clock tower and ramparts along the Iton River.

DIEPPE (pop. 35,894) has been an important port since the Middle Ages; today it is the fifth largest port in France. Some of Canada's first European settlers came from Dieppe. It is the closest Channel port to Paris, only 103 miles away. Dieppe is popular with the English, who often cross the Channel to shop in its supermarkets. Besides a mile-long beach and a casino, there are several impressive Gothic churches and a municipal museum with nineteenth- and twentieth-century paintings, carved ivories (once a specialty of the town), and artifacts of ethnography, archaeology, and maritime history. There is also a *War Museum* commemorating the Canadian landings in 1942; half the landing force was either killed or wounded here.

GIVERNY (pop. 548) is located between Rouen and Paris; it is the home of Claude Monet, one of the leading Impressionists. Here he painted his most famous series of works, including the Water Lilies. Monet's flower-filled garden home was opened to the public in 1980 and attracts nearly

400,000 visitors each year. In 1992 a new *American Impressionists Museum* opened nearby; it will surely increase the number of visitors who come to Giverny.

SELECT BIBLIOGRAPHY

Auger, P., and J. Granier. *Le Guide du pays de Caux.* Paris: La Manufacture, 1990.
Gay, François-J. "Haute Normandie," in André Gamblin, ed., *La France dans ses régions,* vol. 1. Paris: SEDES, 1994.
Guermond, Y. "Haute Normandie," in Y. Lacoste, ed., *Géopolitiques des régions françaises,* vol. 2. Paris: Fayard, 1986.

Chapter 18

PAYS DE LA LOIRE

REGIONAL GEOGRAPHY

Once the playground of kings, queens, and other aristocrats, Pays de la Loire extends from the eastern boundary of Brittany to the northwestern tip of Poitou-Charentes. A portion of Pays de la Loire borders the Atlantic Ocean. The region comprises 19,804 square miles, 5.9 percent of the surface area of France, and includes five departments: Loire-Atlantique, Maine-et-Loire, Mayenne, Sarthe, and the Vendée. The capital is Nantes.

The principal geographical elements of the region are its rivers, especially the famed Loire, and the Atlantic coastline. The beautiful Loire valley, where the French aristocracy once built chateaux—especially between the fifteenth and eighteenth centuries—as a testament to their wealth and power, runs through the region and the neighboring region of the Centre. Other rivers include the Mayenne, the Sarthe, the Sèvre Nantaise, and the Sèvre Niortaise. The Atlantic coastline provides an important access to the sea. The region's geography is conducive to agriculture; indeed, for centuries the Pays de la Loire has been known for its rural and agricultural character.

The climate along the coast is maritime, and thus variable. The Atlantic coast, however, is influenced by the Gulf Stream and therefore the weather is relatively mild, with few hot spells and little frost. Even inland, the weather is relatively mild.

HISTORY

The history of Pays de la Loire is closely tied to the history of the old territories, notably Brittany, Anjou, Maine, and Poitou. The Pays de la

PAYS DE LA LOIRE

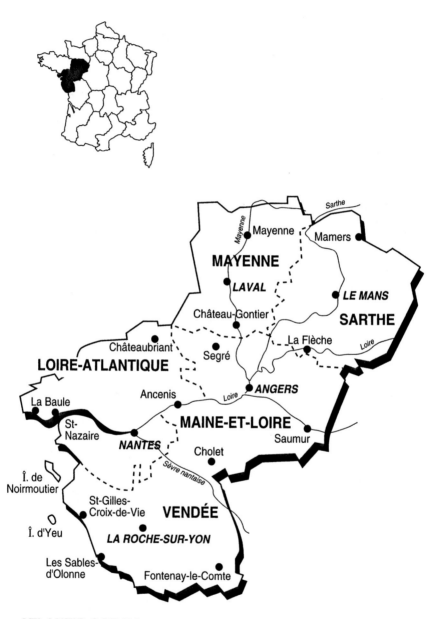

MAYENNE

Sarthe

Mayenne

Mamers

LAVAL

LE MANS

SARTHE

Château-Gontier

La Flèche

Loire

Châteaubriant

Segré

LOIRE-ATLANTIQUE

Ancenis

Loire

ANGERS

La Baule

St-Nazaire

MAINE-ET-LOIRE

NANTES

Saumur

Cholet

Sèvre nantaise

Î. de
Noirmoutier

St-Gilles-
Croix-de-Vie

VENDÉE

Î. d'Yeu

LA ROCHE-SUR-YON

Les Sables-
d'Olonne

Fontenay-le-Comte

ATLANTIC OCEAN

Loire was formally created in 1956 when five departments with a relatively strong identity of their own were organized into one administrative unit. In the past, parts of what is now the Pays de la Loire were attached to Brittany, Anjou, Maine, and Poitou. Thus it is instructive to approach the history of this region from the perspective of its cities and towns.

Nantes was once part of Brittany. The city was the capital of a Gallic tribe called the Namnetae. Until the fifteenth century, Nantes had a long history of struggling to maintain its independence against the Romans, and then subsequently the Normans, the English, and the French. During the Middle Ages, Nantes served for a time as the capital of the Duchy of Brittany, which in 1532 fell to the French crown. The famous Edict of Nantes, signed by Henry IV in 1598, granted religious freedom to the Protestants. Owing to its port, by the sixteenth century Nantes flourished as a commercial town. During the eighteenth century the city was France's most important center in the slave trade. In the nineteenth century, as seagoing vessels became larger and could not sail up the Loire, trade declined in Nantes. Consequently an outer harbor was built at St.-Nazaire, and new industries had to be developed in Nantes.

The town of Angers was once the capital of the territory known as Anjou, which was located on both sides of the Loire River near Angers. In Gallo-Roman times the city was occupied by a tribe known as the Andecair. The Normans occupied the town in the ninth century but were driven out by Charles the Bald. Under the Counts of Anjou—the Foulques dynasty— the city began to flourish in the ninth century. The twelfth century was the great era of Angevin architecture, especially the domed Angevin (or Plantagenet) vault. During the Middle Ages in general Anjou developed into an important feudal state, extending its territory through conquest and dynastic marriage.

The city and the surrounding area played a significant role in a major conflict between France and England. Geoffroy V (1129–1151) was the first to carry the name Plantagenet. His son, Henry II, married Eleanor of Aquitaine, who had been divorced by the French king; Henry was the first Plantagenet to become king of England. Anjou thus came under English control, initiating a long period of conflict between France and England.

In the history of Angers the best-known ruler is Duke René I (1409– 1480), also Count of Provence. Although he suffered defeat by losing the remaining Italian territories of Anjou, he was a great patron of the arts and transformed the city into a cultural capital. When René I died, Anjou fell to the French crown. Today it is the chief town in the department of Maine-et-Loire.

Le Mans was once the capital of the medieval territory known as Maine. It was an important town even in Roman times. During the fourth century it became the seat of the bishop's office. Le Mans now serves as the capital of the department of the Sarthe. It is known for its rich historical tradition and its famous car-racing circuit.

The department of the Vendée was once part of what is now Poitou-Charentes. The Vendée and the area between the Garonne and Loire Rivers represented the Roman province of Aquitainia (later known as Aquitaine and Guyenne). After the fall of Rome in the fifth century, Aquitaine broke up into a number of relatively independent states. Historically the Vendée area is known for its resistance to centralized authority. In 1793 during the French Revolution, a royalist revolt of significant proportions began in the Vendée against the revolutionary government in Paris. Today the area is known for its beautiful beaches and its resorts. (For more details on the history of this region, consult the chapters on Brittany, Centre, Poitou-Charentes, and Aquitaine.)

RECENT POLITICS

Politically, the region has moved to the right. This was revealed in the 1992 regional and cantonal elections, in which the UPF (Union for France—an alliance between the gaullist RPR, or Rally for the Republic, and the UDF, or Union for French Democracy) conserved an absolute majority. In the 1992 vote on the Maastricht Treaty the region was divided, with the departments of Loire-Atlantique, Maine-et-Loire, and the western portion of Mayenne voting in favor of speeding up Common Market integration, whereas the remainder of the region voted no. This vote suggested an east-west split in the region on the question of the Common Market. The 1993 legislative elections confirmed the hold of the right and the weakening of the Socialist party (PS) in the Pays de la Loire. The 1993 elections reversed twenty-five years of socialist progress in the region. In 1967, for instance, the PS had roughly 10 percent of the region's vote, but by 1988 the figure had risen to 25 percent. In the 1993 elections, however, the PS captured only 11 percent of the vote and saw its representation in Parliament slide from seven to two deputies. The right, on the other hand, won twenty-eight seats in the same elections. The Ecologists gained less than expected. Yet the extreme right-wing National Front (FN) made small and steady gains in the region.

In recent years the Pays de la Loire has seen the rise of a new political candidate, Philippe de Villiers from the Vendée. De Villiers is a nationalist who in various elections has won significant vote totals in the larger cities and towns, especially from wealthier voters. He is president of a party known as the Movement for France. He is also president of the general council of the Vendée. He was elected to the National Assembly in 1988 and 1993 but resigned after his election in 1994 to the European Parliament. Running in the 1995 presidential contest with eight other candidates, he won 4.8 percent of the vote in the first round. Also in the first round of the presidential race, the right-wing candidates in general outdistanced the left in all departments. The extremist National Front won 11.97 percent of the vote. In the second round the gaullist candidate Jacques Chirac, the eventual victor, captured all departments in the region except for Sarthe, which the socialist candidate Lionel Jospin won. The June 1995 municipal elections that followed saw the center-right UDF capture Laval, whereas the socialists maintained control over Nantes.

POPULATION

In recent decades the Pays de la Loire has witnessed a birthrate of 1.82, higher than the national average. This is one of the key reasons why the population has expanded. In 1975 the population totaled 2,767,000 inhabitants; yet by 1993 it stood at 3,095,000, roughly 5.4 percent of the total population of France. The population density is below the national average, 96.5 inhabitants per square kilometer (156.33 per square mile), as compared to 105.7 per square kilometer (171.23 per square mile) for France as a whole.

Besides an elevated birthrate, the region is characterized by its youthful population. Whereas those age 60 and over make up slightly below 20 percent of the population (19.7% is the national average), those age 19 and younger comprise 28.5 percent of the region's population, above the 26.8 percent average for France. In 1982 almost 32 percent were age 19 or under. Immigrants comprise a very small part of the region's population, 1.4 percent, as compared to the 6.3 percent national average.

The rural character of the Pays de la Loire is clearly evident. Only 62.5 percent of the population is considered urban, well below the 76.4 percent average for France. Life expectancy parallels the national norm, 77.2 years. Roughly 25.1 percent of all households are single-person households, below the 27.1 percent average for France as a whole.

Another salient characteristic of the population is that it is less educated than the national norm. Approximately 9.4 percent of the region's inhabitants hold only a high school degree, and 8.2 percent possess an advanced degree (10.5% and 11.2%, respectively, are the national norms). Of the work force, 9.6 percent—well above the 5.3 percent national average—are employed in agriculture, and 28.7 percent work in industry (slightly above the national average). Yet representation in the service sector is weak as compared to the national norm; 61.7 percent are employed in the service sector in the Pays de la Loire, whereas the average for France is 67.8 percent. The employment rate is above the national average, with 13.1 percent of the region's inhabitants being out of work. The unemployment rate among women runs at 12.9 percent, also above the average for France.

ECONOMY

Traditionally the economy has focused on agriculture. Today the agricultural sector produces milk, cattle, poultry, and eggs. As noted previously, the percentage of the work force employed in agriculture is almost double the national average. Yet over the past thirty years the Pays de la Loire has witnessed increasing industrial development, and today industry in the region is centered around the production of leather, shoes, electronic equipment, household electronics, rubber, and plastics. Naval works are also important, especially at St.-Nazaire.

Several factors characterize the economy of the Pays de la Loire. First, production per worker is lower than the national average. Second, the educational levels and training of the work force are weak. Third, there has been relatively little international focus in the region. Fourth, small and medium-size enterprises play an important role. Fifth, investment in industry has been weaker than in France as a whole. These characteristics help explain the persistence of the rural and agricultural face of the Pays de la Loire.

Yet the region possesses a number of strong points with respect to future economic development—namely, the extent of its agro-food business, the potential for tourism, and the quality of life in general. Moreover, the infrastructure has been improved, especially with (1) the completion and planned completion of new segments of the autoroute, (2) the construction of a ring road (*périphérique*) around Nantes, the region's capital, (3) plans to extend the high-speed TGV rail line further into the region, and (4) a planned international airport (Notre Dame-des-Landes) north of Nantes. Yet although the coastline of the Vendée is attracting retirees and Nantes is attracting the young, the region is now beginning to witness a negative migratory trend. All in all, the region's economy is in the process of change.

The three largest towns are Nantes with 244,995 inhabitants (greater Nantes 496,078), Angers with 141,404 (greater Angers 208,282), and Le Mans with 145,502. Approximately 19.1 percent of the work force is found in Nantes, 8.1 percent in Angers, and 8 percent in Le Mans. The four largest employers are the regional hospital in Nantes, Renault Le Mans, Chantiers de l'Atlantique (naval works), and the regional hospital in Angers.

CULTURE

For a long time the Pays de la Loire has had a reputation for being rural, agricultural, and religious. The pastoral countryside and the splendor of the Loire, France's longest river, attracted castle-builders in previous centuries as well as a host of writers. Today the region attracts tourists who are discovering what the wealthy, the powerful, and the literati discovered long ago. According to the locals, the Valley of the Loire, especially around Tours in the neighboring region of the Centre, is where the purest and most accent-free French of any spot in the nation is spoken.

The Loire valley and nearby areas in the Pays de la Loire are home to a number of significant writers and have attracted others who have been inspired by this beautiful region. The irreverent humanist **François Rabelais** (1494–1553), who heralded the Renaissance in France, was born in the neighboring region of the Centre (the ancient territory known as Touraine). Some of his best satirical novels, such as *Gargantua* and *Pantagruel,* are set in part in the Loire valley on the border between the Pays de la Loire and the Centre. Although these two novels cover various areas of France and the world at large, the author's Loire homeland is an important setting in his work.

The lyric poet **Joachim du Bellay** (1522–1560) was born near Angers. Even though he had an unhappy childhood, he wrote about the countryside around Angers with great affection, especially when as a young man he spent four years in Rome (1553–1557) as an assistant to his brother, a cardinal. His poems recall the gentleness of the region's landscape.

The great writer **Honoré de Balzac** (1799–1859) was born in the neighboring region, the Centre, in Tours. Some of his ninety-plus novels were inspired by the Loire valley (e.g., *Le Lys dans la vallée* [The Lily of the Valley]). The Loire valley in both the Pays de la Loire and the Centre were very familiar to Balzac. **Jules Verne** (1828–1905), the noted science fiction writer and one of the most translated French-born authors in history, was born in Nantes. Verne authored such books as *Le Voyage au centre de la terre* (1864, Journey to the Center of the Earth) and *Vingt mille lieues sous les mers* (1870, Twenty Thousand Leagues under the Sea). Many other writers found inspiration along the Loire in the neighboring Centre (see Chapter 6 for additional details).

The cuisine reflects the different traditions of the Pays de la Loire. The cuisine in Nantes and the department of the Loire-Atlantique is similar to that enjoyed in the region of Brittany (see Chapter 4). In the Vendée the cuisine resembles that of Poitou-Charentes (see Chapter 20). The cuisine of the remainder of the Pays de la Loire—Maine-et-Loire, Mayenne, Sarthe— does not lack gastronomic specialties. Vegetables are plentiful and excellent here, such as asparagus, green beans, swiss chard, and mushrooms. The area is known for various forms of potted meat called *rillettes,* especially around Le Mans. Normally made of pork, *rillettes* can also be made of rabbit or goose. Le Mans is famous for its capons as well. This area, too, produces superb Reinette apples. The Maine-et-Loire is France's leading producer of apples. The cattle of this area produce a succulent beef. A celebrated regional beef dish is *cul-de-veau à l'angevine.* Freshwater fish is also popular, such as eel, pike, and gudgeon. There are various fish pâtés and fried fish dishes. Below is a recipe for a dish that is typical of the Loire valley; ideally it should be made with whitebait, bite-sized fish that are easy to cook.

FRITURE DE LA LOIRE
(Deep-Fried Fish)

1 lb. whitebait or flounder fillets cut into bite-sized pieces	salt and freshly ground black pepper to taste
2 cups vegetable oil	lemon wedges
¼ cup milk	tartar sauce
1 cup flour	

Preheat oil to 375°F in deep-fryer. Rinse fish pieces and dry them with paper towels. Put fish in bowl and toss with milk. Place flour on a dish and pat fish onto it until coated. Place half the fish pieces in the fryer for 2 minutes, shaking the basket. Drain on paper towels. Fry remaining fish in the same way.

Add salt and pepper to taste; serve with lemon wedges and tartar sauce. Serves 3 to 4.

ARCHITECTURE AND NOTEWORTHY SITES

Houses in Maine-et-Loire, Mayenne, and Sarthe are distinguished by the diversity of the material used, such as tufa, limestone, or schist. In the nineteenth century, brick was often used in Mayenne. Rural houses are often rectangular in shape. In both Mayenne and Sarthe one can find timberframe houses. Also, in these three departments the roofs are double-pitched with large overhangs. Slate is a common roofing material.

The architecture in Loire-Atlantique resembles that of Brittany (see Chapter 4), whereas the architecture in the Vendée is similar to that of Poitou-Charentes (see Chapter 20).

NANTES (pop. 244,995; greater Nantes 496,078), a university town and France's seventh largest urban area, is the main city in western France, linking the Atlantic with the remainder of the country. Its vineyards produce quality wine, especially the white Gros Plant and the Muscadet. In the city the Gothic *Cathédrale Saint Pierre et Saint Paul* was built over a 400-year period. In this church is the tomb of François II, Duke of Brittany from 1458 to 1488, and his wife; the tomb is considered a masterpiece of Renaissance art. The chateau of the Dukes of Brittany, found in Nantes, dates from 1466. In 1598, Henry IV considered the Edict of Nantes here. The *Musée des Beaux-Arts* is a renowned fine arts museum that includes the work of Georges de la Tour. There is also a superb natural history museum. The *Musée Dobrée* displays antiquities, art, armaments, furniture, and artifacts dating to the Egyptians. The city also has a Jules Verne museum; this science fiction writer (1828–1905) was born in Nantes. The *Jardin des Plantes* is an exceptional botanical garden.

ANGERS (pop. 141,404; greater Angers 208,282) is a center for flowers and the arts, a tradition dating to the time of Duke René I; it is also an important market for fruits, vegetables, and the wine of Anjou. Angers is also an industrial center where modern electronics and computer facilities coexist with traditional Angevin activities such as slate quarrying and umbrella manufacturing. The city is the capital of Maine-et-Loire. Many parts of Angers's chateau date to the rule of René I, who once ruled an empire that included Sicily and Piedmont and who also wrote novels and poems. Inside the chateau is one of the city's main attractions, the *Apocalypse Tapestry* woven from wool and gold thread between 1375 and 1380. The tapestry was ordered by Louis I, Duke of Anjou, to demonstrate to his brother, Charles V, that they were equals. The tapestry is considered a masterpiece of medieval art. The *Musée Jean Lurçat* houses a contemporary tapestry that depicts a journey through human destiny. The *Musée des Beaux-Arts* displays contemporary artwork as well as work dating to the fifteenth century. The *Musée David d'Angers* exhibits the sculpture of this nineteenth-century artist. The *Musée Pincé* exhibits an eclectic collection of Greek, Roman, Egyptian, and Chinese artifacts.

LE MANS (pop. 145,502), which lies halfway between Paris and Nantes, is known for more than the 24-hour car-racing event that was first held here in 1923. The city was important in Roman times and is steeped in history. Today it is the capital of Sarthe and has attracted a number of large banks, insurance companies, and the Renault car industry. The *Place de la République* is a beautiful square where one finds the Law Courts, an old monastic building, and the Church of the Visitation, dating to the 1730s. The eleventh-century *Cathédral St. Julien* is a good example of Gothic architecture and contains superb stained-glass windows. The Old Town reflects the Middle Ages and the Renaissance. At the *Maison de la Reine Bérengère* one finds artifacts of the history, art, and popular traditions of the ancient territory of Maine. The *Musée de Tessé* has a variety of exhibitions. Le Mans also has a Gallo-Roman fortress from the third and fourth centuries.

LAVAL (pop. 50,473), a town with a reputation for being nonconformist, is the capital of Mayenne. It is also the home of a number of significant personalities: Ambroise Paré (1509–1590), a father of modern surgery; Henri Rousseau (1844–1910), a renowned artist; Alfred Jarry (1873–1907), a satirist and a precursor of surrealism; and Alain Gerbault (1893–1941), a solo yachtsman. The Old Town has a number of sixteenth-century houses. Laval's chateau was once the home of the Counts of Laval. The town has an imposing cathedral with a Romanesque nave. The Church of St. Vénéraud is known for its beautiful stained glass.

LES SABLES-D'OLONNE (pop. 15,830) is a beach resort in the Vendée.

A quiet town for most of the year, during July and August the town attracts thousands of sun worshippers. Here, as elsewhere on the Atlantic coast, vacationers can enjoy surfing as well.

LA BAULE (pop. 14,845), in the department of Loire-Atlantique, is a popular seaside resort that claims one of the most beautiful beaches in Europe. La Baule became a resort in the 1880s and today is on a par with other Atlantic resorts, such as Royan and Biarritz. It attracts a sophisticated clientele.

SELECT BIBLIOGRAPHY

Martin, J.-C. *La Vendée de la mémoire (1800–1980)*. Paris: Seuil, 1989.

Renard, J. "Pays de la Loire," in Y. Lacoste, ed., *Géopolitiques des régions françaises,* vol. 2. Paris: Fayard, 1986.

Vigarié, André. "Pays de la Loire," in André Gamblin, ed., *La France dans ses régions*, vol. 2. Paris: SEDES, 1994.

Chapter 19

PICARDY
(Picardie)

REGIONAL GEOGRAPHY

Picardy is located to the north of Paris and the Île-de-France, and to the south of Nord-Pas-de-Calais. The region is bordered on the west by Upper Normandy and on the east by Champagne-Ardenne. The northwest corner fronts the English Channel. A small portion of the northeastern corner of the region is contiguous with Belgium. Picardy comprises 11,975 square miles, 3.6 percent of the surface area of France, and includes three departments: Somme, Oise, and Aisne. The regional capital is Amiens.

The region's geography is marked by the absence of dramatic hills. Only near the northeast, north, west, southwest, and southeastern borders do significant hills rise to more than 650 feet. The land is ideal for farming; indeed, the region is a major agricultural producer. Several important rivers run through Picardy: the Marne, the Somme, and the Oise.

The climate of Picardy is temperate, with prevailing winds often blowing from the west and the northwest. Although winter and spring are usually wet, summer is a pleasant season despite the inevitable cloudy periods. The average maximum temperature in summer is 70° F. In autumn the weather is changeable but the temperature is mild.

HISTORY

In its earliest history, Picardy was inhabited by Celtic tribes in numerous villages. The Romans referred to Picardy and the north of France as Belgium. Christianity began to spread here in the fourth century. Between the fourth and sixth centuries the Franks continued their expansion into the

PICARDY
(PICARDIE)

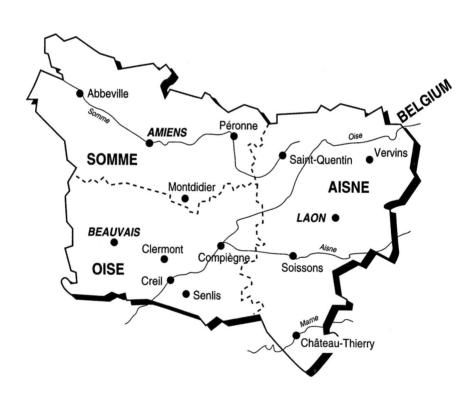

region and established larger communities. By the seventh century numerous abbeys had been founded; these served as centers of learning and trade and attracted the local population. In the eighth century Charlemagne subdivided his kingdom, including Picardy, into domains administered by counts. The power of these regional landholders increased in time and central royal power diminished.

Following the Viking invasions of the ninth century and the return of a sense of security during the tenth to the twelfth centuries, agricultural activity expanded—especially the cultivation of wheat. Along with this development in agriculture an urban upper class began to appear. At this time, too, Gothic architecture developed. The large cathedral at Amiens was one expression of this development. Until the fourteenth century Picardy was under the control of the Count of Flanders; late in the fourteenth century it came under the control of the Duchy of Burgundy. With the exception of Picardy, in 1477 the possessions of the House of Burgundy passed to the Austrian Hapsburgs and then to the Spanish Hapsburgs. Picardy itself was annexed by Louis XI to France in 1477.

From the time of annexation by France until the twentieth century, this region enjoyed a relatively pastoral existence. To a large degree, the Industrial Revolution missed Picardy and ensured that it would have an agricultural and rural character. However, the two world wars were particularly destructive, with many casualties and considerable physical damage. One of the bloodiest engagements of World War I was the First Battle of the Somme, which was waged in villages and woodlands near Amiens. When this long battle ended, casualties on all sides totaled a staggering 1.2 million. The battle has come to symbolize the meaningless slaughter of war. Since the end of World War II, the region has been slow to develop. Living in the shadow of Paris, Picardy is still a region of passage between the capital, the northernmost region of the country, and the English Channel.

RECENT POLITICS

Picardy has often voted against the power elite of Paris. A case in point was the referendum on the Maastricht Treaty in September 1992. Roughly 57 percent of the voters in Picardy voted against the referendum seeking to accelerate the integration of the European Economic Community (EEC, Common Market). The vote reflected the region's attachment to an independent French tradition, rejection of Paris and Brussels (seat of the executive arm of the Common Market), and the penetration of parties opposed to a more integrated Europe. In the 1993 legislative elections the voters in Picardy abandoned the Socialist party (PS) in large numbers, reducing the number of PS deputies in Parliament from ten to two. The biggest winner was the gaullist Rally for the Republic (RPR), which won more than 40 percent of the vote in alliance with the center-right Union for French Democracy (UDF). Both the French Communist party (PCF) and the extreme right-wing National Front (FN) benefited from a protest vote against the political elite in Paris and in the region itself. The PCF captured roughly 10 percent of the vote; the FN won more than 13 percent. In three races in the department of Oise, the FN captured more than 30 percent of the vote in contests with RPR and UDF candidates. During the first round of the 1995 presidential contest the left won all departments in the region except for Oise, which favored right-wing candidates and even gave the extremist Jean-Marie Le Pen of the FN 20.48 percent of its vote (Le Pen averaged 17.8% in the region and 15% nationwide). In the second round of the 1995 race the socialist candidate Lionel Jospin won all departments in Picardy with the exception of Oise, which voted in favor of the gaullist candidate Jacques Chirac, who emerged victorious on the national level. The June 1995 municipal elections saw the PS retain control over Creil while the UDF retained control in Amiens. The RPR, however, won the city hall of St. Quentin.

POPULATION

The population of Picardy has increased since World War II and especially over the past twenty years. In 1975 it stood at 1,679,000; in 1993 it was 1,835,000. Today, Picardy represents 3.2 percent of the population of France. The relatively high birthrate in the region, 1.92, is slightly higher than the average for all regions of France (1.73). Migration out of the region varies by age group but is strong among those age 15–25 and particularly in the department of Oise, which is situated relatively close to Paris. The Île-de-France, dominated by Paris, attracts many seeking job training and employment. The population density of Picardy is 94.6 inhabitants per square kilometer (153.25 per square mile), less than the 105.7 national average (171.23 per square mile).

Owing to its high birthrate, the population is relatively young. Those age 60 and over represent 17.7 percent of the population, less than the 19.7 percent average for France. On the other hand, those age 19 or younger constitute 29.8 percent of the population, above the 26.8 percent average for the nation. Over the past decade there has been a shift in population toward municipalities centered around urban areas and a loss of population in towns of 5,000 to 10,000—a rather unique phenomenon for France. Immigrants make up 4.2 percent of the population, below the national average of 6.3 percent.

The urban population is 60.9 percent, well below the 76.4 percent national average. Owing in part to the region's rural and agricultural character, there are many municipalities—nearly 2,300—and many of these are small. Life expectancy is 75.4 years, less than the 77.2 average for France.

Roughly 21.7 percent of all households are single-family households, well below the 27.1 percent national average.

As one might expect in an agriculturally oriented region, educational levels and the size of the service sector are below national averages. Approximately 8.8 percent of the inhabitants hold only a high school degree (10.5% for France) and 8 percent possess an advanced degree (11.2% nationally). Of the work force, 5.9 percent are in agriculture, 33 percent in industry, and 61 percent in the service sector. The unemployment rate currently runs at 13.5 percent, ahead of the national average of more than 12 percent. Roughly 13.7 percent of women in the region are unemployed.

ECONOMY

Economically, the region is one of contrasts. The northern part of Picardy, including Amiens (the region's capital), is relatively isolated economically; the southern part is coming increasingly under the influence of nearby Paris. The transportation system within the region is satisfactory but not evenly developed. For example, some areas of the Somme and Aisne have inadequate access. In this regard Amiens is some distance from an autoroute, connected only by a long expressway.

Industry in Picardy is relatively well developed, especially in metalworking, auto parts, bicycles, aeronautics, agricultural machinery, and textiles. Yet many traditional sectors pose a barrier to future development. For example, cottage industries are quite numerous. Moreover, the service sector has been late in developing, especially in finance, insurance, and business services.

Picardy is known as a major agricultural region, representing roughly 5 percent of the total agriculture and fishing of France. Agriculture here is highly mechanized and the average farm exceeds 100 acres, larger than the average size of a farm in France. Picardy is the largest producer of beets, especially sugar beets, in the nation. Wheat accounts for 42 percent of the cultivated area of the region. Barley, potatoes, and green vegetables are also produced. Animal husbandry has declined somewhat in recent years, owing in part to European Economic Community policies. Given the orientation of the regional economy, it is not surprising that the canning industry and the confectionery industry are potentially strong and could be further developed.

The three largest towns are Amiens with 131,872 inhabitants, Saint-Quentin with 60,644, and Beauvais with 54,190. Approximately 12.2 percent of the work force is centered in Amiens, 5.1 percent in Saint-Quentin, and 5.8 percent in Creil. The four largest employers are the regional hospital in Amiens, the specialized hospital in Clermont, Usines Chausson (automobile construction), and Sollac (steel).

Future development of the region is hampered by a number of factors.

First, the old industries in the region and the family-centered cottage industries (ranging from artisans to seasonal labor) limit economic development and contribute to the migration of young people toward large cities such as Paris. Second, the lack of educational and training centers is problematic. Although there is a university at Amiens, very few centers prepare workers for the future—the technological university at Compiègne is one of the few exceptions. On the positive side, Picardy has attracted international investment and is the tenth most internationalized region in France. Indeed, international firms have moved into areas such as automobile equipment and parts, various assembly industries, chemical industries, cosmetics, and the agro-food industry. Moreover, improved links with Paris and the north (not to mention Europe in general), and the region's strategic location (Amiens itself is located in the middle of a triangle connecting Paris, London, and Brussels) are distinct advantages. Yet Picardy is not well known by tourists, even though it possesses a rich historical and cultural heritage.

CULTURE

Picardy has two pronounced cultures: rural and urban. Its wealth of cathedrals, basilicas, abbeys, simple churches, city halls, and churches from the Gothic era attest to its proud past. In fact, the British art critic and philosopher **John Ruskin** (1819–1900) wrote a book about the cathedral at Amiens and referred to it as "the Parthenon of Gothic architecture." Ruskin's book, *The Bible of Amiens* (1880), was even translated into French by the writer Marcel Proust (1871–1922).

Not only has its architecture stunned many observers, but over the centuries the region has produced a large number of internationally known figures in the arts, science, and politics. Born here were the playwright **Jean-Baptiste Racine** (1639–1699), the poet and fabulist **Jean de La Fontaine** (1621–1695), the orientalist **Antoine Galland** (1646–1715, translator of the Koran and *A Thousand and One Nights*), the writer **Pierre Choderlos de Laclos** (1741–1803), the general and artillery expert **Jean-Baptiste Gribeauval** (1715–1789), the military pharmacist **Antoine Parmentier** (1737–1813), the naturalist **Jean-Baptiste Lamarck** (1744–1829), the revolutionary leader and publicist **Camille Desmoulins** (1760–1794), the left-wing revolutionary **François-Noël Babeuf** (1760–1797), the philosopher **Marquis de Condorcet** (1743–1794), and the writer **Alexandre Dumas** (1802–1870, author of *Les Trois Mousquetaires* (The Three Musketeers) and *Le Comte de Monte-Cristo* (The Count of Monte Cristo). Given the region's rich cultural history, the continuous economic decline it has experienced since the nineteenth century has in some ways strengthened the regional identity of Picardy among its inhabitants.

In the twentieth century, the region has become known as a battle site that witnessed more than its share of human carnage. East of Amiens is the British war memorial at Thiepval, a 150-foot red-brick arch that is visible across the wheat plains of the Somme. On the arch are inscribed the names of 73,000 British soldiers who perished in 1916 at the Somme battles and who have no known gravesite. This battlefield also played a part in F. Scott Fitzgerald's (1896–1940) novel *Tender Is the Night*.

The cuisine of Picardy is quite similar to that elsewhere in northern France. There is an abundance of fresh fish and a large variety of salted and pickled fish, such as *pilchards* (sardines) and *harengs saur* (smoke-dried herring); shrimp, cockles, and mussels abound also. The freshwater eel is found in many *pâtés*. A sea plant known as *passe-pierre* (sea fennel) is a relatively new favorite. Oysters from the North Sea are plentiful and superb. A dish called *waterzoï* (freshwater fish or chicken stew) is popular, as are french fries with mussels, as well as *andouillettes* (chitterlings sausage). Endive is common, and chicory blended with coffee is consumed frequently. Below is a typical recipe from the region.

CARBONNADE DE BŒUF À LA FLAMANDES
(Beef and Onions Braised in Beer)

⅓ cup oil

2 tbs. butter

2 lbs. beef chuck eye roast, cut into cubes

3 onions, thinly sliced

5 tbs. flour

16 oz. beer

1 cup beef broth

salt and freshly ground black pepper to taste

bouquet garni composed of 1 sprig thyme, 1 bay leaf, 6 sprigs parsley, bound together

Preheat oven to 400°F. Heat half the oil with the butter in a frying pan, add the beef cubes, and brown well over high heat. If necessary, brown the cubes in two batches. Heat remaining oil in an ovenproof casserole. Add onions and sauté over low heat, stirring frequently, for 15 minutes or until soft. Raise heat and brown onions slightly; then stir in flour. Bake in oven, stirring often, for 10 minutes to brown the flour. Remove from oven; stir in beer, broth, salt and pepper, and bouquet garni. Add meat, and bring to a boil on the top of the stove. Return the casserole to the oven and simmer uncovered, stirring often, for 2½ hours or until the meat is very tender when pricked with a fork. When cooked, discard bouquet garni. Serves 4.

ARCHITECTURE AND NOTEWORTHY SITES

In Picardy and the north of France in general, protection from the wind is an architectural concern in the construction of large and small buildings. Houses are often single-storey and are built on the side of a hill protected by a windbreak of trees. Farms and outbuildings are normally grouped around a small courtyard. Roofs are generally of wood, tile, or slate shingles. Brick is the most common building material. Various colors of brick are used for decorative purposes; other decorative techniques include (1) blending of pebbles, stones, and mortar, or (2) varying the brick arrangement. In the past, houses followed a rectangular plan that included a main room accessible from the street; on one side of the main room was the bake house, which led to the bedrooms, and the other side led to the stables and farm buildings.

AMIENS (pop. 131,872), the capital of Picardy, sits along the Somme River. It is near the site of one of the bloodiest battles of World War I, the Battle of the Somme. Amiens is the birthplace of the author Pierre Choderlos de Laclos (1741–1803), who wrote *Les Liaisons dangereuses* (Dangerous Liaisons). The science fiction writer Jules Verne (1828–1905) chose Amiens as his adopted home. The *Cathédrale Notre Dame,* located here, is the largest cathedral in France. This monumental Gothic structure is known for its unity of style, owing principally to the fact that it was constructed in only fifty years. The main doorway of the cathedral has a detailed figure of Jesus. The *Musée d'Art Local et d'Histoire* features furniture and art from the time of Louis XV. The *Musée de Picardie* is known for its local prehistory, Gallo-Roman and Mediterranean archaeology, medieval art, and ceramics from the revolutionary period. The *Centre de Documentation Jules Verne* features the life and work of the visionary science fiction writer who foresaw certain important developments in science and technology, such as the submarine, space travel, and television. Verne authored such novels as *Around the World in Eighty Days, Journey to the Center of the Earth,* and *20,000 Leagues under the Sea.* At the *Centre de Documentation Jules Verne* one can see the site where this famous novelist wrote some of his most important works and view exhibits on his life and craft. *Les Hortillonnages* is a market area approximately one-half mile northwest of the city that has supplied Amiens with vegetables since the Middle Ages. The Battle of the Somme site is nearby; the village of Albert was the first line of the offensive when the assault was launched during World War I.

SAINT-QUENTIN (pop. 60,644) a town that had to be almost entirely rebuilt after World War I, today has several interesting buildings, such as the elegant *Hôtel de Ville* that dates to the fourteenth century and the *théâtre.* Luckily, there is remaining a twelfth- to fifteenth-century basilica with an elegant interior. There is also a major collection, housed in the

Musée Antoine-Lécuyer, of the pastels of Quentin de La Tour (1704–1788), an artist who was born and who died here. The *Musée Antoine-Lécuyer* also exhibits other paintings and porcelain. Also in Saint-Quentin is a unique *Museum of Entomology* with a collection of 600,000 European butterflies.

COMPIÈGNE (pop. 41,869) served as a country retreat for the French rulers from the Capetian dynasty (987–1328) to the time of Napoleon III (1852–1870). There is an eighteenth-century chateau designed by the architects to Louis XV, Jacques and Jacques-Ange Gabriel. For car enthusiasts there is the *Musée de la Voiture.* The *Musée Vivenel* displays Greek vases, statues, and enamels. Here one also finds the entrance to the Compiègne forest, one of the largest and most beautiful in France.

LAON (pop. 26,490), built on an isolated hill overlooking the Champagne plain, has some of the best monuments in northern France. There is an upper and a lower town; the upper town is lined with narrow medieval streets and exquisite houses. The cathedral was begun in 1155 and is one of the first Gothic buildings to be built in France; it incorporated new architectural ideas that inspired aspects of Notre-Dame in Paris and the cathedrals in Reims and Chartres. The town's museum has a number of Greek and Roman antiquities. The *Porte d'Ardon* is a thirteenth-century gateway and rampart walk.

ABBEVILLE (pop. 23,787) is considered a beautiful little town in the Somme valley. It is built around a town hall with a square white belfry. The centuries-old *Château de Bagatelle* is also noteworthy.

SENLIS (pop. 14,439) is a charming, quiet country town only 31 miles from Paris. Here one finds a famous Gothic church, the first in a series of churches devoted to the Virgin. There are also Gallo-Roman fortifications with sixteen towers. Senlis possesses the *Musée d'Art et Archéologie,* a museum of fine arts (the *Hôtel de Vermandois*), and even a hunting museum (the *Musée de la Vénerie*). Near Senlis is the forest of Ermenonville, which is known for its beautiful flowers, picturesque ruins, museum, and park.

SELECT BIBLIOGRAPHY

Bonneton, Christine. *Picardie.* Paris: Encyclopédies Régionales, 1992.

Calame, François, and Robert Fossier. *Picardie.* Paris: A Die, 1994.

Flament, Emile. "Picardie," in André Gamblin, ed., *La France dans ses régions,* vol. 1. Paris: SEDES, 1994.

Grand atlas de la France: Région Nord-Pas-de-Calais et Picardie. Lausanne: Éditions Grammont SA, 1987.

Sellier, J. "La Picardie," in Y. Lacoste, ed., *Géopolitiques des régions françaises,* vol. 1. Paris: Fayard, 1986.

POITOU-CHARENTES

Bressuire

Châtellerault

Parthenay

POITIERS

Vienne

**DEUX-
SÈVRES**

NIORT

VIENNE

Montmorillon

Île de Ré

LA ROCHELLE

Rochefort

St-Jean-
d'Angély

Confolens

Île
d'Oléron

Charente

Saintes

Charente

Royan

Cognac

Jarnac

**CHARENTE-
MARITIME**

ANGOULÊME

Jonzac

CHARENTE

ATLANTIC OCEAN

Chapter 20

POITOU-CHARENTES

REGIONAL GEOGRAPHY

The Poitou-Charentes region is located in the west-southwest portion of France, roughly midway down France's Atlantic coast. The western border of this region fronts the Atlantic Ocean. It comprises 15,932 square miles, approximately 4.7 percent of the surface area of France. The region includes four departments: Deux-Sèvres, Vienne, Charente-Maritime, and Charente. The regional capital is Poitiers.

The geography of this agricultural region is characterized by gently rolling hills. The highest altitude, 1,132 feet above sea level, is found at Montrollet in Charente. Yet the geography is not uniform; for example, the sedimentary formations of the Paris Basin and the Aquitaine Basin converge in this region. Moreover, the coastline has rocky sections as well as sandy and marshy sections. The Charente River links much of the interior with the Atlantic Ocean. The geography permits the region to yield only ordinary wine; however, superb spirits are produced here, namely cognac.

The climate is mild and sunny. Poitou-Charentes receives over 2,000 hours of sunlight per year, nearly as much as Ajaccio Bay in Corsica. The average temperature in July and August ranges from 64.4° to 73.4°F. The proximity to the Atlantic moderates the weather. The countryside is known for its nimbus of light and its luminous mist.

HISTORY

Lascaux cave people lived in some of the valleys of this region around 15,000 B.C. The area near Angoulême was inhabited only when Neolithic people began settling in the region around 12,000 B.C. The Megalithic civilization that followed (6,000–4,000 B.C.) left numerous dolmens, prehistoric stone structures, and covered passages in Poitou. An important wave of Celts settled in the region around 600 B.C. In 56 B.C. the Pictons, originally from northern Britain, first encountered the Roman general Crassus and his legions. Following the Roman takeover of the region, an imperial legate resided in Poitiers and Roman civilization flourished.

In the fourth century A.D., Bishop Hilaire spread Christianity in the area around Poitiers. Yet in the fifth century Visigoths came to dominate this area and established their capital in Toulouse (Midi-Pyrénées region). Their invasion was halted by Clovis's victory in 507. In the seventh century Poitiers was part of the Duchy of Aquitaine. At the same time, Arab armies invaded the region. However, Charles Martel confronted the Arab forces and defeated them near Poitiers in 732. Shortly thereafter the region witnessed a Scandinavian invasion, during which time the local nobility fortified their domains.

Beginning in the tenth century many churches and abbeys were built. This development was aided, of course, as the pilgrimage route developed to Spain's Santiago de Compostela, where the tomb of the apostle St. James is located. However, three centuries of political strife weakened the development of the Church in Poitou-Charentes. When Louis VII married Eleanor of Aquitaine and later repudiated her, a political battle arose for control over Aquitaine and its dependent areas by the houses of Valois and Plantagenet. The situation became particularly tense when Eleanor married the Plantagenet who would later be crowned Henry II, King of England. In 1204, when Eleanor of Aquitaine died, Philippe Auguste annexed Poitou for France; the area around Angoulême, however, was not annexed for another hundred years.

During the Hundred Years War the English made significant inroads in the region. Yet throughout this long conflict some degree of prosperity existed in the region as northern European merchants visited the area to secure wine and salt. This development aided the growth of the port city of La Rochelle, later a bastion of Protestantism. King Charles VII began a re-conquest of the region from the English, culminating in the victorious Battle of Castillon in 1453.

Economic development in Poitou-Charentes was greatly aided by the discovery of the New World and subsequent commerce with this area. Northern Europeans visiting the region for trade helped to spread the ideas of the Reformation. The religious reformer John Calvin taught in the Poitiers area and in Angoulême. Religious disputes were frequent here and elsewhere in France until the Edict of Nantes (1598) provided Protestants with places of refuge, one of which was La Rochelle. However, in 1627 Louis XIII laid siege to La Rochelle and his troops razed it to the ground. Revocation of the Edict of Nantes in 1685 forced many Protestants to flee the region. During the next century La Rochelle and other cities—such as Angoulême, Rochefort, and Niort—witnessed important urban development.

In earlier centuries the area now known as the Vendée was considered part of this region (the Vendée is at this time a department of the Pays de la Loire). In 1793 the Vendée, viewed as backward and reactionary by the revolutionary government in Paris, revolted against military conscription. The Vendée was not successfully pacified until the early years of Napoleon's Empire.

Although World War II brought physical destruction to the region, the post–World War II period has seen important construction projects in Poitou-Charentes. Several cities here—namely, La Rochelle and Royan—were final pockets of German resistance during the war and suffered heavy damage. Reconstruction and many public work projects followed after the war. Moreover, bridges were built to link the islands offshore to the mainland, and an Aquitaine highway was devised to link the region to Paris and the nation's major road network. In recent years, high-speed TGV train service was inaugurated from Paris to La Rochelle.

RECENT POLITICS

Since the 1992 regional elections Poitou-Charentes has seen the reemergence of the center and the right, at the expense of the left. The Socialist party (PS) won only 15.5 percent of the vote in the 1992 elections, as compared to 32 percent in 1986. The Ecologists made gains owing to concerns about the availability and quality of the water supply. The extremist and xenophobic National Front (FN) also made gains, winning 10 percent of the vote.

In the September 1992 referendum on the Maastricht Treaty to accelerate European Economic Community (EEC, Common Market) integration, 50.2 percent of the voters approved the measure (51.04% approved it on the national level). The "yes" vote in the region came mainly from urban areas, with the best scores coming from cities with a strong service sector such as Poitiers and Niort.

Parliamentary elections in 1993 confirmed the advancement of the center and the right. In the first round of voting, the center-right Union for French Democracy (UDF) and the gaullist Rally for the Republic (RPR) won 45.6 percent and 52.6 percent of the vote, respectively. The FN, on the other hand, won more than 10 percent of the vote in Charente-Maritime. Although the Ecologists did not do as well as hoped, the PS and the French Communist party (PCF) lost many voters. When the elections were over the PS had only two deputies remaining in Parliament from the region, one from Charente and one from Deux-Sèvres.

In the 1995 presidential elections, the left-wing candidates won a majority of votes only in the department of Charente, a rural department that is the birthplace of former socialist president François Mitterrand (1981–1995). Jean-Marie Le Pen representing the FN captured 9.85 percent of the vote in the region, below his 15 percent national average. In the second round of the contest the socialist candidate Lionel Jospin won only Charente in his battle against the gaullist Jacques Chirac, the eventual winner. Although the right made headway in the 1995 municipal elections, the former socialist prime minister Edith Cresson (1991–1993), the first female prime minister of France, easily won the mayor's race in Châtellerault in Vienne. Cresson won in large measure because of the traditional division on the right in her area. The PS maintained control as well in Niort and Poitiers; the diverse left maintained power in La Rochelle. The UDF retained power in Angoulême in the 1995 municipal elections.

POPULATION

Since 1975 the population of Poitou-Charentes has increased only slightly. In 1975 it stood at 1,528,000 inhabitants; in 1993 it was only 1,602,000, making the region sixteenth in population in the nation. Historically, at least for more than a century, population growth in the region has been weak. For example, the maximum total population in 1881 was not reached again until 1975. Nevertheless, population growth fell by 0.21 percent between 1982 and 1990. Today the region's birthrate, 1.65, is below the national average (1.73). For the past twenty years the rural population has seen an increase, owing in part to (1) new statistical ways of defining rural and urban, and (2) an influx of retirees. At the same time, the agricultural population fell 15 percent between 1986 and 1991, aiding the cities and their peripheries. The population density of Poitou-Charentes is 62.1 inhabitants per square kilometer (100.6 per square mile), considerably less than the national average of 105.7 inhabitants per square kilometer (171.23 per square mile).

The abundance of retirees in the region elevates the average age of the population. Roughly one out of four in the region is 60 years of age or older (one out of five is the national average); one out of four is 19 years of age or younger. The department of Vienne is less aged than the rest of the region because Poitiers, the regional capital, attracts young people seeking training, education, and jobs. Immigrants make up only a small percentage of the population, 1.6 percent, as compared to 6.3 percent for France as a whole.

The size of the urban population is considerably smaller than the national average, with 50.8 percent in Poitou-Charentes living in an urban setting (the average for France is 76.4 percent). Life expectancy, however, is slightly longer than the national average. Those residing in the region can expect to live an average of 77.9 years (77.2 years for France as a whole).

Approximately 24.1 percent of all households are single-person households, as compared to the national average of 27.1 percent.

Educational levels and the composition of the work force reflect the elderly character of the population. Approximately 9.3 percent of the inhabitants hold only a high school degree and 7.6 percent possess an advanced degree (10.5% and 11.2%, respectively, are the national averages). The agricultural work force is more than double the national average, with 13 percent of the region's work force in agriculture. The region ranks seventh in terms of rural population in France. Roughly 24.9 percent work in industry (2% below the national norm) and 62.1 percent in the service sector (67.8% for all of France). The unemployment rate is 13.3 percent, above the national average of more than 12 percent. Unemployment among women is 15.1 percent.

ECONOMY

During the nineteenth century the sea and pasturelands aided the economic development of Poitou-Charentes. In the mid-nineteenth century the development of seaside resorts and the planting of vegetation to stabilize the sand dunes paid off handsomely. For example, the wealthy middle class from Bordeaux began to visit the seaside resort of Royan and its casino. The oyster industry developed in the port city of La Rochelle, and it emerged once again as a fishing center (Louis XIII had razed it in 1627). When the wine disease phylloxera destroyed the region's vineyards between 1876 and 1882, dairy production developed and provided new income. The first agricultural cooperative opened in Surgères in 1888.

Today, even though Poitou-Charentes has a rural and agricultural character, industry in the region is diversified. The region produces agro-food products, wood products, clothing, construction materials, electric materials, automobile parts and equipment, railroad equipment, aeronautical parts, and paper products. Industries in the region are small and medium-sized enterprises; yet among the twenty largest commercial firms, there are only ten industrial concerns.

The rural and agricultural character helps explain why 14 percent of the gross domestic product comes from the agro-food industry. In fact, the region is one of the world's leading producers of cognac. The cognac industry alone—centered principally in Charente and notably around Angoulême—exports 94 percent of its production to such countries as the United States, the United Kingdom, Germany, Japan, and Thailand. This industry employs 100,000 people and represents three-fourths of the total value of all French exports of spirits. In Charente one finds distilleries such as Martel, Hennessy, Rémy-Martin, and Courvoisier. These distilleries produce roughly 250 million bottles of cognac annually. (The agricultural sector also is engaged in milk production and cattle breeding.)

La Rochelle holds the distinction of being the eighth busiest port in France. It receives imports of petroleum products, wood, minerals, and fertilizers, and it exports cereals and other agricultural products. Even though La Rochelle benefits from the tourist industry, its unemployment rate is close to 16 percent.

An increase in the number of foreigners who have purchased secondary residences has contributed to the affluence of the region's coastline. Moreover, the arrival of new industries and the growth of the retirement community have placed a new emphasis on tourism and the health industry. In fact, in the regional economy the health industry plays a significant role: among the twenty largest businesses in Poitou-Charentes, there are seven hospitals.

Between La Rochelle and Poitou is the city of Niort. The headquarters of several large insurance companies (representing approximately 12,000 jobs) are located here. Niort is also the home of the third largest French mail-order firm, CAMIF. Although the unemployment rate in Niort is 12 percent, income is 8 percent above the national average owing in part to the presence of the insurance industry.

The regional capital, Poitiers, is among the smallest of all regional capitals. A large number of jobs are found here in the service sector, especially nonretail and research positions. The city's prestigious university was founded in 1431 by Charles VII. The mathematician René Descartes (1596–1650) and the poet Joachim du Bellay (1522–1560) once taught on its faculty. Today the university has an enrollment of 23,000 students; 50 research laboratories are part of the university, 20 of which are attached to the National Center for Scientific Research (CNRS).

The three largest towns in the region are Poitiers with 78,894 inhabitants, La Rochelle with 71,094, and Niort with 57,012. Approximately 10 percent of the work force is centered in Poitiers, 8.9 percent in Angoulême, and 8.3 percent in La Rochelle. The four largest employers are the hospitals at Poitiers, La Rochelle, and Niort, and Heuliez Automobiles (manufacturers of automobile bodies).

The future economic development of this region, what some have called a region "*douce et profonde*" (gentle and traditional), may well be tied to the integration of Poitou-Charentes to the remainder of France. Even though the arrival of the high-speed TGV rail line has reduced travel time from Paris to Poitiers to one hour and fifteen minutes (and only slightly longer to La Rochelle and the coast), the region must still overcome obstacles. One is the long history of competition, not cooperation, between such towns as Poitiers, La Rochelle, Niort, and Angoulême. Another obstacle is the fact that to the north and south lie two major cities in other regions—Nantes (Pays de la Loire) and Bordeaux (Aquitaine)—that compete with Poitou-Charentes. An example of intra-regional competition occurred in 1991 when La Rochelle announced the opening of its own university; certain groups in Poitiers maintained that La Rochelle was attempting to compete with the university of the region's capital. A third obstacle is the relatively weak level of training and qualifications for jobs, and the relatively low number of managers and engineers. Consequently, salaries in the region are 13 percent below the national average. Although young people have tended to leave this region, in recent years a number have returned after acquiring job training elsewhere and being attracted to a regional lifestyle that is less costly than the national average. Placing more emphasis on educating the work force and overcoming intra-city competition appear to be two keys to strengthening the economic future of Poitou-Charentes. In this regard, the region recently decided to launch a program of advanced technological institutes.

CULTURE

One might imagine that Poitou-Charentes is the France of postcards, with a countryside that is very gentle in appearance and traditional as well. However, along the coast one finds the sights, sounds, and images of a more modern France. With excellent high-speed train service from Paris, the region is now more accessible to those seeking to discover its beauty and charm.

A number of individuals have written on the culture and traditions of Poitou-Charentes. **Honoré de Balzac**'s (1799–1850) *Les Illusions perdues* (1837, Lost Illusions) is set in the cognac-producing region of Angoulême. This great French writer sojourned in Angoulême between 1831 and 1833 and collected material there for his *Comédie humaine,* a work that examined, among other things, the differences and conflicts between the lower and newly industrialized sectors of Angoulême and the bourgeois upper town. Balzac himself was of provincial origin and sometimes weaved into his novels the theme of the opposition between Paris and the provinces. However, he was proud of his ability to adapt to Parisian life and sometimes criticized the provincial elite in his works.

The region's coastal areas, too, have inspired several writers. The contemporary feminist writer **Marguérite Duras** (1914–1996) situated her novel *Moderato cantabile* in the beachside resort of Royan, south of La Rochelle. Between Royan and La Rochelle is Rochefort, where **Pierre Loti** (1850–1923) was born. Loti became a naval officer, traveled extensively, and developed exotic oriental tastes. Many of his novels (e.g., the well-known *Pecheur d'Islande* [An Iceland Fisherman]) deal with the sea and the harsh realities of seafaring life.

La Rochelle has helped to develop a few writers as well. The Existential philosopher **Jean-Paul Sartre** (1905–1980) attended school here. **Georges Simenon** (1903–1989), the popular Belgian-born French author of detective stories, lived in this costal town for a while. Simenon described La Rochelle in his work *Le Voyageur*. **Eugéne Fromentin** (1820–1876), an artist and art critic, was born in La Rochelle. He authored a romantic novel, *Dominique,* that focuses on a never-consummated love relationship.

The British writer **Charles Morgan,** a true Francophile, wrote a novel called *The Voyage* that deals with the area around the town of Cognac. The book was better received in France than it was in Britain.

The centuries-old art of Poitou-Charentes is characterized by joyous figures on church portals and the mysticism of frescoes on Romanesque churches. Moreover, manor houses and chateaux in the countryside suggest the wealth and tastes of the region's inhabitants. Refinement is also found in the gentle simmered dishes that are well known among both ordinary food lovers and gourmands.

Seafood, poultry, and beef dishes are popular in Poitou-Charentes. The seafood dishes include oysters, mussels, shrimp, eel, lobster, trout, stuffed carp, sardines, salmon, and shad. *Chaudrée* is the region's version of fish soup. Poultry dishes include *Bressuire* hen, and goose prepared with chestnuts. Meat dishes include ribs of beef and veal. Popular vegetables are beans from the marshy area, salad dressed with walnut oil, and stuffed lettuce. More than fifty types of goat's milk cheese are produced. Included among the sweets are *angélique* from Niort, sugar-preserved chestnuts, cheesecake, *duchesse de l'Angoumois* (a chocolate dessert), and nougatine and macaroons. Below is a recipe for a soup that can be served hot or cold; it makes an excellent accompaniment to many meals.

SOUPE À L'OSEILLE
(Sorrel Soup from Poitou)

½ lb. fresh sorrel, or 1 bunch watercress	4 medium potatoes, peeled and cubed (about 3 cups)
salt and freshly ground black pepper to taste	2 large eggs
	¾ cup heavy cream

Wash and spin dry the sorrel, and then pull off the stems.

In a saucepan over low heat, combine the sorrel and 1 teaspoon of water. Stir occasionally and cook until most of the liquid is absorbed. Add 1½ quarts of water and salt and pepper to taste. Bring water to a boil; add potatoes and cook over low heat for 15 to 20 minutes. Leave the mixture as is, or purée it in a food processor.

Combine eggs and heavy cream in a warmed soup tureen, and mix until blended. Add a portion of the potato and sorrel mixture and blend well. Pour in remaining potato and sorrel mixture. Serve immediately or cold. Serves 4–6.

ARCHITECTURE AND NOTEWORTHY SITES

In the rural areas, especially around Poitiers, houses tend to be widely separated; some local villages comprise sixty or more rather isolated dwellings. Houses in Charente tend to be symmetrical and single-storied. Limestone is the usual building material. Sometimes a low wall at the front of the house surrounds a flower garden. Off the coast, the island houses have white-washed exteriors with painted shutters and colorful flowers.

POITIERS (pop. 78,894) is a city rich in architecture and monuments, especially Christian. St. Hilaire was elected Bishop of Poitiers in the fourth century A.D. and played a leading role in the conversion of Gaul. Poitiers clearly reflects its important role in the rise and spread of Christianity. The *Église Notre-Dame-la-Grande* was a major sanctuary for pilgrims during the Middle Ages. It is an excellent example of local Romanesque architecture that emerged around 1140; there is rich ornamentation on the facade. The *Église St. Hilaire-le-Grande* dates from the eleventh and twelfth centuries. This Romanesque edifice was a significant staging post for pilgrims on route to Santiago de Compostela in Spain. The *Baptistère St. Jean* is one of France's oldest Christian monuments. The *Musée Ste. Croix* displays artifacts of classical and medieval archaeology and fine arts. On the former ramparts one finds the *Parc de Blossac,* offering a view over the Clain valley. *Futuroscope,* the European Park of the Moving Image, is located 7.5 miles north of Poitiers. The park is a leisure complex that uses the latest advances in visual image technology in various cinemas.

LA ROCHELLE (pop. 71,094) was a formidable seaport during the fourteenth through seventeenth centuries. The city's ship owners were among the first to establish trade links with the New World. A significant number of French settlers who migrated to Canada, including the founders of Montreal, set sail from this port in the seventeenth century. As noted earlier, the city was a Protestant stronghold and was besieged by Louis XIII. In the fourteenth century the city built two towers to protect the port; between these two towers a large chain was stretched to safeguard the harbor's entrance. The towers still remain today. There is also an imposing clock tower that dates from the fourteenth century. For a contrast to many of France's Catholic churches, one can visit the *Temple Protestant* that served the Protestant community from 1563 to 1628 when the city was besieged. The City Hall has a flamboyant Gothic outer wall from the fifteenth century and a Renaissance courtyard from the sixteenth. The *Musée du Nouveau Monde* displays artifacts of early French exploration and settlement of the New World, including Quebec and Louisiana. The *Musée de la Dernière Guerre,* housed in a German bunker, shows life during the German Occupation. Given the city's important status as a seaport, it also has a maritime museum, an aquarium, and an oceanographic museum. The largest pleasure-craft port on the European Atlantic seaboard is found at Les Minimes, less than 2 miles south of the city, where there is also a beach. In mid-July of each year the city hosts a week-long festival called *Francofolies* that brings together musicians and artists from other parts of the French-speaking world. At the end of June a ten-day international film festival is held as well.

NIORT (pop. 57,012) has become the center of the insurance business; half the town's residents work in the service sector. The town was once a cloth and leather center. The church of *Notre-Dame* is known for its tapestries. Niort also has an interesting museum for arts and local customs, the *Musée Ethnographique du Donjon,* an archaeological museum at the *Hôtel du Pilori,* and a fine arts museum (the *Musée des Beaux-Arts*). A pleasant botanical garden is terraced along the Sèvre River.

ANGOULÊME (pop. 42,876) is situated on the Charente River and on a hilltop surrounded by ramparts. A commercial and industrial center, the town is considered one of the main towns of western France. Although the castle of the Counts of Angoulême no longer exists, two of its towers dating to the thirteenth and fifteenth centuries are still standing. In the old quarter are houses from the Renaissance and Louis XIV's era. The twelfth-century cathedral has an interesting facade and a tall Romanesque bell tower. There is the *Musée archéologique de la Charente* and a fine art museum, the *Musée Municipal.*

SAINTES (pop. 25,874), in addition to being one of the richest small towns in France in terms of monuments and museums, has become a large regional market and a center for craft work and industry. The town is situated on the Charente River. Here one finds ruins of Roman baths, a Roman amphitheater, and an arch—Germanicus's Arch—erected in A.D. 19 to honor the Roman emperor Tiberius. The *Ste. Marie* church was built during the eleventh and twelfth centuries; it has an interesting doorway, facade, and bell tower. The *Musée Dupuy Mestreau* displays artifacts of history, regional arts, and traditions.

COGNAC (pop. 19,528) is a town transformed by the brandy trade. It was once a small craft post where François I was born in 1494. When the process of brandy distillation was discovered in the seventeenth century, the town changed radically and warehouses for wine and spirits opened along the river. Here one can visit the wine cellars that have generated prosperity for the town and the surrounding area. Nearby is the small town of Jarnac (pop. 4,786), the birthplace of former president François Mitterrand (1981–1995). Jarnac is also the home of the well-known Courvoisier distillery, which can be visited.

ÎLE D'OLERON (pop. 16,841) sits less than 2 miles off the coast to the west of Rochefort. It is France's largest Atlantic island, comprising 47 square miles. On the western coast of the island are massive sand dunes, some almost 100 feet high. Flowers grow well here in the mild climate. In February the island hosts a mimosa festival. Fishing, oyster farming, and tourism are main industries. The Île d'Oleron is connected to the mainland by a viaduct.

ROYAN (pop. 16,837), a beach resort, was established in the nineteenth century. It has a number of beaches, bays, and parks. It was rebuilt after suffering damage in World War II. Royan is the largest seaside resort between Biarritz in Aquitaine and La Baule in Brittany.

ÎLE DE RÉ (pop. 11,396) is situated off the coast to the west of La Rochelle; the island is 17.5 miles long and 2–3 miles wide. It produces wine, vegetables, and oysters. Tourism is also a key industry. The island is popular with sun and beach worshippers.

SELECT BIBLIOGRAPHY

Arlaud, Samuel. "Poitou-Charentes," in André Gamblin, ed., *La France dans ses régions,* vol 2. Paris: SEDES, 1994.

Labande, E.-R. *Histoire du Poitou, du Limousin et du pays charentais.* Toulouse: Privat, 1976.

Luneau, J. "Poitou-Charentes," in Y. Lacoste, ed., *Géopolitiques des régions françaises,* vol. 2. Paris: Fayard, 1986.

PROVENCE
(PROVENCE-ALPES-CÔTE D'AZUR)

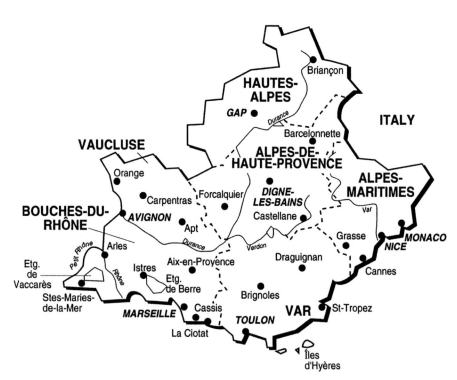

Chapter 21

PROVENCE
(Provence-Alpes-Côte d'Azur)

REGIONAL GEOGRAPHY

Located in the southeastern corner of France, this region—officially known as Provence-Alpes-Côte d'Azur but hereafter referred to as Provence—stretches from the Italian border to the Camargue, the salt marshes west of Marseille. The famous French Riviera is located here between Marseille and the Italian frontier. The region borders both sides of the Rhône River and extends just north of Orange. It comprises 19,383 square miles, 5.8 percent of the surface area of France, and includes six departments: Alpes-de-Haute-Provence, Hautes-Alpes, Alpes-Maritimes, Bouches-du-Rhône, Var, and Vaucluse. The region's capital is Marseille.

In terms of geography, Provence is quite varied. On the Mediterranean coast are beautiful beaches—normally pebbled, not sand—as well as the marshes of the Camargue, which is actually a delta of the Rhône River. The Rhône and the Petit Rhône flow through the western portion of the region. To the west of Arles lies the Gorges d'Ardèche, created by the often overflowing Ardèche River. To the east of the Rhône are the region's well-known mountains: Mont Ventoux (painted by Paul Cézanne and other artists), the Baronnies, the Vaucluse plateau, the Lubéron range, and the Alpilles. In the eastern part of the region is the spectacular canyon known as the Gorges du Verdon.

The Mediterranean climate of Provence is ideal, especially along the Côte d'Azur. It varies somewhat according to altitude and exposure. There can be heavy rains in spring and autumn; winter is extremely mild along the coast; summer is usually hot and dry. The region is especially known for its bright, sunny skies. In fact, for several centuries painters such as Vincent

Van Gogh, Pablo Picasso, and Paul Cézanne have been intrigued by the quality of its light. However, the region is susceptible to the Mistral, a strong wind that blows down the Rhône valley. Flying roof tiles and up-rooted trees are common when the Mistral blows at peak velocity, some-times approaching 100 miles per hour. It has also been known to fan forest fires. Nevertheless, the mistral has a positive side: it clears away the clouds and contributes to the big, bright sky that is so characteristic of this popular region.

HISTORY

Provence was inhabited by the Ligurians, the Celts, and the Greeks cen-turies before the birth of Christ. It began to flourish, however, after Julius Caesar conquered the area in the first century A.D. and integrated it into the Roman Empire. Well-preserved feats of Roman architecture and engi-neering, such as arenas, theaters, aqueducts, and arches, are still visible in towns such as Arles and Orange.

Following the fall of the Roman Empire in 476, Provence was invaded by the Visigoths, Burgundians, and Ostrogoths. For a time the Arabs con-trolled the Iberian Peninsula and parts of southern France; yet they were defeated and driven out during the eighth century by Charles Martel. In time the Franks peacefully integrated the region, creating a Territory of Provence that was tied to Burgundy and ruled by counts and viscounts. In 972 William the Liberator (who won his title by taking a provençal fort from the Saracens) instituted the first dynasty of the Counts of Provence. For centuries it remained a distinct area, passing by marriage to the Counts of Catalonia and later to the House of Anjou. During the fourteenth cen-tury the Church—under French popes—moved papal headquarters from Rome to Avignon. In 1481 Charles de Maine bequeathed the region to King Louis XI of France. Nevertheless, Avignon remained under papal con-trol until the French Revolution of 1789.

The sixteenth and seventeenth centuries witnessed important economic changes in Provence. Agriculture changed drastically as wine and mulberry production and the silk industry spread. Yet sheep and corn remained the heart of the economy. During this period shipbuilding developed as well, with Toulon becoming the largest naval port on the Mediterranean (it was surpassed by Marseille during the eighteenth century). Other thriving in-dustries were tanning, paper-making, textiles, pottery, and roof tiles. How-ever, disaster struck Provence in 1720 with the outbreak of plague; Marseille alone lost 38,000 people—half the population at the time—and Provence as a whole lost 100,000 inhabitants.

Following the French Revolution, political reorganization took place in the region. In 1860 Savoy and Nice were annexed to France in return for

Napoleon III's support for Italian independence. In the following years, France purchased Menton and Roquebrune from the Prince of Monaco.

During the nineteenth century the opening of the Paris-Lyon-Marseille rail line, coupled with the popularity of Nice as a winter resort for the British and Russian aristocracy, transformed the Côte d'Azur into a premier resort destination. Even today the Riviera is world-famous as a place of leisure, especially during the summer.

RECENT POLITICS

Over the past decade the right—especially the extreme right of the xenophobic and nationalistic National Front (FN)—has made gains in Provence. Even though the traditional right—the gaullist Rally for the Republic (RPR) and the Union for French Democracy (UDF)—cooperated with the FN on the regional level between 1986 and 1992, intense rivalry brought an end to this cooperation in the 1992 regional elections. The 1993 legislative elections revealed the discontent of the electorate in Provence and the depth of the economic crisis. Compared to the 1992 regional elections, in the 1993 parliamentary elections the traditional right saw its share of the votes increase from 32 percent to 35 percent, the extreme right regressed from 24 percent to 21 percent, the presidential majority (the Socialist party) fell from 23 percent to 15 percent, the Ecologists stabilized their votes at around 10.7 percent, and the French Communist party (PCF) jumped from 8.6 percent to 11.5 percent. Abstentions in the 1993 election increased to 36 percent (29% in 1992). Before the election the left (the socialists, the communists, and their supporters) had seventeen deputies in Parliament from this region; but in 1993 its representation fell to only five, as the right saw its representation in the National Assembly rise from twenty-three to thirty-five. In the past Provence had been a stronghold of the left. Yet after the death in 1986 of the socialist mayor of Marseille, Gaston Defferre, the left has had difficulty mobilizing the region's voters. The socialist entrepreneur Bernard Tapie, owner of the famed Marseille soccer team, has tried to rally the left; however, Tapie and his soccer team have suffered from serious scandals. Consequently the right, including the extreme right, has emerged as a powerful force in Provence.

The 1995 presidential and municipal elections confirmed this trend. In the first round of the presidential contest the leftist candidates out-scored the right in only two departments: Alpes-de-Haute Provence and Bouches-du-Rhône. Also in the first round the National Front's candidate, Jean-Marie Le Pen, won an average of almost 20 percent of the vote in the region. In the second round the gaullist candidate Jacques Chirac, running against the socialist Lionel Jospin, captured all six departments in the region. Chirac also won on the national level and succeeded François Mitterrand as president of France. The June 1995 municipal elections that followed saw the National Front win the city halls of Toulon, Orange, and Marignane (an aerospace industry center north of Marseille). Toulon is the first city of over 100,000 inhabitants to be controlled by the National Front. Moreover, a former FN member and friend of Le Pen's, Jacques Peyrat, was elected mayor of Nice. Following the municipal elections some people in France called for a boycott of the towns captured by the extremist FN. In the same election the center-right UDF took control of Marseille after forty-eight years of leftist rule; the RPR won Avignon. The socialists, however, captured Arles and retained power in Vitrolles.

POPULATION

For a long while Provence has absorbed various migrations. In 1962 some 400,000 French settlers in North Africa migrated to the region following the granting of independence to Algeria. This was followed by a general stream of immigrants from North Africa. Migration to Provence has also come from within France (especially older people seeking a milder climate to enjoy in their retirement years) and from the international community. Consequently, the diverse population is one of the main characteristics of the region today.

Over the past fifteen years the population of Provence has increased steadily. In 1975 it stood at 3,676,000; by 1993 it had climbed to 4,380,000, roughly 7.6 percent of the total population of France. Over the past century the number of people living in the region has doubled. In recent decades the increase is attributed to immigration; for example, between 1982 and 1990 it contributed to three-quarters of the population increase. The birthrate, 1.79, approximates the national average of 1.73. Population density in Provence is considerably higher than the average for France as a whole. Today there are 139.5 inhabitants per square kilometer (225.99 per square mile); the average for France is 105.7 per square kilometer (171.23 per square mile).

Because the region has become a favorite area for retirees, the population is more elderly than the national average. Those 60 years of age or older make up 22.7 percent of the population (19.7% is the national average), and those 19 years old or younger make up 24.8 percent of all inhabitants (26.8% is the national average). Foreign immigrants make up roughly 7 percent of the population—slightly higher than the national average of 6.3 percent—with relatively heavy immigrant concentrations along the Mediterranean coast.

The urban population in Provence is above the national average, and life expectancy mirrors the nation as a whole. The urban population stands at 89.8 percent (76.4% is the average for France). Life expectancy is 77 years of age, as compared to 77.2 years for France as a whole. Roughly 28.3

percent of all households in Provence are single-family households, above the 27.1 percent average for the nation.

Educational levels are higher than the national averages, and in the region's work force there is a large service sector. Approximately 11.9 percent of those residing in Provence hold a high school diploma, and 11.6 percent possess an advanced degree (10.5% and 11.2%, respectively, are the national averages). Of the work force, a mere 2.8 percent are in agriculture (5.3% for France as a whole), 19.3 percent are in industry (below the 26.9% national average), and 77.9 percent are in the service sector (67.8% for France as a whole). Unemployment is higher in Provence than in France as a whole, with roughly 16.1 percent being out of work in the region. Unemployment among women is 15.5 percent.

ECONOMY

Tourism and leisure activities—coupled with industry, especially around Fos-sur-Mer near Marseille and the high-tech research center Sophia-Antipolis near Cannes and Nice—account for many of the new jobs that have been created in the region. The increase in the service industry, the influx of retired people, and the arrival of many young and well-trained workers strengthen the possibility for more job creation in the future.

There are several unique characteristics of the region's economy. First, there is a large service sector. In fact, the region has the third largest service sector in all of France, after the Île de France and Rhône-Alpes. Jobs are increasing faster in this sector than in other sectors of the economy; many jobs are related to hotels, cafés, restaurants, business services, and the health industry. Second, many jobs are concentrated in specific areas—for instance, more than 100,000 jobs are located along the Mediterranean coast. In Marseille there are roughly 335,000, in Nice 208,400, in Toulon 168,200, and in Cannes-Antibes 127,300. Also, along the coast a considerable part of industry is owned by groups outside the region and by foreign concerns. Major activities in Provence include shipworks at Marseille and the electronics industry in the department of Alpes-Maritimes, especially around Cannes and Nice. The area further inland is less developed, with employment zones ranging from 20,000 to 50,000 jobs.

The busiest port in France is Marseille, which handled more than 90 million tons of goods in 1991. It is generally ranked the second or third busiest port in Europe. It benefits from its location right on the Mediterranean and its proximity to the industrial area Fos-sur-Mer, which has metallurgy and petrochemical industries.

Agriculture plays a very small role in the region's economy, mainly in the production of fruit, vegetables, and flowers. The numerous outdoor markets in the region offer clear evidence of this specialization.

The three largest towns are Marseille with 800,500 inhabitants (Marseille–Aix-en-Provence 1,230,936), Nice with 342,439 (greater Nice 516,740), and Toulon with 167,619 (greater Toulon 437,553). These three towns rank among the nine largest in France. Roughly 31 percent of the work force of the region is found in Marseille–Aix-en-Provence (Aix is a famous university town just north of Marseille), 13 percent in Nice, and 9.8 percent in Toulon. The four largest employers in Provence are Direction Construction Armes Naval, Aérospatiale (aeronautics), SOLLAC (metallurgy), and the Commissariat à l'Énergie Atomique.

Although a large percentage of jobs is located near the coast where economic development has been the greatest, there is less economic opportunity inland. The beautiful coastline and high-tech industries of the Côte d'Azur, especially at Sophia-Antipolis above Cannes, give this area a California-like facade. Along the coast it is estimated that one-fourth of all tourists come from abroad. (Recently, tourism has declined in Provence, while Languedoc-Roussillon and the Atlantic coast have witnessed large increases in tourism.) Clearly, the economic challenge is to continue the development of the region (especially the inland area) and to aid the poor (especially the immigrant population) in cities such as Marseille. Economically as well as socially and geographically, Provence is a region of contrasts.

CULTURE

During the Middle Ages *occitan* was spoken in the south of France and French was spoken in the north. *Occitan* was referred to as *langue d'oc—languedoc* and *provençal* in its medieval literary form. *Provençal* was the literary language of southern France and northern Spain from the twelfth to the thirteenth centuries. In the south of France, including Provence, occitan is still spoken, especially by older people in rural areas.

In the mid-nineteenth century a movement known as the *Félibrige* sought to revive provençal literature. A key member of this movement was **Frédéric Mistral** (1830–1914). Besides writing poems, short stories, and other works, he edited a provençal language periodical and worked on a provençal dictionary. In 1904 Mistral received the Nobel Prize for literature. In the twentieth century, the novels of **Marcel Pagnol** (1895–1974) have helped to maintain an interest in Provençal folklore. Several of his novels have been made into films and released under the titles *Jean de Florette* and *Manon des Sources*. (Pagnol himself made the original version of these films in 1953).

Provence has attracted and inspired a large number of writers and artists. One such writer was **Alphonse Daudet** (1840–1897). Although he was born in Nîmes and lived in Paris, he often stayed with friends near Arles. He is known for a number of works, including the romantic drama *L'Arlésienne* and the trilogy *Tartarin de Tarascon* that caricatures the exuberant and boastful provençal character. He is also known for *Lettres de mon moulin*

(1866, Letters from My Mill), a collection of quaint tales that schoolchildren read.

Pagnol, mentioned above, was a great storyteller, filmmaker, and playwright in addition to being a novelist. Many of his stories are set near the small town of Aubagne to the east of Marseille (Aubagne today is the home of the French Foreign Legion.) Based on his life in Aubagne as a youth, his best-selling trilogy of memoirs, *Souvenirs d'enfance,* recounts provençal life in the south of France. Many of his works portray the lives of a picturesque, but backward, witty, and less-than-efficient peasantry.

Jean Giono (1895–1970), son of a provençal cobbler and a man of little formal education, sketched interesting portraits of the landscape and the natural world in his novels. Many of his works suggest that it is the simple peasant who is blessed with the riches of life, not the educated or city folk. One of his best-known works is the Pan trilogy, which tells of peasants battling with nature in beautiful settings. Besides focusing on themes of nature and ecology, Giono, who fought in the trenches in World War I, also espoused pacifism, especially in his novel *Le Grand Troupeau* (1931, The Large Flock). The Pétain regime during the war years exploited his back-to-nature campaign for propaganda purposes.

Another writer from Provence is **Henri Bosco** (1888–1978), who was born in Avignon. His work in many ways resembles that of Giono. Bosco examines men and women and their relationship to the landscape and their struggles. *Le Mas Théotime* (Farmhouse in Provence) is probably his best-known work.

One twentieth-century writer from the region who is held in high regard is **René Char** (1907–1988). Born near Avignon, he spent most of his life there with some periods in Paris. He began as a surrealist but broke with the movement and developed his own style of verse and prose poems, which are sometimes rather obscure.

A number of other writers have been inspired by Provence. The astrologer and prophet **Michel de Nostradamus** was born in St. Rémy in 1503 and lived for a long while in Salon de Provence. The nineteenth-century writer **Emile Zola** (1840–1902) spent his boyhood in Aix-en-Provence, which is featured in one of his novels. The famous Existentialist **Albert Camus** (1913–1960) spent the last years of his life just north of Aix.

A number of places in Provence, but especially Avignon, have inspired a number of foreign writers. The Italian poet and scholar **Petrarch** (1304–1374) lived in Avignon and the surrounding area during his youth. Avignon, its environs, and a French woman whom he met in the area inspired some of his best works, such as his Italian poems. In the contemporary period the British author **Lawrence Durrell** (1912–1991) has written about Avignon and the region in general. His *Monsieur* and *Prince of Darkness* reveal many of the charming aspects of this sun-baked town with its tile roofs, narrow walkways, and natural simplicity.

The famous beachfront of Provence has attracted both French and foreign writers for decades. French writers who spent time on the Côte d'Azur include **Prosper Mérimée** (1803–1870), **Guy de Maupassant** (1850–1893), **André Gide** (1869–1951), and **Albert Camus** (1913–1960). In recent years the socialist politician and historian **Max Gallo** (b. 1932) has written a trilogy of novels entitled *La Baie des Anges* that focuses on his native Nice. The first novel of the well-known contemporary writer **Françoise Sagan** (b. 1935) was set on the Côte d'Azur.

The beauty of the coast has also attracted foreign writers. The English writer **Tobias Smollett** (1721–1771) spent several months on the Riviera between 1763 and 1765 and then wrote *Travels through France and Italy*. In the nineteenth century the German philosopher **Friedrich Nietzsche** (1844–1900) often stayed in Nice. In the twentieth century the English author **Somerset Maugham** (1874–1965) lived on the Riviera for forty years. The English novelist **D.H. Lawrence** (1885–1930) went to the Côte d'Azur for health reasons and stayed in Bandol and Vence, where he eventually died. The American writer **F. Scott Fitzgerald** (1896–1940) also knew the pleasures of the coast; his work *Tender Is the Night* (1934) is set on the Riviera. The New Zealand–born British writer **Katherine Mansfield** (1888–1923) also spent time in Bandol and Menton near the Italian border. The English writers **Anthony Burgess** (b. 1917) and **Graham Greene** (1904–1991) both resided on the Côte d'Azur. In recent years, the British advertising executive-turned-writer **Peter Mayle** (b. 1939) lived in Provence and wrote highly romanticized accounts of life in the inland areas of the region. Mayle's *A Year in Provence* and *Toujours Provence* were both runaway best-sellers. His works have helped to popularize Provence within the English-speaking world.

The beauty, climate, and brilliant blue sky of Provence, among other factors, have also attracted artists. Some who have lived in the region include **Paul Cézanne** (1839–1906), **Pablo Picasso** (1881–1973), **Vincent Van Gogh** (1853–1890), and **Pierre Bonnard** (1867–1947). Cézanne, born in Aix, is known for his landscapes—especially of Mont Ste. Victoire near his place of birth—his still-lifes, and occasional portraits. His simple style, emphasizing the relationship of forms and color, contributed to the rise of cubism. Picasso, although born in Spain, after World War II spent much of his life in Provence. Influenced by Cézanne and the form of African masks, he broke up forms and presented them in angular designs. Picasso, along with his collaborator Georges Braque (1882–1963), created a revolutionary art form known as cubism. One of Picasso's best-known works is *Guernica*, a mural protesting the German bombing of the Basque capital of Guernica during the Spanish Civil War. Van Gogh, the Dutch post-Impressionist, spent a number of years near Arles and painted the people and countryside scenes of this area. One of his well-known paintings inspired by Provence is his portrait of the postman Joseph-Etienne Roulin (1889).

Today Provence is also known for its festivals, especially summer festivals, that feature music, dance, and theater. The best-known festivals are held at Aix, Avignon, Arles, and Orange. These productions are normally of high quality and attract visitors from the rest of France and from abroad. At other times of the year there are additional festivals that have contributed to the region's reputation. In May, Cannes hosts the famous International Film Festival. Nice sponsors the Carnaval de Nice at Mardi Gras.

A typical male pastime in Provence is *pétanque*, a game that is played in the south in general and throughout France. The ideal climate, especially along the coast, makes this a great favorite in the south. Pétanque is a form of lawn bowling, but it is played on a natural dirt or gravel surface. Most cities, towns, and villages in Provence, as well as the rest of France, have an area where men of all ages gather to roll steel balls toward a small rubber target some distance away. The game can be played by two individuals or by teams.

Other pastimes include sunbathing, café sitting, and dining. The beautiful Côte d'Azur makes Provence ideal for sun worshippers. Beaches stretch from the Italian border to Marseille (e.g., those below the *Promenade des Anglais* at Nice or the small *Plage Bestuan* at Cassis near Marseille). Most of the beaches are public, but some are private where one can rent a beach pad or chaise lounge and be served drinks by a roving waiter. The beaches along the Côte d'Azur are pebbled, not sand; only east of Marseille to the Spanish border can sun worshippers find sand beaches. It is not uncommon for women to bathe topless along the Côte d'Azur. There are a few nudist beaches as well.

When in Provence, one sometimes wonders if the inhabitants invented and perfected the art of café sitting. The climate and the brilliant blue sky of this region make it an excellent area in which to partake of a café, many of which have outdoor tables. One of the most beautiful café streets in all of France is the Cour Mirabeau in the university town of Aix. It is lined with large arching trees, ancient fountains, and numerous sidewalk cafés where one can sit for hours and watch the world pass by—indeed, in Aix one finds people from all over the world who come to see the charm of this pleasant town and region.

Enjoying the regional cuisine is another favorite pastime in Provence. It is one of the things that have made this region the most popular in France. Two principal ingredients in much of provençal cooking are olive oil and tomatoes. Dishes listed as *à la provençal* are prepared with garlic-seasoned tomatoes. The region is sometimes referred to as "the garden of France" because of the abundance of locally grown fruit (grapes, cherries, strawberries, figs, apricots, plums, peaches, pears, quince, and melons), vegetables (artichokes, tomatoes, squash, onions, etc.), and spices (garlic and a variety of herbs). Truffles are also found here. Vegetables comprise the traditional staple diet, served as either gratins, in salads, or filled with meat. *Soupe au pistou* is also popular; it is made with summer vegetables, vermicelli, and *pistou*—a garlic, basil, cheese, and olive oil paste. *Ratatouille* is a well-known dish from the region; it is made by stewing together tomatoes, eggplant, squash, green peppers, garlic, and various herbs. A famous fish stew found in the region is *bouillabaisse*, which is made of several kinds of fish cooked in a broth with onions, tomatoes, saffron, and other herbs. One normally adds small pieces of toast and *rouille*, a spicy sauce, to this fish stew. *Bouillabaisse* is often served as a main course. Seafood in general is popular along the coast, especially a variety of fish, mussels, and oysters. Also popular, especially in Marseille, is a variety of couscous, a rice-like grain from North Africa that is topped with vegetables and meat. Meat dishes in general are often served as a *daube*, braised with garlic, bay or clover, and vegetables.

The region's best-known and finest vineyard is Chateauneuf-du-Pape, which produces a full-bodied red wine high in alcoholic content. This wine is produced near Orange. Côte du Rhône, another red wine, is produced along a 125-mile stretch that extends from near Marseille to just south of Lyon. From Aix to the Var River one finds Côte de Provence, an ordinary wine that comes in reds, rosés, and whites. Another favorite drink is *pastis*, a licorice-flavored *apéritif*. Below is a recipe for *ratatouille*, which some consider to be "the taste of Provence." It is served hot as a vegetable garnish or cold as a first course during the summer.

RATATOUILLE NIÇOISE
(Ratatouille Nice-Style)

1 medium eggplant	1 bay leaf
3 medium zucchini	1 sprig fresh thyme or ¼ tsp. dried thyme
1 medium red bell pepper	
1 medium green bell pepper	1 tbs. chopped fresh basil
8 tbs. olive oil	1 tbs. rosemary leaves
2 large onions, sliced	1 tbs. tomato paste
1 lb. tomatoes, peeled, seeded, and diced	salt and freshly ground black pepper to taste
3 cloves of garlic, finely chopped	

Cut eggplant and zucchini into slices, 1½ inches long and ¼ inch wide. Slice off ends of peppers and take out ribs and seeds. Cut peppers the same size as eggplant and zucchini.

In a large frying pan heat 3 tablespoons of olive oil over high heat. Add eggplant and zucchini and sauté until golden brown. Using slotted spoon, remove from pan and drain on paper towels.

In a large saucepan heat remaining 5 tablespoons of olive oil over low heat. Add onions and peppers and cook until soft. Add tomatoes, garlic, herbs, tomato paste, and sautéed zucchini and eggplant. Season with salt and pepper. Without stirring, simmer over low heat for approximately 20 minutes. Serves 4–6.

ARCHITECTURE AND NOTEWORTHY SITES

Dwellings in Provence are often clustered in country towns on the plain or perched on the side of mountains. This pattern of habitation is related to the notion that highly clustered towns and villages are more defensible than other patterns. Many houses in Provence villages have been restored by foreigners or the French themselves seeking a secondary residence or a vacation house. In many village houses in the region one finds on the first floor a living room/dining room/kitchen combination; on the second floor are the bedrooms. In traditional villages in the region and in similar villages throughout France, the house is the woman's domain, whereas the village square, café, and *pétanque (boule)* field are the man's domains.

Isolated dwellings are normally called *mas, bastides,* or *domaines.* A *mas* is a house with a small plot of land; on the plain the *mas* is usually two storeys, but three storeys in the hills. A *domaine* is larger than a *mas;* it is a large estate that includes the farmhouse itself and several outbuildings, staff quarters, workshops, and the like. A *bastide* is traditionally a prosperous city dweller's house. Many *bastides* are located near towns on the western coast of the region and near Aix.

Many dwellings in Provence are made of stone and are faced with a plaster material called *crépi.* Brightly painted shutters often adorn houses in the region. Tile roofs are standard, as in the south of France in general.

Somewhat unique to the region is the *cabanon,* a shed or shack built as temporary habitation or as storage space, or as a place simply to escape domestic order.

MARSEILLE (pop. 800,500; Marseille-Aix 1,230,936) is France's third largest city after Paris and Lyon. This port city, the gateway to North Africa, is not beautiful and sophisticated like Paris, but it is interesting. A walk down *Le Canebière,* the main traffic artery of central Marseille, reveals the social and ethnic diversity of the city. In atmosphere Marseille is atypical of Provence, mainly because of its diverse population. Many who reside in Marseille are immigrants or descendants of immigrants (North Africans, Muslims, *pieds-noirs* [former colonists from Algeria], West Africans, Indo-Chinese, Jews, Greeks, Italians, Armenians, Spanish, and others). The crime rate is relatively high in Marseille, and racial tensions are sometimes pronounced. In this regard the extreme right does well in elections here, often winning more than 20 percent of the vote. The varied social and ethnic composition, the long history of the city (founded in 600 B.C. by Greek mariners from Asia Minor), and the bustling old port make Marseille an interesting place to visit. Noteworthy museums include the *Centre de la Vieille Charité,* which has a good permanent collection and thought-provoking temporary exhibits. At the *Musée du Vieux Marseille* one can see provençal household items, including playing cards (the city has long been known for the production of playing cards) and photos of this port city under German occupation. The *Musée des Docks Romains* displays first-century A.D. Roman warehouses and docks. Perched on the highest point in the city and just south of the old port is the *Basilique Notre Dame de la Garde,* an enormous nineteenth-century Romano-Byzantine basilica. Panoramic views are found here. The main beach, *Plage Gaston Defferre* (named after the city's long-time socialist mayor), is 2.5 miles south of the city.

NICE (pop. 342,439; greater Nice 516,740), founded in 350 B.C. by Greek seafarers, is considered the capital of the Riviera. Popular during the Victorian era as a winter resort for the British and other European aristocracies, Nice today is known as a summer resort par excellence. Besides possessing beaches that attract many French and international tourists, a number of well-known casinos, and a charming old town, Nice is blessed with fine museums. The *Musée d'Art Moderne* features French and American avant-garde works since the 1960s. The *Musée Matisse* has a fine collection of works by Henri Matisse (1869–1954), who moved to the Côte d'Azur in the 1920s. The *Musée Chagall* (Marc Chagall) is also located in Nice, as well as the *Musée des Beaux-Arts Jules Chéret.* The *Musée Masseno* has an electric collection of paintings, furniture, ceramics, and the like. In Nice, too, is the *Musée d'Art Naif,* which features naive art from around the world. There is also the *Musée d'Archéologie* and the nearby *Gallo-Roman Ruins.* Near Nice is the picturesque hilltop village of St. Paul de Vence, home to a number of artists and writers; nearby is the famous *Fondation Maeght,* an important center for contemporary art that features works by artists such as Braque, Bonnard, Matisse, and Miro. (Across the bay from Nice is Antibes, a beautiful little seaside town that has attracted many artists over the years. The *Musée Picasso* in Antibes contains paintings, lithographs, drawings, and ceramics by this cubist painter and memorabilia from his life.) In Nice itself, a lively carnival known as the *Carnaval de Nice* is held at Mardi Gras. In France, Nice is known for more than its festival, art, beaches, and climate. In recent years the city has developed a reputation for its right-wing political climate. Like Marseille, Nice is one of the strongholds of Jean-Marie Le Pen's extremist National Front. Moreover, the city's municipal government has known its share of corruption. In 1992, for instance, mayor Jacques Médcin fled to Uruguay prior to his conviction in absentia for the misuse of public funds.

TOULON (pop. 167,619; greater Toulon 437,553) is the home base of France's Mediterranean fleet. The city suffered heavy bombardment in World War II. Although Toulon is not known for its museums and cultural life, it is known for its rugby team. In many ways, Toulon is atypical of cities and towns along the Côte d'Azur.

AIX-EN-PROVENCE (123,842) is a beautiful and sophisticated university town with a student population of roughly 30,000. Outside of Paris some of the most expensive real estate in France is found around Aix. The town was founded by the Romans in 123 B.C. as a military camp on the site of thermal springs. Today it is known as a town of fountains, art, and students. The main thoroughfare is called the *Cour Mirabeau*, after the orator and politician the Comte de Mirabeau (1749–1791) who played a key role in the early phase of the French Revolution. Mirabeau and the painter Paul Cézanne were both natives of Aix. Cézanne's studio can be visited here. The *Musée Granet* exhibits Celtic statues and Roman artifacts; works of Italian, Dutch, and French artists from the sixteenth to the nineteenth centuries; and some of Cézanne's paintings. The *Musée du Vieil Aix* has a collection of artifacts and documents relating to the history of the town. There are several colorful outdoor markets in Aix, including a flower market. And, of course, in the summer Aix sponsors a well-known festival of music, theater, and dance.

AVIGNON (pop. 86,939) is known as a city of art and culture, a reputation that it has had since the papal offices were located here in the fourteenth century. The city is walled, surrounded by 2.7 miles of ramparts that date to the fourteenth century. The chief attraction is the *Palace of the Popes,* a large Gothic structure built during the fourteenth century for the pontifical court. The *Musée du Petit Palais,* which once served as the palace for bishops and archbishops in the fourteenth and fifteenth centuries, contains notable Italian religious paintings from the thirteenth to the sixteenth centuries. The *Cathédrale Notre Dame des Doms* is a Romanesque church with an elaborately decorated interior; several popes are entombed here. The *Pont St. Bénézet* is a fabled twelfth-century bridge, only partially intact, that stretches out into the Rhône River. The bridge was immortalized as the *Pont d'Avignon* in a nursery rhyme. *Le Rocher des Doms* is a beautiful park with views of Mont Ventoux, the fortifications of Villeneuve-les-Avignon (known as the "city of cardinals" because many cardinals built large residences here), and the Pont St. Bénézet.

ARLES (pop. 52,058) attracted the painters Van Gogh and Picasso, not to mention many others. Van Gogh spent the final years of his life here, and Picasso liked the town so much that he donated a collection of drawings to Arles. The *arènes* in the town is one of the best-preserved Roman amphitheaters in France; bullfights are staged here. Another Roman site is the *Théâtre Antique,* now used for summer festivals. The *Musée Réattu* contains contemporary art and some of the works of Henri Rousseau

(1844–1910). The *Fondation Van Gogh* has works of over 700 artists, poets, and composers who have contributed original works to the memory of the Dutch master. The *Musée Arlaten* is a superb folk museum founded at the end of the nineteenth century by the writer and provençal nationalist Frédéric Mistral. The *Musée d'Art Chrétien* has the finest collection of Christian sarcophagi outside the Vatican Museum in Rome. Arles, too, holds an international photography festival in June.

ORANGE (pop. 26,964) is best known for its Roman ruins. The *Théâtre Antique* is considered the best-preserved Roman theater in France; summer festivals are held here. The *Musée Lapidaire* houses artifacts unearthed from the theater site. The *Arc de Triomphe,* completed in 26 A.D., is situated on the ancient *via Agrippa* that once connected Arles to Lyon.

CASSIS (pop. 7,967) is considered by some to be among the most beautiful small towns in France. Situated on the coast approximately thirty minutes to the east of Marseille, Cassis was once a lively fishing village. Although fishing still prevails, Cassis has become a tourist mecca. A favorite pastime is to walk along the *calanques* (fiords) outside of the town; or to take a boat cruise to the *calanques,* where there are small marinas and beaches, not to mention occasional mountain climbers practicing their skills on the side of cliffs at water's edge. Cassis, too, produces a very good white wine that is excellent with seafood dishes.

ST.-TROPEZ (pop. 5,754) is a beautiful, chic, and wealthy town on the Mediterranean; it was made famous, in part, by French actress Brigitte Bardot. The *Musée de l'Annociade* displays a collection of neo-Impressionist and Fauvist paintings. Within the vicinity of St. Tropez are several beautiful beaches. The town now has a reputation as the playground of the rich and famous.

SELECT BIBLIOGRAPHY

Christofferson, Thomas. "Marseille," in Wayne Northcutt, ed., *Historical Dictionary of the French Fourth and Fifth Republics, 1946–1991.* Westport, CT: Greenwood Press, 1992.

Guiral, P. *La Provence de 1900 à nos jours.* Toulouse: Privat, 1978.

Langevin, P. *L'Économie provençale.* Aix-en-Provence: Edisud, 1983.

Wolkowitsch, Maurice. *Provence-Alpes-Côte d'Azur.* Paris: PUF, 1984.

―――. "Provence-Alpes-Côte d'Azur," in André Gamblin, ed., *La France dans ses régions,* vol. 2. Paris: SEDES, 1994.

Wylie, Laurence. *Village in the Vaucluse.* New York: Harper, 1964.

Chapter 22

RHÔNE-ALPES

REGIONAL GEOGRAPHY

This vast region, the second largest in France, representing 26,974 square miles and 8 percent of the surface area of the nation, is located in the southeastern portion of the hexagon. Roughly one-third of the region lies to the west of the Rhône River and two-thirds to the east of the Rhône. The eastern border of Rhône-Alpes is adjacent to the Italian frontier; the northeastern border is adjacent to Switzerland. The northern border is formed by the regions of Burgundy and Franche-Comté; the southern border is bounded by Languedoc-Roussillon and Provence-Alpes-Côte d'Azur. Eight departments make up the region: Ain, Ardèche, Drôme, Isère, Loire, Rhône, Savoie (hereafter Savoy), and Haute-Savoie (hereafter Upper Savoy). The capital is Lyon.

This region lacks geographical unity. It contains the Saône and Rhône valleys, which make travel and communication relatively easy between Northern Europe and the Mediterranean. The eastern and northeastern part of the region encompasses the high peaks of the French Alps. To the west are the high elevations of the Monts du Forez and the Massif Central. The southernmost part of Rhône-Alpes is the gateway to the Mediterranean.

Given this geographical diversity, the climate varies greatly from one area to another. Around Lyon and low-lying areas, fog and overcast skies are common. The forested mountain areas have wet and brisk weather, with harsh winters. The southern part of the region has a somewhat Mediterranean climate. The French often say that the Mediterranean climate begins at Valence, a town in the southern section of Rhône-Alpes.

RHÔNE-ALPES

HISTORY

Because this region covers a large area and is an amalgamation of three older regions—Lyon-Bresse, Dauphiné, and Savoy—our discussion of the history of Rhône-Alpes will focus on three distinct parts.

Lyon-Bresse

In 43 B.C. Roman colonists settled in Lyon, in the area once known as Lyon-Bresse, which had been settled more than 2,000 years earlier. In 16 B.C. Lyon was made the capital of Gaul, and the population soon reached 100,000. Many early Christians sought protection in the city; yet many were martyred, 18,000 alone in A.D. 197. Following the fall of the Roman Empire in the fifth century and the dissolution of Charlemagne's Frankish Empire in the ninth century, Lyon and the surrounding area were incorporated into the kingdom of Provence and subsequently integrated, together with Burgundy, into the Holy Roman Empire. At this time Church architecture, Romanesque in styling, began to flourish. Lyon itself expanded as an important trade center. In 1240 Lyon formed the first municipality in France; it won protection from the French crown toward the end of the thirteenth century.

At the commencement of the fifteenth century, a number of refugees from civil wars in Italian city-republics fled to Lyon. These individuals introduced the silk industry to the city, an industry that later flourished. After Louis XI granted the city the privilege of four free fairs each year, Florentine merchant bankers and German printers opened offices in Lyon. Moreover, the city's stock market opened in 1506, making it the oldest in France. At this time Lyon was wealthier than Paris and even had a larger population.

Given the work ethic in Lyon, when the Protestant Reformation broke out in the early sixteenth century it found acceptance in the city. However, reprisals against Protestants during the 1540s forced many to flee to Geneva and elsewhere. It was in this atmosphere that the first recorded workers' strike occurred in 1539–1542; the first strikers were printers.

Despite the early labor unrest, the first workers' organizations were formed in Lyon in the eighteenth century in the silk mills. Also in the eighteenth century, coal mines were put into commercial production in 1759 in the St.-Étienne area southwest of Lyon.

After the French Revolution of 1789, Lyon developed a tradition of invention, innovation, and industry. The first balloon ascent was made at Brotteaux in 1784, followed soon after by the launching on the Rhône of an early form of the steamship. In 1804 Joseph-Marie Jacquard's loom revolutionized textile weaving. When violent workers' revolts hit the area in the 1830s, many mill owners moved their operations to the countryside where there was an abundance of cheap labor. Given the fuel supply in and around St.-Étienne, metalworking thrived there. The area also has a tradition of resistance, especially Lyon. During World War II, Lyon was the capital of the Resistance movement against the Nazis.

In the post–World War II period Lyon has continued to develop as a center of industry, business, and commerce. Between 1950 and 1970, the major problems for the city were population increase and economic expansion. As industry expanded during this period, an increasing number of foreign immigrants—mainly from North Africa—settled in Lyon. This was accompanied in the 1960s by a significant number of repatriates from Algeria after the country won its independence from France in 1962. Today, approximately 12 percent of the city's population are foreign nationals.

Over the past two decades economic growth has slowed and the population has leveled off somewhat. The city opened a new metro system in 1978, and since 1984 the high-speed TGV train makes the journey to and from Paris in a mere two hours, instead of the four hours by conventional train service. The city, too, has opened a major retail and office complex at Le Part-Dieu, where 15,000 people work. Lyon, like the Rhône-Alpes region as a whole, is now attempting to promote a European image rather than simply a French image. The city is the undisputed capital of Rhône-Alpes and the nation's second city after Paris.

Dauphiné

The area known as the Dauphiné at one time covered what is now the southern section of the Rhône-Alpes region, namely, the departments of Isère and Drôme. The Celts, ancestors of the Gauls, began to settle here around 650 B.C. The Allobroges, the best-known tribe of this area, developed a reputation for their resistance to the Romans. The Roman occupation of this area lasted for 575 years, from 121 B.C. until the fifth century A.D. During this period Vienne, just south of Lyon, became a wealthy and brilliant city where both commerce and industry flourished.

Following the fall of the Roman Empire in the fifth century and the beginning of the Middle Ages, various seigneurs (lords) dominated others through either alliance or force. Guiguer le Vieux, the Comte d'Albon, founded the Dauphiné; his descendants continued a policy of expansion. In the fourteenth century Humbert II, last of the Dauphiné line, sold his domains to the King of France. The agreement, the *Transport du Dauphiné,* stipulated that the eldest son of the king should control the Dauphiné. This is why the crown prince in France—the king to be—was referred to as the *Dauphin.* After acquiring this region, the crown administered it well. Fortunately it had a diversified economy: cattle, arable farmland, wine, fruit, hemp, wood, and wool. In general, the Dauphiné was favorable to the Protestant Reformation.

A parliament emerged in the region in 1453, an outgrowth of Humbert's Delphinal Council. This new parliament, known as the Parliament of Grenoble, played a major role in the early phase of the French Revolution because of its resistance to the crown. When leaders of the Revolution divided France into departments, the Dauphiné was carved up into three departments: Isère, Drôme, and Hautes-Alpes.

During the nineteenth century, economic change came to the region. New roads and railways were built, including the Paris-Marseille rail line that passed through Valence. In 1869 water power was first used to operate a paper mill. This new energy source enhanced the rise of Grenoble, along with the later development of the electrochemical and metallurgical industries. Grenoble, France's second high-tech center after Toulouse, is the leading city in the area.

Today the area once known as the Dauphiné has a reputation for imaginative research and invention. Tenacity and resistance are sometimes associated with inhabitants of this part of France.

Savoy

Savoy, too, has an interesting history. The people from this area are referred to as Savoyards and often speak in a centuries-old dialect. Shepherd tribes from north of Italy inhabited Savoy beginning in the Bronze Age. The Gauls appeared during the Iron Age. The communities of this area were united and referred to as the Allobroges. They were conquered by the Romans between 122 B.C. and 118 B.C. Strategically, the area was important to the Romans because it served as a natural communication link between the valleys of northwestern Italy and the valleys of the Rhône.

Following the fall of the Roman Empire, Savoy came under the control of Lothair and then Burgundy. In 1032 the Holy Roman Empire gained control of the area. The first representative of the House of Savoy was Humbert aux Blanches Mains. This dynasty became as important to the area as the Capetian dynasty (987–1328) was to France. The ruling family in Savoy created a strong and sovereign state that exploited the geography of the area, a crossroads of Europe. Eventually the Blanches Mains came to control the northern and southern slopes of Savoy, becoming the gatekeepers of the Alps. During the twelfth and thirteenth centuries, monastic orders spread in the area.

In the thirteenth and fourteenth centuries the power of Savoy grew. For instance, the Counts of Savoy owned Geneva and Turin, as well as key mountain passes that facilitated European communication. This small but well-governed state played a significant role in the affairs of Europe.

In 1416 Amadeus VIII became Duke of Savoy and soon proved to be the greatest leader of his dynasty. Under this duke and his followers, Annecy and Chambéry and their abbeys became centers of artistic activity.

Furthermore, the Dukes of Savoy gained control of Nice and an area in Italy known as Piedmont. At this time the Dukes of Savoy began to play France off against the Hapsburg Empire. Because of the power of Savoy, in 1536 François I of France invaded the duchy. Duke Emmanuel-Philibert later restored Savoy to its former power and status. However, for protection, the capital was moved from Chambéry to Turin, further away from France. Consequently, Piedmont became more important than Savoy.

The Dukes of Savoy resisted repeated efforts by the French to take possession of this mainly French-speaking area. Louis XIV invaded it twice. Under the Treaty of Utrecht (1713), at the end of the Spanish War of Succession (1701–1714), Savoy was on the "correct" side and Duke Victor-Amédée received the crown of Sicily, but then soon exchanged it for the crown of Sardinia. Savoy was annexed by France during the Revolution of 1789 but was returned twenty-three years later.

In 1815 under the Treaty of Paris, which ended the French Revolution and the Napoleonic era, King Victor Emmanuel of Italy won back Sardinia and Savoy. This ushered in a conservative era that included strict police controls. In 1848 the king granted a constitution that permitted a two-chamber parliament, but Savoy's representation was to be based on its physical size and not its historical past; this led to discontent in Savoy, and many began to look toward the French emperor Napoleon III (1852–1870). Fortunately, Count Camillo Benso di Cavour (1810–1861), who was one of the architects of Italian unification, promised Napoleon III that if the French drove the Austrians from Italy, France would be given both Savoy and Nice. In 1868 the Savoyards voted to unite with France. Later, two departments were created, Savoy and Upper Savoy, which became integrated into the development of France. In the 1870s a railway was completed across the Alps; at this time roads were also improved and tourism developed. With the development of hydro-electricity, heavy industry also began to appear in the area. Nevertheless, economic development today lags behind the rest of the Rhône-Alpes region.

RECENT POLITICS

The politics of Rhône-Alpes in the 1990s have conformed somewhat to the rightward swing in the rest of France. In many ways the 1993 legislative elections in Rhône-Alpes echoed the 1992 regional elections. In 1993 the right—the gaullist Rally for the Republic (RPR) and the Union for French Democracy (UDF)—consolidated their gains, winning 39.52 percent of the vote. The presidential majority, the Socialist party (PS), captured only 16.92 percent. Moreover, many well-known socialist leaders were defeated in these elections. In 1993 the Ecologists won 11.92 percent of the vote, and the French Communist party (PCF) garnered 7.96 percent. The extreme right, the National Front (FN), won 14.96 percent in the same elections.

In terms of representation in the National Assembly, these results meant that the socialists would have only three seats, as compared to the RPR and UDF's forty-two seats.

In the 1995 presidential election, left-wing candidates outscored the right in only one department in the region, Isère. The National Front candidate, Jean-Marie Le Pen, captured 17.79 percent of the vote in the first round, above his 15 percent national average. In the second round of the presidential contest, only Isère voted in favor of the socialist candidate Lionel Jospin; the other seven departments voted in favor of the gaullist Jacques Chirac, who became the new president of France. However, in the June 1995 municipal elections that followed, the socialists won control over Grenoble. Lyon and St.-Étienne, on the other hand, remained controlled by the UDF and the right.

There are several key politicians from the region. One is Raymond Barre, an economics professor-turned-politician who served as prime minister (1976–1981) under the presidency of Valéry Giscard d'Estaing (UDF). In 1978 Barre was first elected as a deputy from the Rhône to the National Assembly. He was a presidential candidate in 1988 but came in a distant third behind the socialist François Mitterrand and the gaullist Jacques Chirac. He headed a successful list of candidates in the 1995 municipal elections. Barre is known for his independent stances on issues facing the nation.

Another key politician from the region is Michel Noir, a neo-gaullist who was elected mayor of Lyon in 1989 and a long-time deputy in the National Assembly. In the late 1980s he became one of the "renovators" in the RPR and declared publicly that the party would do better to lose elections than to lose its soul by making electoral alliance with Jean-Marie Le Pen's extremist National Front. He also publicly criticized the structure and the evolution of the party. In December 1990 he resigned from the party and from his position as deputy in the National Assembly.

POPULATION

Not only is Rhône-Alpes a large region in terms of geography, but it is the second most populated region in France, containing 9.5 percent of the nation's population. For the past fifteen years there has been a relatively steady increase in its numbers. In 1975 the population stood at 4,781,000; by 1993 the population had climbed to 5,474,000. From 1982 to 1990 the population grew at a rate of 0.8 percent per year. In recent years the excess of births as compared to deaths has accounted for two-thirds of the population increase. The birthrate is currently 1.81, as compared to a national average of 1.73. Another part of the increase is owing to migration into the region: next to the south of France, this region is the most attractive to newcomers, especially those seeking employment. The population density is 125.3 inhabitants per square kilometer (202.98 inhabitants per square mile), slightly more than the density rate for all of France (105.7 per square kilometer/171.23 per square mile).

Compared to France as a whole, Rhône-Alpes has a relatively young population. Those age 60 and older make up 18.3 percent of the population, below the 19.7 percent average for France. On the other hand, those age 19 and younger comprise 27.5 percent of all inhabitants (26.8% is the average for France). The immigrant population, 7.9 percent, is higher than the national average of 6.3 percent.

The urban population conforms exactly to the national average of 76.4 percent. Life expectancy is 77.4 years, slightly more than the national norm. Approximately 27 percent of all households are single-person households, almost the same as the national average.

Educational levels and the work force are telling aspects of this growing area. Roughly 11.1 percent of all inhabitants possess a high school diploma (10.5% for France as a whole), and 12.1 percent hold an advanced degree (above the 11.2% average for the entire nation). Of the work force, the agricultural sector is relatively small, with 4.1 percent involved in farming—slightly less than the national average of 5.3 percent. Yet 30.2 percent of the work force is found in industry, as compared to 26.9 percent for France as a whole. The service sector comprises 65.7 percent of the work force, approximately 3 percent less than the national average. Unemployment is roughly 12 percent in the region, approximately the same as the national average. Roughly 12.7 percent of women are out of work in Rhône-Alpes.

ECONOMY

The diversified economy of Rhône-Alpes holds several key advantages that may strengthen its economic development in the future: a strong industrial base that attracts a highly qualified service sector, a grouping of dense urban areas (Lyon, St.-Étienne, Grenoble), and exceptional natural spaces—such as the Alps—that permit the development of an important tourist industry.

To a large degree, the industrial tradition of Rhône-Alpes is related to plentiful energy resources. The chemical and related industries are well developed, ranging from petrochemicals to pharmaceuticals. The region also specializes in the production of aluminum, nuclear fuel, metallurgy, and metalworks in general. It is the principal center for plastics in France. The region also produces heavy equipment, especially for the industrial and transportation industries. The electronics industry is also well developed here. Although consumer products are produced in Rhône-Alpes, such as textiles and clothing, leather goods and shoes, and winter sports equipment, this dimension of the economy is less developed than the sectors noted above.

The diversification of industry helps explain why for years the unemployment rate has been slightly less than the national average. Unemployment in the region has been the highest in places such as Savoy, where at times it has reached 25 percent. In other departments that lack a strong industrial base, such as Drôme and Ardèche, unemployment has exceeded the regional average.

The three largest towns are Lyon with 415,487 inhabitants (greater Lyon 1,262,223), St.-Étienne with 199,396 (greater St.-Étienne 313,338), and Grenoble with 116,872 (greater Grenoble 404,733). Roughly 27.8 percent of the region's work force is found in Lyon, 8.9 percent in Grenoble, and 5.8 percent in St.-Étienne. The four largest employers are Renault V. I. Vénissieux, SNR Roulements, GIAT Industries Roanne (armaments), and Sextant Avionique (avionics).

Given the location of Rhône-Alpes next to the Swiss and Italian borders, the region is orienting itself more toward the European Economic Community (Common Market) than toward Paris. Its large towns and well-trained work force, coupled with the presence of several important universities (e.g., at Lyon and Grenoble), enhance the possibility that this region will continue to be dynamic. The risk, however, is that the regional economic development will be uneven, with dynamic growth possible in key cities such as Lyon, St.-Étienne, and Grenoble, but stagnation possible in the more mountainous and more sparsely populated areas such as Savoy. Two Winter Olympic Games have been held in the region, the latest in 1992 at Albertville in Savoy. Many in the region hoped that the latest Games would call international attention to Savoy and spur tourism. Despite the difficulties in developing Savoy, the economic future of the region looks bright.

CULTURE

The capital of this region, Lyon, has a long tradition of scientific inquiry, a literary tradition, and a glorious culinary tradition. The eighteenth-century physicist **André-Marie Ampère** (1775–1836) was from Lyon. Ampère did work on electric current; the basic unit of electric current is named after him. Lyon also houses the *Institut Lumière,* which honors the **Lumière brothers** Louis (1864–1948) and Auguste (1862–1954), pioneers in motion picture photography. The great humanist and writer **François Rabelais** (1494–1553) worked in the Lyon hospital, and it was in Lyon that he published *Pantagruel.* Both *Pantagruel* and its sequel, *Gargantua,* have many references to Lyon. **Antoine de Saint Exupéry** (1900–1944), author of *Le Petit Prince,* was born in Lyon. During World War II, Lyon became a center for writers and journalists working with the Resistance. In recent times the city has been revealed through cinema more than through literature, especially in two films by **Bertrand Tavernier** (b. 1941) about his native Lyon. Tavernier's films are entitled *L'Horloger de Saint-Paul* and *Une Semaine de Vacances*. Besides its scientific and literary traditions, Lyon is known for its culinary arts. It is the home of some of France's best restaurants and chefs, such as **Fernand Point** and **Paul Bocuse.**

Several famous writers and thinkers were born in this region of France or spent an important period of their lives here. The eighteenth-century Enlightenment philosopher and author **Jean-Jacques Rousseau** (1712–1778), usually associated with France but actually born in Geneva, spent twelve years off and on in Annecy, Chambéry, and Les Charmettes with his mistress, Madame Warens. Rousseau discussed his relationship with Madame Warens in his *Confessions*. Rousseau's *Contrat social* advocates a social contract between those who govern and those who are governed, an idea that challenged the "divine right" of kings and weakened the legitimacy of kingship in prerevolutionary France.

François-Marie Voltaire (1694–1778), another major thinker from the French Enlightenment period, spent time in the region. During the last eighteen years of his life Voltaire lived at the chateau at Ferney, 4 miles west of Geneva. He moved to Ferney from Geneva to avoid harassment by Calvinist authorities in Switzerland. He fell in love with the area and spent a large sum of money restoring his chateau. He enjoyed hosting other European writers, thinkers, and artists and developed a reputation of sorts as "The Innkeeper of Europe." Voltaire devoted his life to the ideas of tolerance, justice and freedom; his ideas helped foster the Revolution of 1789.

The young poet **Alphonse de Lamartine** (1790–1869) had an unhappy love affair in Savoy. His famous poem "*Le Lac,*" named for the beautiful Lac du Bouget, was inspired by his affair with Julie Charles, the wife of a Parisian physician. Lamartine was also a politician.

Several very well known writers are associated with Rhône-Alpes. The novelist and biographer **Henri Stendhal** (1783–1842), famous for his novel *Le Rouge et le noir* (The Red and the Black) was born in Grenoble. *La Vie de Henri Brulard,* his boyhood autobiography, tells how he despised his Royalist father and the bourgeoisie of Grenoble. The writer **Alphonse Daudet** (1840–1897) wrote an autobiographical novel *Le Petit Chose* (The Small Thing) about his early years in Lyon, where he was less than happy. His father was forced to close his silk factory in the Midi (the south of France) and move to Lyon. Daudet's novel discusses the life of a young man who felt he was an exile in fog-ridden Lyon. The village of Brangues, near Aix-le-Bain, was the home for a number of years of the writer **Paul Claudel** (1868–1955). Claudel is buried on the grounds of his chateau.

The noted American writer **Gertrude Stein** (1874–1946) also spent a memorable period in this region. Encouraged to flee Nazi Occupied Paris during the war years because of her Jewish heritage, she and her companion, Alice B. Toklas, and Stein's poodle went to the village of Culoz west of Annecy and remained there from 1943 to 1945. She discussed her experience in the region in her book entitled *Wars I Have Seen*.

The regional costumes worn by women in Savoy in the high Alpine valleys have no equal in either color or cut. Although they vary from valley to valley, they have the same accessories: a multicolored shawl, and a golden or silver cross hanging from a metal heart by a black velvet ribbon. Characteristic of this costume is a black dress and a black embroidered apron with bright stripes. There is also a three-pointed black headdress embroidered and laced with gold. One point of the headdress goes over the forehead; the other two points go over the temples. The costume is only worn on festival days and for traditional celebrations.

Rhône-Alpes is known for its culinary excellence, especially the area around Lyon. Even the sixteenth-century author Rabelais paid tribute to the region's culinary pleasures. Traditional regional cooking does not attempt to change basic flavor; the French saying "Let things taste as they are" was never so true as it is in Lyon regional cooking. The basic ingredients for cooking are found here: poultry, butter, cheese, freshwater fish, mushrooms, and wine. Home-style dishes from the Lyon area include sausages; potted pork and pâté in a pastry crust; and salads made with a mushroom known as sheep's feet, with dandelions, sippets and herring, or dandelions and coddled eggs. Also typical of Lyon regional cuisine is poached mousse of pike with a hot butter sauce, tripe, pig's tail, chicken with slices of truffles under the skin, and cardoons with marrow. Specialties of Forez and Bugey include freshwater crayfish, roasted game, and duck braised in red wine. The Beaujolais wine region stretches just north of Lyon; consequently it is not surprising that Beaujolais is a favorite in and around Lyon. Burgundy wine vineyards are in close proximity to the Lyon area; they are also popular. Chocolate truffles and other chocolate concoctions are popular desserts.

In the departments of Isère and Drôme, *gratins*, a dish consisting of browned crumbs and butter and often with melted grated cheese, are extremely popular; the best known is the potato-based *gratin dauphinois*. The list of possible gratins is unending. Delicacies such as olives grow around Nyons and Dignes. Truffles are also found in these departments. A local pastry is *la pogne*, a cross between a brioche and a tart that is garnished with fruit or squash. The town of Montélimar is the nougat capital of France (nougat is a confection made from a sugar or honey paste into which nuts are mixed). Numerous liqueurs are found here, such as *chartreuse* and *génépi*.

The mountainous Savoy produces a much heartier cuisine. Fondues and *raclette* (a Swiss dish consisting of cheese melted and served on boiled potatoes) are popular in this area. The Savoy also produces relatively well-known cheeses, such as Reblochon and Beaufort. It also produces several good white and red wines.

Below is a recipe for a dish typical of the Savoy area.

SOUPE SAVOYARDE
(Winter Vegetable Soup)

2 tbs. butter or oil	2 cups lukewarm water
1 large onion, chopped	salt and freshly ground black
1 lb. leeks, trimmed, split, and sliced	pepper to taste
	2½ cups milk
1 small turnip, quartered and sliced	12 small round croûtes (pieces of bread crust), sautéed in butter
1 small celery root, quartered and sliced	Gruyère cheese, cut into 6 thin slices
2 large potatoes, peeled and quartered	

Heat the butter or oil in a soup pot, add onion, and cook over low heat until onion is soft but not browned. Stir in the leeks, turnip, and celery root; cover tightly and cook over low heat, stirring occasionally, for 20 minutes or until softened. Add potatoes, lukewarm water, and salt and pepper. Simmer for 15 minutes or until potatoes are nearly tender. In a separate pan bring the milk to a boil, add it to the soup, and cover and simmer for 15 minutes, or until vegetables are very tender. Taste for seasoning. Put the croûtes in a soup tureen or individual soup bowls and top them with slices of cheese. Pour the soup over them and serve immediately so that the croûtes remain crisp. Serves 6.

ARCHITECTURE AND NOTEWORTHY SITES

Around Lyon the past is reflected not so much in the monuments but in the rural and domestic architecture. In the Dombes area (an area near Lyon that is dotted with ponds), low farmhouses with pebble-dashed earthen walls are quite common. In the Beaujolais area, houses are constructed of *pierres dorées* (limestone pebbles with a significant content of yellow ochre that appears golden) and Mediterranean-style tiled roofs. Also, around Bresse (northeast of Lyon) one finds timber-faced balconied houses.

In the departments of the Drôme and Isère, especially at higher elevations, the village houses often have protecting ramparts and are perched, giving the appearance of a miniature town. Somewhat typical of this area is the Roman bell tower built of stone, normally surrounded by the town hall, school, and cemetery. In general, more stone is used in this area than in Savoy. Near Briançon are large stone houses with two or three floors; sometimes they are decorated with beautiful arcaded balconies. In the Drôme, the southernmost department of the region, the houses have a more Mediterranean appearance.

In the mountainous Savoy one rarely finds a single group of houses. Villages normally consist of several hamlets spread around a village center. Houses are positioned to take maximum advantage of the sunshine, and open spaces are small to provide protection from the cold. Buildings are massively constructed; wooden galleries and balconies are common. Roofs tend to be of wooden tiles, grey slate (especially in the north), or stone tiles (mainly in the south).

LYON (pop. 415,487; greater Lyon 1,262,223) is France's second largest city; it has been a commercial and industrial center for centuries. The city is divided into nine *arrondissements,* or quarters. Lyon has a relatively large immigrant population and racial tensions have flared in recent years, much like in Marseille. Although the city has a reputation for being a bit staid, Lyon has a rich cultural life and outstanding museums. The old section of the city is filled with narrow streets lined with over 300 medieval and Renaissance houses. The *Place Bellecour,* one of the largest public squares in Europe, was laid out in the seventeenth century; an equestrian statue of Louis XIV stands in the middle of the Place. During the Reign of Terror in the French Revolution, a large number of Lyonnais were executed at the Place Bellecour. The *Cathédrale Saint Jean* was begun in the twelfth century and has a fourteenth-century astronomical clock. The *Basilique Notre Dame de Fourvière* was completed in the late nineteenth century; similar to the *Sacré Coeur* in Paris, it was constructed as a way of rejuvenating the nation following the disastrous Franco-Prussian War of 1870 that completed the unification of Germany. The basilica offers the visitor a panoramic view of Lyon. *The Musée Gallo-Romain* has a superb collection of Roman artifacts, including a four-wheeled vehicle from around 700 B.C., as well as several impressive mosaics. There are also two rebuilt Roman theaters next to the museum; the largest is used for concerts. The *Musée des Beaux-Arts,* an excellent fine arts museum, has approximately ninety rooms of paintings and sculpture from practically all periods of European art. The *Musée Historique des Tissus* is a museum of the history of textiles. It includes silks, tapestries, and lace produced in Lyon, and textiles from other countries. Also in Lyon is the *Musée de l'Imprimerie,* which features the history of printing—a technology that has been perfected in Lyon since the late fifteenth century. Some of the first books ever printed are on display here, including a page from the *Gutenberg Bible* (1450s). Throughout the year, a visitor to the city can see the Guignol puppet shows at the *Place de l'Observatoire.* An important part of Lyon and France's wartime history can be viewed at the *Centre d'Histoire de la Résistance et de la Déportation.* During World War II, Lyon's notorious Gestapo chief, Clause

Barbie, operated here. The Centre commemorates French resistance to the German Occupation and the thousands of French citizens—including some 76,000 Jews—who were deported to Hitler's concentration camps.

GRENOBLE (pop. 116,872; greater Grenoble 404,733) is considered France's second high-tech center, after Toulouse. Nuclear and micro-electronic research is important here. Grenoble is also the undisputed capital of the French Alps. The city is exceptionally clean and therefore has the feel of a Swiss city. Grenoble first emerged as a dynamic city in the 1960s under the socialist mayor Hubert Dubedout. The university, established in 1339, has an enrollment of approximately 36,000 students, including many from abroad. Being located close to Alpine skiing, Grenoble hosted the 1968 Winter Olympic Games. For spectacular views of the Grenoble area, one can visit the *Fort de la Bastille,* built in the sixteenth century to control entry into the city. The *Musée des Beaux-Arts* possesses an excellent collection of paintings and sculpture; there are works of the Flemish artist Peter Paul Rubens (1577–1640) as well as Henri Matisse (1869–1954), Marc Chagall (1887–1985), Fernand Léger (1881–1955), Pablo Picasso (1881–1973), Amedeo Modigliani (1884–1920), and others. This museum is considered one of the best in the French provinces. The *Musée Dauphinois* displays the crafts and history of the area, especially that of the mountain people. The city, too, has an interesting Old Town.

ST.-ÉTIENNE (pop. 199,396; greater St.-Étienne 313,338) sits at the foot of Mt. Pilat. This is an industrial city that possesses a number of important industries, such as metallurgy, arms, tools, and milling machinery. The city not only has an active cultural life but also enjoys more than 2,000 hours of sunshine annually. The *Palais des Arts* houses a museum of art and industry and a mining museum. There is also a museum of old St.-Étienne and a botanical garden. The city has a historic quarter as well.

ANNECY (pop. 49,644) is the upscale capital of Upper Savoy. Located on the northern edge of *Lac d'Annecy,* it is an excellent spot for water sports, hiking, cycling, and skiing. Visits to the Old Town, the lake, and the town's gardens—notably the *Jardin de l'Europe*—are essential. The *Musée d'Histoire d'Annecy et de la Haute-Savoie* features the history and culture of the area. The *Musée d'Annecy* is housed in the thirteenth- to sixteenth-century chateau that overlooks the town. In addition to a permanent collection, local artisanship and miscellaneous objects are on display.

CHAMONIX (pop. 9,701) offers not just excellent skiing, with more than 125 miles of downhill and cross-country ski trails, but some of the most spectacular scenery in the French Alps. It is also the mountain-climbing capital of France; for hiking enthusiasts, there are 131 miles of hiking trails. The highest aerial tramway in the world is located here, stretching from Chamonix to the *Aiguille du Midi,* a singular spire of rock extending 5 miles across glaciers and snow fields from the peak of Mont Blanc. (Mont

Blanc, meaning "white mountain," is normally covered with snow and ice throughout the year.) One can also take an excursion to see *La Mer de Glace,* a famous glacier that can be reached by railway. The *Réserve des Aiguilles Rouges,* 7 miles outside of Chamonix, is a nature reserve that has a variety of Alpine vegetation. The *Musée Alpin* in Chamonix displays the history of mountain climbing and other Alpine sports. The *Mont Blanc tunnel* allows motorists to pass through an impressive mountain that separates France and Italy. Opened in 1965, this tunnel aided the development of Chamonix as a resort.

SELECT BIBLIOGRAPHY

Labasse, J. O. Brachet, and P. Bachot. "Rhône-Alpes," in Y. Lacoste, ed., *Géopolitiques des régions françaises,* vol. 3. Paris: Fayard, 1986.

Latreille, A. *Histoire de Lyon et des Lyonnais.* Toulouse: Privat, 1988.

Lebeau, René. "Rhône-Alpes," in André Gamblin, ed., *La France dans ses régions,* vol. 1. Paris: SEDES, 1994.

Lequin, Y. *Rhône-Alpes, 500 années Lumière.* Paris: Plon, 1991.

Tuppen, John N. "Core-Periphery in Metropolitan Development and Planning: Socio-Economic Change in Lyon since 1960," *Geoforum* 17 (1986).

———. "Lyon," in Wayne Northcutt, ed., *Historical Dictionary of the French Fourth and Fifth Republics, 1946–1991.* Westport, CT: Greenwood Press, 1992.

CHRONOLOGY

ANCIENT PERIOD

B.C.

4,670 Flourishing of Megalithic civilization in Brittany (Carnac) and Corsica for more than 2,500 years.

8th cent. Arrival of Celtic tribes from Central Europe; Celtic tribes construct fortified settlements.

600 Marseille, Aléria (Corsica), and other cities are founded by the Greeks.

2d cent. Celtic culture is overtaken by Germanic and Roman culture. In 122 B.C. Romans are established in Aix-en-Provence; in 118 B.C. in Narbonne.

58–52 Gallic Wars of Julius Caesar.

A.D.

1st cent. Roman rule in Gaul is consolidated and expanded.

5th cent. Monasteries are established by St. Martin and St. Honorat, strengthening Christian beliefs.

MEROVINGIANS, 418–751

451 King of Salian Franks, Merovius, defeats Attila the Hun. Dynasty is named after victorious Frankish king.

476 Roman Empire falls in the west and barbarian tribes take over Gaul.

496 Clovis, King of the Franks, is baptized at Reims.

507	Clovis defeats the Visigoths.
732	Charles Martel defeats invading Arab armies near Poitiers.

CAROLINGIANS, 751–986

751	Pepin the Short establishes a new dynasty.
800	Charlemagne is crowned Emperor of the West.
843	Carolingian Empire is divided under the Treaty of Verdun; sons of Louis I are awarded territories, with Charles the Bald obtaining area approximating modern France.
910	Great Abbey at Cluny is established.
911	Duchy of Normandy is established by treaty between Charles the Simple and Viking chief Rollo.

CAPETIANS, 987–1328

987	Hugues Capet is made King.
1066	Duke of Normandy defeats English at Battle of Hastings and becomes King of England, although still a vassal of the French king.
1095	First Crusade is announced at Clermond-Ferrand.
1137	Louis VII marries Eleanor of Aquitaine. He later repudiates her and sets in motion a long conflict between England and France, especially when she marries a Plantagenet to be crowned Henry II, King of England.
1209	Beginning of Albigensian Crusade, called by Pope Innocent III against the Albigensians, or Cathars, a religious sect in the south in Languedoc.
1214	Victorious Battle of Bouvines fosters French patriotism.
1244	200 Cathars are burnt at the funerary pyre at Montségur.

HOUSE OF VALOIS, 1328–1589

1337–1453	Hundred Years War, political and dynastic battle between Capetians and Plantagenets over rule of France; conflict extends over six reigns.
1539	François I promulgates Ordinance of Villers-Cotterets, requiring the maintaining of parish registers of births and deaths and mandatory use of French instead of Latin in legal affairs.
1541	John Calvin (born in Noyon) publishes *Institutes of the Christian Religion.*
1562–1598	Wars of Religion.

HOUSE OF BOURBON, 1589–1792

1589–1610   Henry IV consolidates power in France and sponsors architects to work on a number of great projects (e.g., the Louvre and the Place des Vosges in Paris).

1610   Louis XIII becomes King; his reign is marked by flourishing trade, an aristocratic rebellion, Descartes's *Discourse on Method,* and Vincent de Paul's pioneering efforts in social welfare.

1624   Richelieu, the king's first minister, reduces Protestant influence.

1634   Founding of the *Académie Française.*

1643–1715   Louis XIV, the Sun King, begins a 72-year reign, consolidating and centralizing power in France, constructing Versailles, and engaging European powers in long periods of war.

1715–1774   Reign of Louis XV sees a monarchy marked by indecision and corruption. Lorraine is annexed in 1766; Corsica in 1769.

1774–1792   Reign of Louis XVI confronts alarming state debt.

REVOLUTIONARY PERIOD, 1789–1799

1789   Fall of the Bastille and beginning of the French Revolution.

1792   Republic is proclaimed.

1793   King Louis XVI is executed.

1793–1794   Reign of Terror.

1795–1799   Directory rules France.

NAPOLEONIC PERIOD, 1799–1815

1799   Rise of Napoleon to power, named First Consul.

1804   Napoleon is crowned Emperor of the French in Notre-Dame cathedral; introduces the Napoleonic Code, which codifies the country's legal system.

1806   Napoleon launches the Continental System to blockade the British and to cripple their economy.

1808   Napoleon's forces are entrenched in the Peninsula War.

1812   Napoleon invades Russia.

1813   Battle of Leipzig leads to fall of Napoleon.

THE RESTORATION, 1815–1830

1815   The Hundred Days: Napoleon escapes exile on island of Elba and returns to France; finally is defeated in Belgium at Waterloo. Congress of Vienna restores principle of legitimacy and balance of power. Louis XVIII begins his reign and is followed by Charles X (1824–1830).

THE JULY MONARCHY, 1830–1848

1830–1848	Reign of Louis-Philippe, after reactionary King Charles X sparks revolt.

SECOND REPUBLIC AND EMPIRE, 1848–1870

1848	Napoleon III is elected President of the Second Republic.
1852	Formation of the Second Empire, with Napoleon III as emperor.
1869	Freedom of the press is assured.
1870	Franco-Prussian War leads to defeat of France at Sedan; uprising in the capital; Third Republic is proclaimed.

THE THIRD REPUBLIC, 1870–1946

1871	Paris Commune. Under Treaty of Frankfort, France cedes Alsace and part of Lorraine to Germany.
1881	Jules Ferry makes primary education secular, free, and compulsory.
1884	Recognition of trade unions.
1885	Eiffel Tower is inaugurated.
1894	Franco-Russian Treaty allows France to break free from Germany's diplomatic isolation of the French nation.
1895	Dreyfus Affair splits the nation when a Jewish General Staff Captain is unjustly imprisoned.
1904	Entente Cordiale with Britain.
1914	Outbreak of World War I.
1934	Threatening extreme right-wing demonstrations.
1936	Formation of Léon Blum's Popular Front Government.
1939	Outbreak of World War II.
1940	Fall of France; northern France and the Atlantic seaboard are occupied, while a "French State" created in Vichy collaborates with the Nazis. General Charles de Gaulle forms a Free French movement and inspires the Resistance.
1942	All of France is occupied by the Germans; French fleet is scuttled at Toulon.
1944	Allies begin Normandy invasion in June.
1945	Germans surrender.

THE FOURTH REPUBLIC, 1946–1958

1954	French military defeat at Dien Bien Phu in Vietnam.
1956	France abandons Indo-China and grants Morocco and Tunisia independence.

1958   Algerian crisis leads to downfall of the Fourth Republic and the
                  formation of the Fifth Republic by de Gaulle.

FIFTH REPUBLIC, 1958–

1958   De Gaulle assumes presidency of the Fifth Republic; formation
                  of the European Economic Community (EEC, Common Mar-
                  ket).

1962   Referendum establishes universal suffrage for the presidency.

1965   De Gaulle wins run-off election against François Mitterand and
                  begins his second term.

1968   Student-work revolt cripples the gaullist regime.

1969   De Gaulle retires to write his memoirs. Georges Pompidou is
                  elected President.

1974–1981   Presidency of Valéry Giscard d'Estaing.

1981–1995   Presidency of socialist François Mitterrand (re-elected in 1988).
                  In 1981 socialists win absolute majority in the National As-
                  sembly. High-speed TGV train service is inaugurated between
                  Paris and Marseille, with other routes opened later.

1986   Right-wing victory in parliamentary elections. *Cohabitation* gov-
                  ernment between a socialist president and a gaullist prime min-
                  ister, Jacques Chirac.

1988   Re-election of President Mitterrand.

1992   Narrow victory for the referendum on the Maastricht Treaty call-
                  ing for an acceleration of EEC integration.

1993   Parliamentary elections produce right-wing government led by
                  Prime Minister Edouard Balladur.

1995   Jacques Chirac, mayor of Paris, is elected President. Socialist can-
                  didate Lionel Jospin and National Front candidate Jean-Marie
                  Le Pen make strong showings. Municipal elections in June see
                  socialists holding their ground and even winning six *arron-
                  dissements* in Paris—Chirac's fiefdom—and the National
                  Front winning the mayorship in Toulon, Orange, and Marig-
                  nane in the south of France. In the summer a new terrorist
                  wave begins in France; Chirac re-launched French nuclear test-
                  ing in the South Pacific amid international protest.

1996   In late January Chirac announced a halt to nuclear tests in French
                  Polynesia. During this same period, Chirac announced that
                  France would re-enter NATO and that the French government
                  would make significant cuts in its military budget. The French
                  president is seeking a stronger European pillar in NATO.

THE RULERS OF FRANCE SINCE A.D. 987

CAPETIAN DYNASTY

Hugh Capet, 987–996
Robert II the Pious, 996–1031
Henry I, 1031–1060
Philip I, 1060–1108
Louis VI the Fat, 1108–1137
Louis VII the Young, 1137–1180
Philip II, 1180–1223
Louis VIII the Lion, 1223–1226
Louis IX (St. Louis), 1226–1270
Philip III the Bold, 1270–1285
Philip IV the Fair, 1285–1314
Louis X the Quarreler, 1314–1316
Philip V the Tall, 1316–1322
Charles IV the Fair, 1322–1328

HOUSE OF VALOIS

Philip VI, 1328–1350
John II the Good, 1350–1364
Charles V the Wise, 1364–1380
Charles VI the Well-Beloved, 1380–1422

Charles VII, 1422–1461
Louis XI, 1461–1483
Charles VIII, 1483–1498
Louis XII, 1498–1515
Francis I, 1515–1547
Henry II, 1547–1559
Francis II, 1559–1560
Charles IX, 1560–1574
Henry III, 1574–1589

HOUSE OF BOURBON

Henry IV of Navarre, 1589–1610
Louis XIII, 1610–1643
Louis XIV, 1643–1715
Louis XV, 1715–1774
Louis XVI, 1774–1792

FIRST REPUBLIC

National Convention, 1792–1795
Directory, 1795–1799

CONSULATE

Napoleon Bonaparte, 1799–1804

FIRST EMPIRE

Napoleon I, 1804–1815

HOUSE OF BOURBON RESTORED

Louis XVIII, 1815–1824
Charles X, 1824–1830

BOURBON-ORLEANS LINE

Louis-Philippe, 1830–1848

SECOND REPUBLIC

Louis Napoleon, 1848–1852

SECOND EMPIRE

Napoleon III (Louis Napoleon), 1852–1870

THIRD REPUBLIC (PRESIDENTS)

Adolphe Thiers, 1871–1873
Maurice de MacMahon, 1873–1879
Jules Grévy, 1879–1887
Sadi Carnot, 1887–1894
Jean Casimir-Périer, 1894–1895
Félix Faure, 1895–1899
Émile Loubet, 1899–1906
Armand Fallières, 1906–1913
Raymond Poincaré, 1913–1920
Paul Deschanel, 1920
Alexandre Millerand, 1920–1924
Gaston Doumergue, 1924–1931
Paul Doumer, 1931–1932
Albert Lebrun, 1932–1940

VICHY GOVERNMENT (CHIEF OF STATE)

Henri Philippe Pétain, 1940–1944

PROVISIONAL GOVERNMENT (PRESIDENTS)

Charles de Gaulle, 1944–1946
Félix Gouin, 1946
Georges Bidault, 1946-1947

FOURTH REPUBLIC (PRESIDENTS)

Vincent Auriol, 1947–1953
René Coty, 1953–1958

FIFTH REPUBLIC (PRESIDENTS)

Charles de Gaulle, 1958–1969
Georges Pompidou, 1969–1974
Valéry Giscard d'Estaing, 1974–1981
François Mitterrand, 1981–1995
Jacques Chirac, 1995–

GENERAL BIBLIOGRAPHY

Andrews, William G., and Stanley Hoffmann, eds. *The Impact of the Fifth Republic on France*. Albany: State University of New York Press, 1981.

Antonetti, P. *Histoire de la Corse*. Paris: Robert Laffont, 1973.

Ardagh, John. *France Today*. London: Penguin Books, 1988.

——. *Writer's France: A Regional Panorama*. London: Hamish Hamilton, 1989.

Auger, P., and J. Granier. *Le Guide du pays de Caux*. Paris: La Manufacture, 1990.

Balabanian, Olivier, and Guy Bouet. *Le Guide du Limousin*. Paris: La Manufacture, 1994.

Baleste, Marcel, et al. *22 régions de programme*. Paris: Masson/Armand Colin, 1995.

Barbey, Adélaide, ed. *France* (Guides Bleus). Paris: Hachette, 1990.

——. *The Hachette Guide to France*. New York: Pantheon Books, 1986.

Becker, Jean-Jacques. *Histoire politique de la France depuis 1945*. Paris: Armand Colin, 1988.

Bell, D. S., and E. Shaw. *The Left in France*. Nottingham: Spokesman, 1983.

Berger, Alain, and Jacques Rouzier. *Vivre et produire en Languedoc-Roussillon: approche économique et humain*. Toulouse: Privat, 1981.

Bernstein, Richard. *Fragile Glory: A Portrait of France and the French*. New York: Alfred A. Knopf, 1990.

Boichard, J. *Encyclopédie de la Franche-Comté*. Lyon: La Manufacture, 1991.

——. *La Franche-Comté*. Paris: PUF, 1985.

Bonneton, Christine. *Picardie*. Paris: Encyclopédies Régionales, 1992.

Borella, François. *Les Partis politiques dans la France d'aujourd'hui*. Paris: Seuil, 1990.

Borne, Dominique. *Histoire de la société française depuis 1945*. Paris: Armand Colin, 1988.

Bouet, G., and A. Fel. *Le Massif Central*. Paris: Flammarion, 1983.

Braudel, Fernand. *Histoire économique du monde méditerranéen, 1450–1650*. Toulouse: Privat, 1973.

———-. *The Identity of France*, 2 vols., trans. Reynolds Sian. New York: Harper-Collins, 1990 and 1992.

Calame, François, and Robert Fossier. *Picardie*. Paris: A Die, 1994.

Clary, D. *La Normandie*. Paris: PUF (Que sais-je?), 1987.

Cobban, Alfred. *A History of Modern France*, 3 vols. London: Penguin, 1963.

Commission nationale consultative des droits de l'homme. *La Lutte contre le racisme et la xénophobie. 1990*. Paris: La Documentation Française, 1991.

Corbett, James. *Through French Windows: An Introduction to France in the Nineties*. Ann Arbor: University of Michigan Press, 1994.

Cordellier, Serge, et al., eds. *L'État de la France, 93–94*. Paris: La Découverte, 1993.

———. *L'État de la France, 95–96*. Paris: La Découverte, 1995.

Crozier, Michel. *The Stalled Society*. New York: Viking Press, 1977.

Dayries, Jean-Jacques, and Michèle Dayries. *La Régionalisation*. Paris: PUF (Que sais-je?), 1986.

Denis, M. N., and C. Veltman. *Le Déclin du dialecte alsacien*. Strasbourg: Presses Universitaires de Strasbourg, 1989.

Domingo, J., et al. *Champagne-Ardenne: une région à la recherche de son identité*. Montreuil-sous-Bois: Bréal, 1987.

Duby, Georges, ed. *Histoire de la France de 1852 à nos jours*. Paris: Larousse, 1988.

———. *Histoire de la France rurale*, 4 vols. Paris: Seuil, 1992.

———. *Histoire de la France urbaine*, 5 vols. Paris: Seuil, 1985.

Dulong, R. *La Questionne breton*. Paris: Presses de la Fondation Nationale des Sciences Politiques, 1975.

Estienne, Pierre. *Les Régions françaises*, 2 vols. Paris: Masson, 1994.

Flatres, P. *La Bretagne*. Paris: PUF, 1986.

Floyd, Keith. *Floyd on France*. London: Citadel Press Books, 1993.

Franey, Pierre, and Richard Flaste. *Pierre Franey's Cooking in France*. New York: Alfred A. Knopf, 1994.

Fried, Eunice. *Burgundy: The Country, the Wines, the People*. New York: Harper & Row, 1986.

Furet, François, Jacques Julliard, and Pierre Rosanvallon. *La République du centre: la fin de l'exception française*. Paris: Calmann-Levy, 1988.

Gamblin, André, ed. *La France dans ses régions*, 2 vols. Paris: SEDES, 1994.

Garnotel, J. *L'Ascension d'une grand agriculture. Champagne pouilleuse—Champagne crayeuse*. Paris: Economica, 1985.

Gaspard, Françoise. *A Small City in France*, trans. Arthur Goldhammer. Cambridge, MA: Harvard University Press, 1995.

Giard, J., and J. Schiebling. *L'Enjeu régionale*. Paris: Éditions Sociales, 1981.

Giblin-Delvallet, B. *La Région, territoires politiques. Le cas du Nord-Pas-de-Calais*. Paris: Fayard, 1990.

Giscard d'Estaing, Valéry. *Démocratie française*. Paris: Fayard, 1976.

Gooch, R. K. *Regionalism in France*. New York: Century Company, 1931. (Publication of the University of Virginia Institute for Research in the Social Sciences.)

Gourevitch, Peter. *Paris and the Provinces*. Berkeley: University of California Press, 1980.

Grand atlas de la France: Région Nord-Pas-de-Calais et Picardie. Lausanne: Éditions Grammont SA, 1987.

Gras, Christian, and Georges Livet. *Régions et régionalisme en France du 18e siècle à nos jours.* Paris: PUF, 1977.

Gras, Solange. *La Révolte des régions d'Europe occidentale: de 1916 à nos jours.* Paris: PUF, 1982.

Gravier, J.-F. *Paris et le désert français en 1972.* Paris: Flammarion, 1972.

Guiral, P. *La Provence de 1900 à nos jours.* Toulouse: Privat, 1978.

Hemingway, Ernest. *A Moveable Feast.* New York: Macmillan, 1971.

Hewitt, Gillian, ed. *France: A Culinary Journey.* San Francisco: Collins Publishers, 1992.

Hilaire, Y.-M., ed. *Histoire du Nord-Pas-de-Calais de 1900 à nos jours.* Toulouse: Privat, 1982.

Hoffmann, Stanley, *Decline or Renewal? France since the 1930s.* New York: Viking Press, 1974.

Hoffmann, Stanley, et al. *In Search of France.* New York: Harper Torchbooks, 1965.

Hollifield, James, and George Ross. *Searching for the New France.* New York: Routledge, 1991.

Howorth, Jolyon, and George Ross, eds. *Contemporary France,* vol. 3. London: Pinter, 1989.

Institut national de la statistique et des études économiques (INSEE). *La France et ses régions.* Paris: INSEE, 1993.

Johnson, Hugh. *The World Atlas of Wine.* New York: Simon & Schuster, 1994.

Johnson, Hugh, and Hubrecht Duijker. *The Wine Atlas of France and Traveller's Guide to the Vineyards.* New York: Simon & Schuster, 1987.

Keating, Michael, and Paul Hainsworth. *Decentralisation and Change in Contemporary France.* Aldershot, UK: Gower Publishing Company Limited, 1986.

Kepel, Gilles. *Les Banlieues de l'Islam.* Paris: Seuil, 1987.

Kesselman, Mark. *The Ambiguous Consensus: A Study of Local Government in France.* New York: Alfred A. Knopf, 1986.

Kuisel, Richard. *Capitalism and the State in Modern France.* Cambridge: Cambridge University Press, 1981.

Labande, E.-R. *Histoire du Poitou, du Limousin et du pays charentais.* Toulouse: Privat, 1976.

Lacoste, Yves, ed. *Géopolitiques des régions françaises,* 3 vols. Paris: Fayard, 1986.

Lacouture, Jean. *De Gaulle: The Rebel, 1890–1944,* trans. Patrick O'Brien. New York: Norton, 1990.

———. *De Gaulle: The Ruler, 1945–1970,* trans. Alan Sheridan. London: Harvill, 1991.

Langevin, P. *L'Économie provençale.* Aix-en-Provence: Edisud, 1983.

Latreille, A. *Histoire de Lyon et des Lyonnais.* Toulouse: Privat, 1988.

Le Moigne, Guy. *L'Immigration en France.* Paris: PUF (Que sais-je?), 1991.

Le Monde. *La France dans ses régions: vingt-six enquêtes sur le pays d'aujourd'hui.* Paris: Le Monde, 1992.

Lequin, Y. *Rhône-Alpes, 500 années Lumière.* Paris: Plon, 1991.

Le Roy Ladurie, Emmanuel. *Montaillou: The Promised Land of Error,* trans. Barbara Brayl. New York: G. Braziller, 1978.

———. *The Peasants of Languedoc*, trans. John Day. Urbana: University of Illinois Press, 1974.

Loubere, Leo. *Radicalism in Mediterranean France: Its Rise and Decline, 1848–1914*. Albany: State University of New York Press, 1974.

Lyness, Stephanie, and Dolores Simon, eds. *Le Cordon Bleu at Home*. New York: William Morrow, 1991.

Machin, Howard. *The Prefect in French Public Administration*. London: Croom Helm, 1977.

Madaule, Jacques. *The Albigensian Crusade: An Historical Essay*, trans. Barbara Wall. New York: Fordam University Press, 1967.

Margadant, Ted W. *Urban Rivalries in the French Revolution*. Princeton, NJ: Princeton University Press, 1992.

Marrus, Michael, and Robert O. Paxton. *Vichy France and the Jews*. New York: Shocken, 1983.

Martin, J.-C. *La Vendée de la mémoire (1800–1980)*. Paris: Seuil, 1989.

Mauratille, G. *Le Limousin*. Paris: Arthaud, 1987.

Mayle, Peter. *A Year in Provence*. New York: Vintage Books, 1991.

———. *Toujours Provence*. New York: Vintage Books, 1991.

Mazataud, P. *L'Auvergne. Géopolitique d'une région*. Paris: Fayard, 1988.

McCarthy, Partick, ed. *The French Socialists in Power, 1981–1986*. Westport, CT: Greenwood Press, 1987.

Mermet, Gérard. *Francoscopie 1993: Qui sont les Français?* Paris: Larousse, 1992.

Michelin. *France*. Watford Herts, UK: Michelin Tyre Public Limited Company, 1994.

———. *France, 1994*. Paris: Michelin, 1994.

———. *Paris*, 6th ed. Harrow, UK: Michelin Tyre Public Limited Company, n.d.

Mossuz-Lavau, Janine, and Mariette Sineau. *Enquête sur les femmes et la politique en France*. Paris: PUF, 1983.

Northcutt, Wayne, ed. *Historical Dictionary of the French Fourth and Fifth Republics, 1946–1991*. Westport, CT: Greenwood Press, 1992.

———. *Mitterrand: A Political Biography*. New York: Holmes & Meier, 1992.

Paris, D., ed. *Nord-Pas-de-Calais: une région d'Europe en mouvement*. Paris: La Documentation Française, 1989.

Parti socialiste. *La France au pluriel*. Paris: Entente, 1981.

Pellaprat, Henri Paul. *The Great Book of French Cuisine*. New York: Vendome Press, 1994.

Perrineau, Pascal, ed. *Régions: le baptême des urnes*. Paris: Pédone, 1987.

Plenel, Edwy, and Alain Rollat. *La République menacée: Dix ans d'effet Le Pen*. Le Monde Éditions, 1992.

Price, Roger. *A Concise History of France*. New York: Cambridge University Press, 1993.

———. *The Modernization of Rural France: Communications Networks and Agricultural Market Structures in Nineteenth Century France*. London: Hutchinson, 1983.

Queyranne, J.-J. *Les Régions et al décentralisation culturelle. Les Conventions de développement cultural régional*. Paris: Documentation Française, 1982.

Reitel, F. *La Lorraine*. Paris: PUF (Que sais-je?), 1982.

Renucci, Janine. *La Corse*. Paris: PUF (Que sais-je?), 1982.

Renzo, Salvadori. *Architect's Guide to Paris*. London: Butterworth Architecture, 1990.

Righter, Evie. *The Best of France: A Cookbook*. San Francisco: Collins Publishers, 1992.

Robert, Jean. *Île-de-France*. Paris: PUF (Que sais-je?), 1994.

Robert, M., ed. *Limousin et Limousins, image régionale et identité culturelle*. Limoges: Lucien Souny, 1988.

Robinson, Daniel, and Leanne Logan. *France*. Berkeley: Lonely Planet Publications, 1994.

Robinson, Jancis, ed. *The Oxford Companion to Wine*. Oxford: Oxford University Press, 1994.

Root, Waverley. *The Food of France*. New York: Vintage Books, 1992.

Roudie, P. *Le Vignoble bordelais*. Toulouse: Privat, 1973.

Roudy, Yvette. *La Femme en marge*. Paris: Flammarion, 1982.

Roussel, Eric. *Georges Pompidou*. Paris: JC Lattès, 1984.

Sainclivier, J. *La Bretagne de 1939 à nos jours*. Rennes: Ouest-France, 1989.

Savary, G. *La Dérive des régions. L'Aquitaine de la décentralisation à l'Europe*. Bordeaux: Vivisques, 1990.

Schain, Martin, and Philip Cerny. *Socialism, the State, and Public Policy in France*. London: Francis Pinter, 1985.

Schmidt, Vivien. *Democratizing France: The Political and Administrative History of Decentralization*. New York: Cambridge University Press, 1990.

Smith, A.D. *The Ethnic Revival*. Cambridge: Cambridge University Press, 1981.

Stoléru, Lionel. *La France à deux vitesses*. Paris: Flammarion, 1982.

Suleiman, Ezra. *Elites in French Society: The Politics of Survival*. Princeton, NJ: Princeton University Press, 1978.

Sweets, John F. *Choices in Vichy France: The French under Nazi Occupation*. New York: Oxford University Press, 1994.

Taguieff, Pierre-André. *Face au racisme*, 2 vols. Paris: La Découverte, 1991.

Thompson, Richard, et al. *Toulouse-Lautrec*. New Haven, CT: Yale University Press, 1991.

Tiersky, Ronald. *France in the New Europe: Changing Yet Steadfast*. Belmont, CA: Wadsworth Publishing, 1994.

Todd, Emmanuel. *The Making of Modern France: Ideology, Politics, and Culture*. London: Basil Blackwell, 1991.

Verrière, Jacques. *La Loire et Paris. La France essentielle de Clovis à nos jours*. Paris: Flammarion, 1990.

Viers, G. *Le Pays basque*. Toulouse: Privat, 1975.

Vogler, B., et al. *L'Alsace, une histoire*. Strasbourg: Oberlin, 1990.

Wall, Irwin. *The United States and the Making of Postwar France, 1945–54*. Cambridge: Cambridge University Press, 1991.

Weber, Eugen. *Peasants into Frenchmen: The Modernization of Rural France, 1870–1914*. Stanford, CA: Stanford University Press, 1976.

Wells, Patricia. *Bistro Cooking*. New York: Workman Publishing, 1989.

Wolff, Philippe. *Histoire de Toulouse*. Toulouse: Privat, 1970.

Wolkowitsch, Maurice. *Provence-Alpes-Côte d'Azur*. Paris: PUF, 1984.

Wright, Gordon. *France in Modern Times: From the Enlightenment to the Present*. New York: Norton, 1987.

———. *Rural Revolution in France*. Oxford: Oxford University Press, 1964.

Wright, Vincent. *The Government and Politics of France.* London: Unwin Hyman, 1989.
Wylie, Laurence. *Village in the Vaucluse.* New York: Harper, 1964.
Zeldin, Theodore. *France 1848–1945,* 4 vols. Oxford: Oxford University Press, 1979–1980.
———. *The French.* New York: Pantheon, 1982.

INDEX

About the Author

WAYNE NORTHCUTT is Professor of History and Coordinator of the International Studies Program at Niagara University in New York. He is the author of *Mitterrand: A Political Biography* (1992) and *The French Socialist and Communist Party Under the Fifth Republic, 1958–1981* (1985). He is also editor of the *Historical Dictionary of the French Fourth and Fifth Republics, 1946–1991* (Greenwood, 1992). Professor Northcutt has published widely on political, social, and intellectual trends in post–World War II France.